1991

Hamlet as Minister and Scourge
and Other Studies in Shakespeare and Milton

HAMLET

AS MINISTER AND SCOURGE

and Other Studies in

SHAKESPEARE

and MILTON

FREDSON
BOWERS

University Press of Virginia

Charlottesville

THE UNIVERSITY PRESS OF VIRGINIA
Copyright © 1989 by the Rector and Visitors
of the University of Virginia

First published 1989

Designed by Janet Anderson

Library of Congress Cataloging-in-Publication Data

Bowers, Fredson Thayer.
   Hamlet as minister and scourge and other studies
in Shakespeare
   and Milton / Fredson Bowers.
      p.   cm.
   ISBN 0–8139–1247–4
   1. Shakespeare, William, 1564–1616—Criticism
and interpretation.
   2. Shakespeare, William, 1564–1616. Hamlet. 3.
Milton, John,
      1608–1674. Samson Agonistes. I. Title.
   PR2976.B56 1989
   822.3'3—dc20   89–16443
                                                        CIP

Printed in the United States of America

TO

Nancy Hale

CONTENTS

PREFACE

THIS IS NOT A PROPER BOOK ABOUT Shakespeare, with a closely related excursus into Milton as a dramatist. Instead it is a collection of separate but thematically linked essays written at different times and initially for different purposes. Starting with "Hamlet as Minister and Scourge," all germinated in seminar teaching at the University of Virginia and then developed as papers for public delivery—some at learned meetings, some as the obligatory repertoire of a Phi Beta Kappa Visiting Scholar, and some at the invitation of friendly universities. Publication followed as requested with little alteration save for the restoration of cuts occasioned by the conventional time limit of fifty minutes, and in some papers the addition of discursive commentary notes, a pleasant vice or virtue according to the point of view.

Despite the varied origin and occasion for these essays, they share a common background from the active teaching of a relatively few plays in the Kittredge manner of close analysis although with a different focus from his. It used to be a standing joke that George Lyman Kittredge's students, inspired, all went out to teach Shakespeare like him—and promptly failed. In fact, failure could be anticipated because Kittredge's extraordinary memory, reaching to total recall, his thorough philological grounding, his wide reading in classical, medieval, and Renaissance culture, and especially the powerful thrust of his associative and analytical mind, all gathered together in one uniquely forceful teacher—these made him inimitable. Nevertheless, he put a stamp on his students that was permanent.

I like to reminisce that I may have escaped the usual fate of his imitators by not having had the opportunity to try my hand at teaching Shakespeare for some years after my degree. In the interval there was time enough to come to terms with my own different capacities, to add to my knowledge of the general Elizabethan drama, and to try to be my own man when it came to investigating Shakespeare. Thus when the opportunity came to initiate an annual series of seminars in Shakespeare, under the pressure of discussion my own interests came to focus on the analysis of Shakespeare's meaning in a somewhat different manner from Kittredge's close verbal explication. It is true that, like him, I selected only five or six plays in a year so that minute attention was possible; and indeed as my seminars developed I reduced this number so that I could spend an entire semester on *Hamlet* alone. It is also true that in seminar we always had our text open before us so that the discussion could proceed extemporaneously as my own or the students' interest lighted on some passage or often only a phrase.

We started, certainly, with what words, and especially the images, actually meant in Elizabethan terms. But this foundation for our study quite naturally expanded to include other matters since Kittredge's notes in his *Sixteen Plays* took care of much of the groundwork. It followed that larger questions of meaning developed from the textual explication, and my instincts drew me to several main areas of analysis to apply to the plays under consideration. Foremost, because of our extended study of *Hamlet*, we were drawn to consider what seemed to Shakespeare to constitute the essential elements and procedures of the tragic form. Then we turned to the unique relationship that drama as a genre establishes between playwright and audience. Since novelistic discourse is forbidden him, a dramatist must build his characters and transfer his intentions (that is, his meaning) in special ways. Aristotle's *Poetics* led to plot as the most important factor with which to start; thus Shakespeare's dramatic structure as a revelatory means of analysis came to the fore. The comparison of

Aristotle's observations with what Shakespeare learned by himself produced as many interesting differences as similarities, especially given Shakespeare's special interest in character which Aristotle placed below plot. It became clear that much of the difference with the Greek was not idiosyncratic, but that it was rooted in the civilization in which each man lived. Thence developed the discussion that takes up various pages of this collection about the profound changes that may be observed between the Sophoclean and the Shakespearean tragic ethos. In the Greek one observed the characters' futile struggles against Fate to no ultimate purpose save stubborn human resistance to the vagaries of indifferent or hostile gods and the darkly sensed force of Fate, especially as represented in the two Oedipus plays. In contrast, Shakespeare's breeding in a Christian world picture which it was unthinkable to modify or reject brought in a quite different conception of the relations between the human and the divine, this leading to an ethic based on free will and its accompanying personal responsibility for action. The attempt to clarify the dramatic results of this striking and basic difference led in turn to the concept of reconciliation as a critical Shakespearean tragic doctrine. The ethical background of Renaissance tragedy having been established as an interpretative tool, sharpened by the comparison with the Greek, the common ties of thought that linked Shakespeare and his original audience brought in the question of the necessary dramatic implementation. Thereby the analysis of dramatic structure as it evolves into ultimate plot seemed to offer a method for examining the various specific means by which Shakespeare conceived his plays—comedies and histories as well as tragedies—and controlled the reactions of his audiences to the understanding of character and action according to his intentions.

The first four essays in this collection endeavor to treat from different points of view the general problems of Shakespeare's ethos and dramatic structure, chiefly tragic but with some consideration of comedy as an illustration of technical differences. Since temperamentally I dislike theory without practice, these opening studies introduce various illustrations, certain of which will reappear in more comprehensive discussion within their proper divisions. *Hamlet, Antony and Cleopatra, King Lear, 1 Henry IV,* and *Much Ado about Nothing* constitute the main frame of reference, but some consideration of *Romeo and Juliet, Macbeth, Coriolanus, All's Well That Ends Well,* and *As You Like It* is included with minor illustration provided from a few other plays. Aristotle and *Oedipus the King* are not neglected.

A block of six essays on *Hamlet* follows, broken down into the special areas of interest previously introduced. The earlier, more generalized survey of tragedy, with a variety of illustrations of its dramatic method, here receives specific application in a narrower focus on *Hamlet,* its special problems and Shakespeare's solutions. Inevitably, some of the crucial accounts of the dramatic action recur in the more specialized analysis when there is a need to restate an earlier argument in order to buttress the return of consideration in another light and in a different situation. In particular, the summing-up in "Dramatic Structure and Criticism: Plot in *Hamlet*" resurveys various previously introduced theses but brought together for another purpose and with a different point of view.

The attempt to arrange a cohering progress of thematic concerns continues after the core group on *Hamlet* when a similar form of structural analysis is applied to *King Lear* and to *1 Henry IV,* a method previously somewhat scanted. *King Henry IV* as a highly developed dramatization of English history is as serious in its genre as is *Hamlet* or *King Lear,* and an examination of the structure of its first part is no less significant for demonstrating the important theme on which Shakespeare built the play. As for *King Lear,* the new argument that it is constructed as essentially a fifth-act tragedy may be helpful in a critical view of the famous storm scene.

One last word. This collection starts with what I believe to be the most important of all—the theme of the hero's reconciliation with his expiatory death, and through him of the audience, to which Shakespeare's *Hamlet* progresses from the climax to its culmination in the catastrophe. In this basic situation as flawed ministers of justice, strong ties exist between Hamlet and Milton's Samson. Earlier I had remarked how one play concerns themes of major interest in the other, although I did not specifically consider this relationship again in the essay on *Samson*. *Samson*, I suggest, is more likely to illuminate *Hamlet* than the reverse. Having opened the collection by a discourse on reconciliation with particular reference to *Hamlet*, I closed it with the theme of reconciliation in *Samson Agonistes*, not as an appendage I hope but as the natural culmination in another masterpiece of my concern with the nature and methods of tragedy—as well as its subject—as a form of art. Although these two essays were written some years apart, it proved to be no accident that at the moment of writing I chose to end both studies with the magnificently simple and moving catharsis in the last lines of *Samson*, when the ultimate understanding of reconciliation is revealed to the participants in the tragedy, both characters and audience.

Hamlet as Minister and Scourge and Other Studies
in Shakespeare and Milton

DEATH IN VICTORY:
Shakespeare's Tragic Reconciliations

A PARADOX of more than casual interest treats the pleasure an audience can be led to take in tragedy, a form that exhibits suffering, and often human defeat, ending in death. The universal response to tragedy and its persistence as a higher form of art—in the recognition that it is a more probing criticism of life—than comedy, does not mean that mankind is naturally sadistic. On the contrary, pain intolerable to witness in real life may in the world of art take on a beauty which creates a sense of contour and of satisfaction superior to that enjoyed by a longed-for outcome in good fortune. The distinction is an important one between the reaction of spectators to events in real life, and to the events of simulated life in drama. Thus it is that actions that in life could not be allowed to pass except over our determined intervention can be viewed in the theater without inciting us to action. Unless we are singularly naïve we do not cry out to Hamlet that the rapier he has just ignored is unbated, or to Othello that the evidence of the handkerchief is false. We may view with concern Antony's attempted suicide after the de-

From *Studies in Honor of DeWitt T. Starnes*, ed. Thomas P. Harrison and James Sledd (Austin: Univ. of Texas Press, 1967); by permission of the publisher © 1967.

ceitful news of Cleopatra's death, but we do not feel that we must
leap on the stage to arrest his sword.

We should, perhaps, be wary of any theory of art that denies
the obvious fact that men *can* take a form of satisfaction in the
disasters that occur to others. Out of our superstitious past, un-
questionably we feel that there is a certain generally fixed portion of ill luck—or evil fate—circulating through the world. If
someone else has absorbed a portion of this ill, so much the less
remains, for the time being, as a threat to ourselves. Although
lightning may strike twice, the odds are against it. If the man
next to us in battle is killed by a bullet, in an obscure sense he
has saved our life by being the one to be killed.

The element of propitiation, then, is not to be neglected as
part of the tragic experience in drama. Just as in ancient religions
the animal-offering became a substitute for human sacrifice (or
so Thomas Mann tells us), so the related *semblance* can be offered
to the gods in the hope that—though undeceived—they will
accept the fiction for the fact and allow their portion of ill will
to expend itself on symbols and not on men. To this extent a
character in a tragedy is a fictively human lightning-rod to draw
off like danger from ourselves. And since we know that the experience is a simulated one, no guilt remains in enjoying our
good fortune at someone else's expense.

Yet drama, if responsive to no deeper emotions in the audience than these, would scarcely have progressed beyond the enactment of sympathetic magic. We need feel no shame that the
tragic experience basically invokes a personal relief that disaster
has channeled itself to a scapegoat and missed our person. We
cannot deny the dark past in this relief, as in all our other emotional and intellectual experiences. But we can be proud that by
the power of sublimation evil can indeed be made good: we can
be reborn into light from primitivistic darkness, and—as an artistic, an aesthetic experience—we can create joy from pain, and
find what can be an ennobling pleasure from the contemplation
of tragic error, suffering, and defeat.

Although any dramatist knows this truism, not all dramatists
are equipped with the intellectual and emotional insight to take
full advantage of the tragic effect that can powerfully influence

an audience. But Shakespeare, as in so much else, was pre-eminent in securing the highest level of artistic experience from the tragic fact. By necessity, the great Shakespearean tragedies, though miraculously unified in their effect, are so complexly constructed that the interplay of character and of action within the particular tragic theme of the fable does not lend itself readily to dissection. Yet a critic must deal with specifics if he is to attack the problem of understanding the inner workings of the artistic experience that is uniquely Shakespearean.

These specifics may be limited and humble in their immediate objective. Perhaps the critic may concern himself with nothing more than an attempt to determine whether Hamlet thought of enterprises as "of great pitch and moment" or of "great pith and moment"; or—of somewhat more interpretative importance—whether he regarded his flesh as "too too sullied" or as "too too solid." One may try to find evidence, for instance, to determine whether "A little more than kin, and less than kind" is truly an aside, as marked by all editors, or else a defiant pun flung at the surrounding courtiers and perhaps overheard by Claudius himself.

The limited objectives of such inquiries should not lead us to undervalue their cumulative effect in the process of understanding Shakespeare's dramatic art, for if his text is corrupt (as with *solid* or *sullied* flesh) or incomplete, what can we know of the details of his precise intentions? Yet these yield in general interest to other types of specific evidence that can be explored for their bearing on a higher dramatic experience that involves the total effect of Shakespeare's plays.

When Aristotle examined Greek tragedy, he did not discuss generalities and abstruse questions of aesthetics. Instead, he engaged himself to an analysis of the most important dramatic specifics there are: the various concrete agents of dramatic technique such as action, character, plot structure, and the exact contribution that each of these specifics makes to the total tragic effect. Among other matters we are told that, for certain well-defined reasons, action is more important than character, and that both are more significant than thought. That the most powerful interest in tragedy lies in the part of the plot known as

Peripeteia or Reversal of Situation, and also in Recognition Scenes. That unity of plot does not consist merely in the unity provided by the hero. That Tragedy is an imitation of events inspiring fear or pity, and that such an effect is best produced by surprise and will be heightened when the surprising events follow one another as cause and effect. Only after all the technical points were settled did Aristotle, as a sequel, proceed to consider the general effect of Tragedy that had been adumbrated in his opening definition, "Tragedy is an imitation of an action, not of narration; through pity and fear effecting the proper purgation [catharsis] of these emotions."

A critic who seeks to understand the workings of Shakespeare's tragic effect may well sit at Aristotle's knee, at least in respect to relating the general to specific questions of dramatic function. That is, we should study the precise use to which Shakespeare puts the essential elements of a tragedy, such as, for example, the cause-and effect relationship of the incidents of the plot to one another. The effect on an audience of certain relationships may be most informative to criticism. A concrete example, of a limited kind, occurs in *Hamlet*. Just before Hamlet obeys his mother's summons to the interview that is to have such fatal consequences in the killing of Polonius, he speaks the fifth soliloquy beginning, "'Tis now the very witching time of night,   When churchyards yawn, and hell itself breathes out   Contagion to this world. Now could I drink hot blood   And do such bitter business as the day   Would quake to look on." Then the mood abruptly changes, with "Soft! Now to my mother!" This is followed by a quite overt piece of exposition aimed squarely at the audience. He will not become a matricide, like Nero. Although he proposes to be cruel, "I will speak daggers to her, but use none." In whatever way he may berate her in his words, he will never seal these threats with actions. In other words, Gertrude's life is safe, no matter what menacing postures he may assume.

The plain purpose of this soliloquy is to prevent the audience from misinterpreting the scene that is to follow. One result of warning the audience what attitude it should take is to increase its appreciation of the exquisite tragic irony of Gertrude's error that, in a sense, leads to her son's death in the catastrophe. *We* know she is in no physical danger, but *she* does not share our special knowledge. Her misinterpretation of Hamlet's thrusting her back into her chair when she was rising to call the guards leads her to shout for help. From behind the arras Polonius cannot know what is happening; he takes her to be in mortal danger from a madman and echoes her cry. Hamlet mistakes the old man for the King, and kills him. The murder of Polonius raises Laertes as a revenger, who is the direct means of Hamlet's death in the catastrophe. The Queen's drinking of the poisoned cup in this final scene is an inadvertent[1] but nevertheless very real expiation for her error which, though temporarily, saves her son's life at the expense of her own and thus enables him to secure a revenge on Claudius.

This whole chain of ironic commentary on human error leading to the important tragic effect of the catastrophe would be radically altered in its significance if, for instance, the audience had shared Gertrude's alarm and had joined in fearing that Hamlet was indeed out of all control and in the process of murdering the Queen. As the soliloquy shows us, Hamlet is basically in complete control of his emotions and is feigning violence according to a previously conceived plan. In turn, this plan is an essential part of the design of the play, which consists in a double

---

1.   Perhaps influenced by Gertrude's promise in the Bad Quarto to assist Hamlet in his revenge on her husband, but perhaps for little other reason than the restless search for novelty such as may bring Ophelia on the stage for her mad scene pregnant, modern directors sometimes have the Queen deliberately sacrifice herself by drinking the poisoned cup to save her son from the plot. This is sentimental nonsense that distorts the proper dramatic effect by removing Shakespeare's irony. Not a piece of evidence exists in the text to support such interpretation. If Gertrude had learned beforehand of the poison, she could readily have warned Hamlet; thus the only place she could have suspected treachery was when Claudius dropped the "pearl" in the cup—but how detect poison then? Moreover, even so, her sacrificial action would have been quite pointless; if she suspected the cup was poisoned she could have overturned it as by accident, or otherwise revealed its deadly nature. That the King inadvertently causes the death of his beloved wife is one of the ironies of the tragedy and an indication of the way that evil destroys itself. Moreover, in this light Gertrude's expiation is more powerful if accidental.

action required by the Ghost: justice to be visited on Claudius; also, the separation of Gertrude from his incestuous marriage bed, an act that is to include the awakening of her conscience as a means of saving her from the sin that will else damn her soul.

This redemption of Gertrude is firmly planned. We hear it introduced in the Ghost's commands to his son; we return to it in the fifth soliloquy that informs us of Hamlet's plans to shame, or threaten, her; we follow its course in Hamlet's rejection of an opportunity to kill the praying Claudius believed to be in a state of grace as yet denied to Gertrude. This temporary rejection of vengeance in some part occurred because of the urgent need to convert his mother while her repentance would still have some validity (that is, as it could be demonstrated by her resisting the temptation to return to Claudius' bed); and we see it crowned with success despite Gertrude's violent opposition and the resulting murder of Polonius. Any exploitation of the sensational in the closet scene would necessarily detract from the audience's understanding of Hamlet's reforming purpose and of the firm manner in which he carries out one part of the Ghost's commands under the gravest difficulties. Indeed, so important was it for the audience to recognize that Hamlet was acting a part for a fixed purpose in his violence to his mother that Shakespeare could not permit any question on this score lest the audience lose sight of or else misinterpret the mainspring of Hamlet's actions. This rigorous control of the audience's response to a scene could not be managed by normal dramatic means. Hence the special quality of the fifth soliloquy that points forward to the order of the succeeding events and unmistakably enforces the interpretation that Shakespeare desired.[2]

Such analysis may suggest the interest of the critical results that can accrue from the study of an author's dramatic technique, in this case the reasons for what seems on the surface to be a relatively clumsy expository soliloquy. The soliloquy by its nature revealed the presence of a dramatic problem that faced Shakespeare in guiding the reactions of his audience to a scene yet to come. When we then examine the reaction he sought to

2. See "Hamlet's Fifth Soliloquy" for a close analysis of this scene.

provoke in us, we can follow in some detail his conscious intention in this closet scene, which turns out to be the climax of the play, the scene that roughly corresponds in a Renaissance five-act tragedy to Aristotle's Reversal of Situation which he asserted held the most powerful emotional interest in a play. When we see how Shakespeare was afraid we might misinterpret this crucial scene, we are led to a clear view of what he considered its dramatic import truly to be, especially in relation to Hamlet's state of mind and to his plans for following the Ghost's commands for revenge. We are offered some additional motivation, also, why Hamlet should have spared Claudius at prayer. Without the soliloquy the ironic tragic error of the climax scene—the interview with his mother—might in large part have been obscured.

In this last connection one cannot over-emphasize the importance of the carefully prepared-for closet scene, since in its ironies lies the most important technical secret of the whole play—the identification of the turning point of the drama, that scene in which, within the framework of a morally determinate action, the hero makes the tragic error, or decision followed by action, that is to cost him his life in the catastrophe. The identification of the climax scene is of singular critical importance, for in it the dramatist must necessarily reveal the true nature of the tragic error, and thus the essential purport of his play as worked out in the action forming the structure of his plot.

If Hamlet's tragic error were his staging of the play-within-a-play that alerted Claudius to his knowledge of his father's murder, then the play means one thing. If Hamlet's tragic error were, instead, his sparing of Claudius at prayer, then as a result of this decision the play would mean something else. But if—as is indeed the truth—the tragic error is the impulsive killing of Polonius in mistake for the King,[3] then we have an important clue to guide us in our interpretation of the plot. A side benefit is the instant removal of all critical misunderstanding that persists in

---

3. For the evidence favoring the selection of the closet scene as climax from among the three possibilities, see "Dramatic Structure and Criticism: Plot in *Hamlet*."

somehow associating Hamlet's tragic end with his delay. Instead, Hamlet's catastrophic death resulted not from inaction but from action, mistaken as its object turned out to be. The main benefit, however, is the relation of the killing of Polonius to Hamlet's immediately succeeding recognition of his error. When Hamlet repents the murder, and recognizes that he has been punished for his impulse by the slaughter of an innocent, even though prying, man, so that he now has become the scourge as well as the minister of divine justice, we have pinpointed for us the exact nature of his fault.

Without question this error is Hamlet's alienation from Heaven by his inability to wait upon a non-criminal revenge that God would in due course have arranged for His minister.[4] We thence derive the critical paradox that Hamlet's inaction is not a weakness, as critics have generally supposed since late eighteenth-century romantic sensibility first took hold, but instead that his inaction has been a strength. Correspondingly, it was the crack in this patience, or fortitude, and his instant springing into action at the cry from behind the arras, that led him in his momentary weakness to commit a crime that on the Elizabethan stage must inevitably be repaid by death.

It is the climax that dictates the peculiar nature of the Shakespearean tragic catastrophe, the action of which always consists in the death of the protagonist, or hero. Moreover, without our understanding the nature of the tragic error that forms the climax, the terms of the catastrophe and its awards of death and of life, in punishment and in commendation, would have no ethical significance. That is, the justice that is dealt out in the catastrophe must (first) be appropriate to the nature of the tragic error and (second) must be linked to it by cause and effect.

A tragic universe is ruled by law in Shakespearean drama. Since the tragic error is some violation of this law, then the ending must show the repair of the break and the return of law.

4. The commission ordering Hamlet's death that he brings back from the English voyage might, for instance, have been enough to unseat Claudius if properly exploited. But the discovery comes too late, after the murder of Polonius; and before Hamlet can plan on utilizing its evidence he is swept up in Claudius' plot and Laertes' revenge.

When the law of reason in Othello, the man, is broken by Iago's insinuations, a form of chaos results in which appearance triumphs over reality: the good is distorted to look like evil, and the evil like good. The demonstration of Desdemona's innocence leads to the corrective justice that Othello administers to himself, and to the retributive justice visited on Iago. (For this important distinction, see "Milton's *Samson Agonistes:* Justice and Reconciliation." Retributive justice is mere punishment, whereas corrective justice has redemption or enlightenment as its purpose.) It is important for us to recognize that the triumph of justice is essential for the return of sanity in *Othello*, the play, and the re-establishment of the rule of reason. That Desdemona is proved to be innocent is not enough. The breach of equity caused by her murder cannot be healed except by the administration of justice on the perpetrators of her death, for otherwise the balance of law will not be restored.

Through his almost exclusive emphasis on the catharsis caused by pity and fear as the end-effect of tragedy, Aristotle neglects the role of justice in producing the tragic experience. In his too narrow view, justice is associated almost exclusively with the satisfaction that an audience feels at the downfall of a villain; hence the opposite view—that it is an essential background for the catharsis—he does not seem to recognize except perhaps by implication, and that only partially, in the discussion of the tragic flaw in a hero of moderate virtue. The satisfaction that he envisages from the exhibition of justice, therefore, would be felt at the fate of Iago, led away to torture and execution, but not at the fate of Othello, which, instead, would provoke the emotions of pity and fear. Similarly, the death of Claudius in *Hamlet* would provide satisfaction at the fall of a criminal; but the death of Hamlet—like that of Samson—would evoke the purgative emotions, a different result. We should feel satisfaction at the punishment of death meted out in *King Lear* to Edmund by his justice-dealing brother Edgar; but other, more complex emotions ought to be felt at the death of Lear.

This Aristotelian view seems to have been fostered by the narrow concept of justice as condign punishment, and not as what we may call "corrective justice." The distinction is a reasonably clear one. Retributive justice never goes beyond the bounds of simple punishment, and thus has no other purpose than to retaliate on the villain by an eye for an eye, a tooth for a tooth. This concept of justice is primitive, and the punishment is simple, because it has no other end in view than mere repayment, or retribution.

On the other hand, corrective justice seeks, even though obscurely, to create an attitude of reform, which is only to say, of repentance, by means of inducing a self-knowledge that was absent in the moment of tragic error. The punishment is not an end in itself, as in retribution, but instead a means to an end. The end, in Shakespeare, is the clarification in the minds of the audience of the issues involved in the tragic dilemma. This clarification on the part of the audience accompanies, and may even be induced by, a corresponding enlightenment and thus the ennoblement of the tragic hero. He may suffer death, but it will be a death in victory. In some way he will have won through and reasserted his indelible humanity, even though the audience accepts his death as just and thereby receives the satisfaction that equity has triumphed.

But more is involved. The tragic hero's death is certainly punishment, of a sort. Yet it is not the retributive, sterile, and hopeless form visited on Iago, or even on Claudius. The audience's satisfaction at viewing the death of Cleopatra, for example, is of a very different sort from that it experiences at knowing Edmund's fate in *King Lear*. Even in the mixed emotions that may accompany the death of Macbeth, who is scarcely an Aristotelian protagonist, a distinction may be felt separating the feelings aroused here from those that follow the death of Claudius.

The reason is not far to seek. The retributive fates assigned to the Shakespearean villains, who like Iago are incapable of alteration from experience, teach them nothing and illustrate little more to the audience than the basic platitude that the wages of sin is death.[5] On the contrary, no one can say that Hamlet goes

5. Since Iago's mind and understanding are not altered by the collapse of his schemes and his arrest, his defiant exit to torture and death teaches the audience nothing except the doctrine that evil will not permanently endure. His

to his death without having in some form been regenerated by his tragic experience.[6] Even Laertes profits from his doom, not to say Macbeth, who discovers more in the process of his defeat than the simple maxim that one should not murder one's king. At the end Lear has other things on his mind than the lesson that a father should not divide a kingdom between two unworthy children.

What the fictive characters in a Shakespearean tragedy end by learning dissolves into what the real-life audience ends by learning. If Cleopatra, or Othello, as dramatic characters learn something from defeat, the audience shares in their self-knowledge. Thus punishment, though still required as payment for tragic error, is not the end-all of the larger idea of equity that permeates the Shakespearean tragic drama. In Christian terms, the one resembles the Old Law of punishment without hope. The other stems from the New Law, which by joining Mercy to Justice establishes a dispensation and an equity in which Hope is one of the triad of intermediaries.

This Shakespearean process of learning, and its transmission to the audience, is dramatic, not didactic. The closest that Hamlet comes to generalizing his state of mind preparatory to his death is that the "readiness is all." However, Hamlet is well aware of his enlarging experience, and this consciousness governs his actions leading to the catastrophe that fulfils him. This is the plain sense of his discussion with Horatio on his return from England, with the conclusion that, although he has no precise plan to visit justice on the King, the interim will be his. Even more it is the plain sense of his rejection of Horatio's prudent advice to obey the omen of the pain about his heart and to decline the offered fencing match.

---

failure to repent and thus to make himself eligible for divine mercy powerfully exemplifies to the audience the depths of his Satanic malignancy, of course.

6.   Northrop Frye would place the regeneration somewhat earlier than I do in "the moment of final suspense," as early indeed as the moment when Hamlet leaps into the grave to grapple with Laertes, crying "This is I, Hamlet the Dane!" (that is, the King). But Frye's grounds are aesthetic, not structural, and I do not fancy them.

The same may be said, on a lesser scale, for Cleopatra, whose death in imitation of Antony is "after the high Roman fashion" and is ritualistically calculated to make Death proud to take her. The bravery she demonstrates in her suicide contrasts with, and expiates, the cowardice she showed in her flight at Actium after she had usurped command from Antony. She has undergone an experience of clarification and of ennoblement, and her death is publicly recognized as a victory over Octavius Caesar.

On the other hand, it may be argued that the artful switch that Shakespeare makes in the audience's view of Antony before and after his defeat is not accompanied by any significant rise in Antony's self-knowledge. That is, under Cleopatra's influence from the start, Antony the political figure behaves progressively in a more irrational manner to the point, almost, of self-destructiveness. And when the blow falls, and he is irreparably defeated at Actium, he seems to learn nothing from his defeat: his actions and emotional motivation remain essentially the same; that is, his reason seems to be no more in control of his passion, or emotions, than before.

Nevertheless, once the audience is released from the pain of viewing his declining political fortunes, and the bottom has been reached, a complete reversal takes place in its attitude to him. Antony the triumvir is ruined, but Antony the individual—still holding to the same scale of values—is shown to surpass material success. The attachment he feels for Cleopatra does not differ after his defeat from before, or, if so, differs only momentarily in his rage when he thinks himself betrayed. What alters is the audience's view of this passion and its consequences, owing to the change in perspective that defeat has brought. When Antony the Roman triumvir and later the Emperor of the East is concerned, his effeminate subjection to Cleopatra that leads him to put personal consideration over the world's public affairs to which he has committed himself—all this appears as Miltonic levity, a tragic unawareness of the true nature of the mighty issues involved. But when these public issues have been decided, and Antony has been stripped of the power that he could not wield, the same traits of generosity, loyalty, and attachment apply only to a private, not to a national situation, and in that personal frame they can be wholly admirable, large-souled, and supremely aware of the issues involved, as in his instantaneous reaction to the false news of Cleopatra's death. Hence Antony in defeat shows himself to be greater, as a man, than the politician Octavius Caesar in victory.

The point is, however: Antony has not truly altered, as Cleopatra is to alter or as Hamlet or Lear alters, as a result of learning from his tragic error, and thereby willing himself not to repeat it. Antony remains himself (one of the ironic phrases of the tragedy). The only difference lies in the application of the same motives to a different situation. The effect of this difference rests on the shift in the audience's point of view as it observes the same scale of values applied to highlight an action in which they are admirable, not fatally inadequate. Something of the same shift, although much less marked, occurs in *Othello*.

Thus some characters, like Hamlet, Lear, and even Macbeth, learn from experience and in the process draw the audience along with them and shape its understanding by their own. As the result of their experience these deliberately set right their tragic error when the catastrophe arrives. Other characters, like Antony, Coriolanus, and perhaps Othello, enter the catastrophe without having digested and understood the nature of their past tragic error in the climax although recognizing its fact. In one way or another, then, Shakespeare prepares the audience, whether it is experiencing the clarification in company with the character or whether, ironically, its knowledge is well in advance of the understanding reached by the protagonist. Which it is will dictate to an extent the kind of play that is being written, and in some part the nature of the catharsis, whether the emotions are moved by sympathy or by irony. But since the whole purpose of a tragic playwright is to induce the necessary catharsis in the emotions of an audience, the means are significant only as they bear on the nature of the end.

The exact import of Aristotle's description of the tragic experience on the audience as "through pity and fear effecting the proper catharsis of these emotions" is much in dispute. The traditional view has been that catharsis means either the "purgation" of the emotions of pity and fear from the minds of the audience, or the "purification" in a moral or ethical sense of these emotions. Either sense would apply to the great close of *Samson Agonistes:*

> *His servants he with new acquist*
> *Of true experience from this great event*
> *With peace and consolation hath dismist,*
> *And calm of mind, all passion spent.*

Without involving ourselves in these vexed definitions, let us accept catharsis as some alteration in the audience of the emotions, transferred to the mind in the form of understanding, from the effect of the pitiful and fearful events portrayed in a tragedy. Pity is the outgoing reaction of the members of the audience applied to the predicament of one or more characters in a play. It is, in a sense, a generous emotion. On the contrary, fear is the inward-turning emotion that is egoistic and not generous in its object. "We pity others where under like circumstances we should fear for ourselves." "Pity turns into fear where the object is so nearly related to us that the suffering seems to be our own." [7] The specific events of the tragedy that are fearful in this sense need not be applied personally in all their details, however. Few members of an audience have had the ghost of a murdered father rise to demand vengeance. At the same time, though few may have had the opportunity to divide the inheritance of a kingdom, the facts of filial ingratitude are current. Hence all members of an audience can participate personally, though with irregular degrees of identification, in the universal fear created by the very fact of human existence led among conflicting duties and often in the face of situations that seem without hope of satisfactory solution.

Aristotle does not say so, but the tragic catastrophe, or dénouement—the untying of the knot—must be the focus for the catharsis. Since the pitiful or fearful events of the play receive their final shape in this catastrophe, it is clear that the ultimate emotional and intellectual resolution of the play must be there

7. S. H. Butcher, *Aristotle's Theory of Poetry and Fine Arts,* 4th ed. (London, 1923), p. 256.

if the dénouement is to lead to the ending in peace, all passion spent.[8] The catastrophe not only concludes the action; in a very important manner it confirms, by re-enforcement or by reversal, the tragic error made in the climax.

Here we enter upon an important difference between the Greek and Shakespearean tragedy. If, with Aristotle, we take *Oedipus the King* as one of the most perfect of Greek dramas, we see the tragedy of a fate-driven man who is not basically responsible for his actions. If Shakespeare had written this tragedy, the wrathful slaying of his father would have been the morally determinate climax of the whole story, from which the ensuing catastrophe followed by cause and effect. To Sophocles, on the contrary, the patricide is only one of a chain of errors; indeed, the incestuous marriage is more likely the hinge on which the tragic action turns. At Colonus, it is interesting to observe, Oedipus defends the slaying in part as an act of self-defense and in part as an act of ignorance—he did not know the stranger was his father. This last is in answer to the Chorus' suggestion that he has suffered from a continuing fault in his tendency to quick anger; and, significantly, his denial is never questioned.[9] The tragic fact, hence, is the pollution of Thebes by a man for whom

8. The "new acquist" that Milton expects his audience to receive from the true experience of the tragic story is by no means confined to the final action of the messenger's narrative of Samson's death-in-victory, and the reception of the news by Manoa and the Chorus; but since in the kommos the narrative causes the recognition of their blindness in comparison to the inner light that moved Samson to his last heroic action, the increase in the understanding of the audience is at least focused on the action of this final scene. Under these circumstances the tragic catastrophe has only a technical relationship to the delightful untying of the knot in comedy. Instead, the chain of cause and effect of the rising tragic action, turning in the climax from good to ill, reaches in the catastrophe the inevitable resolution that, in action, enforces the ethical content of the drama. Although Aristotle may prescribe the Reversal of the Action as the moment of highest emotional intensity, the cathartic effect of tragedy would manifestly be incomplete without a dénouement that leads to the ending in peace.

9. If the audience is to take his denial as a statement of the exact truth, then the action is as stated above. On the contrary, if the Chorus' suggestion is correct that Oedipus has indeed suffered from the tragic fault of irascibility, and it is so recognized by the audience, then he is still blind in the dénouement

disaster has been prophesied and therefore one who is in the grip of a destiny that allows him, in fact, no personal choice.[10]

The distinction is that Oedipus, in the grip of his fate, is not personally responsible for his actions in the Christian sense, because he has no free will. When man is the victim of the gods, as in *Prometheus Bound, Ajax,* or *Oedipus at Colonus,* the suffering can be countered only by stoicism, which is defensive and not redemptive. Greek tragic stoicism merely tries to seal off man's responses to ill and thus to glorify fortitude in adversity, for life would otherwise be intolerable. The greatness of human character is manifested by Promethean resistance to external situations.

On the contrary, Christian thought is based firmly on the supreme principle of free will. No fate but a personal decision made without external duress leads Hamlet, Lear, Othello, Macbeth, Antony, Coriolanus, to embrace error. Since they choose error without external compulsion, they are personally responsible for their tragic decision in a manner incomprehensible to the audience of *Oedipus.* Oedipus' crime was not the slaying of a stranger, but the fact that the stranger turned out to be his father. But Hamlet's crime is the slaying of Claudius in the person of Polo-

---

and any regeneration is arbitrary and anomalous at best. One way or another, the audience cannot be enlightened as Milton expected from *Samson.*

10. Even to put the best face on it, the most we can say is this from Butcher's commentary (*Aristotle's Theory,* pp. 323–24): "If a man is so placed that he is at war with the forces outside him—either the forces of the universe, the fixed conditions of existence, the inevitable laws of life, which constitute 'Fate'; or the forces that reside in other wills that cross and thwart his own—the result may be a tragic conflict. The ancient drama is chiefly, though by no means exclusively, the representation of a conflict thus unwittingly begun, however much purpose may be involved in its later stages. The spectacle of a man struggling with his fate affords ample scope for the display of will power and ethical qualities. The *Oedipus Tyrannus* portrays a tragic conflict none the less moving because the original error which leads to the catstrophe springs from the necessary blindness and infirmity of human nature."

This statement modifies only slightly the narrow concept Aristotle has previously suggested: "The fate of the [Greek] hero is determined by forces outside the control of the human will. A mere error, due to the inherent limitations of man's facilities, brings ruin" (p. 323).

nius behind the arras. The murder is the tragic fact in *Hamlet*, not the identity of the murdered man.

The effect of this distinction is far-reaching. The moral of *Oedipus the King* is expressed in the final words of the Chorus: "Therefore, while our eyes wait to see the destined final day, we must call no one happy who is of mortal race, until he has crossed life's border, free from pain." (It is the same Chorus, we may note, that responds to Oedipus' laments that as a babe he had been released from death and restored to life, with the blunt agreement, "Thou wert better dead than living and blind.") This classical counsel of despair is not the Renaissance message of *Samson Agonistes* that a new and constructive understanding has been given to the participants of the tragedy, and through them to the onlookers, as a result of the interpretation of the tragic happenings, and thus a regenerative peace and consolation can accompany the final view of the catastrophe. The difference is between the law of death and the law of life, between doomed guilt and remediable guilt.[11]

Since death is the ultimate fact of Greek tragedy, justice can be only retributive because no means is provided mankind for resurrection from sin. In horrified retaliation for the pollution that his unwitting crime of incest has brought on Thebes, the blinded Oedipus is expelled from the city, and he acquiesces because he realizes that he is not the child of fortune he had supposed but instead the hated of the gods. It is true that Greek tragedy may refer, in general terms, to learning through suffering; but the lesson is mainly of the unstable nature of human happiness and of the need for endurance under the blows of fortune and the incomprehensible enmity of the gods. There is no enlightenment in this view; man cannot be reborn by such doctrine. It is not redemptive because repentance has no religious significance that can heal tragic error. Whatever healing takes place at Colonus does not result from Oedipus' repentance, for in truth since he acted throughout from ignorance he had noth-

---

11. It would seem evident that the Christian theme of redemption so emphasized in *Samson Agonistes* is Milton's means of setting himself to outgo Greek tragedy, as in *Paradise Lost* the same theme enabled him deliberately to outgo pagan epic tradition.

ing of personal responsibility to repent. Simple endurance ultimately turns the scales. The relaxation of Apollo's hatred is, as a consequence, arbitrary.

Shakespeare was a Christian dramatist writing for a Christian audience, but he was no propagandist and he was not writing religious problem plays. Nevertheless, by the very fact of his birth in Renaissance England he was conditioned to the standard religious ethos. Hence no dim fate oppressing mankind moves through his tragedies, even in *King Lear* I maintain, but instead a personal responsibility for actions in which decisions for good or evil are freely willed, and rewarded or punished accordingly.

In the prayer scene Claudius could have repented and seized on offered mercy if he had been able to will himself to relinquish the fruits of his crime—his crown and queen. He could not give them up, and the Elizabethan audience foresaw his inevitable fate. On the other hand, by the rule of Love, crimes can be expiated if truly repented. Justice will demand the same externals of punishment, but the effects are as different as day from night. Hamlet's soul is accompanied by flights of angels to its rest, although by Elizabethan tragic ethics he must pay the legal penalty of physical death for the slaying of Polonius.[12]

In this sense, the punishment of the tragic catastrophe, since it creates an act of expiation, is a death accompanied by victory, as much the hero's victory over himself as over an adversary in the plot. The death is temporal; the victory is spiritual and eter-

12.   In its crudest aspect, the Elizabethans sought by all means to secure the repentance of a murderer before they hanged him. Justice demanded that he be punished by death of the body; but mercy could accept his soul freed from guilt, especially if he co-operated with the authorities by an exemplary speech from the cart. A hardened criminal, defiant to the last, was also hanged; but if his soul were thereby punished too, and lost, it was because he had denied the offer of mercy and had willed his own damnation by free choice. In its more refined aspects, however, Gertrude expiates her sin by unwittingly drinking the poisoned cup intended for her son (an act that draws its significance from her "conversion" in the closet scene), and Claudius thereby becomes a double murderer. Laertes expiates his poisoning of the rapier and his acceptance of Claudius' plot. And it is evident that Shakespeare is much concerned to emphasize to the audience the release of Hamlet from the spiritual consequences of his blood-guilt.

nal. In this pattern there is no room for Oedipus' plea that he had sinned in ignorance. If the Christian hero is blind, or ignorant, it is because he has made himself so. His error, basically, is his temporary inability to weed falsehood from truth and to see for what it is the deception that is leading him into evil. His deceived free will has relied on appearances, not on reality; and he has not properly used his God-given gift of reason.

Under these conditions the effect of catharsis on a Renaissance audience differs from that on a Greek. Each Christian tragedy by necessity becomes a re-affirmation of God's mercy and justice.[13] This is the lesson of *King Lear* and of *Hamlet*. The Shakespearean tragedy is a tragedy of error; but unlike the Greek it is a tragedy in which error is repaired, in which arbitrary action is meaningless and negative, as set against the willed action that alone is positive and meaningful.[14] Hence the basically external Aristotelian recognition scene is altered in Shakespeare to rep-

13.   Certainly no tragedy in a religiously meaningful world can take as its theme God's injustice. The smaller satisfaction for the Shakespearean audience lay in the mere condemnation of unrepentant crime. The contemporary sensational villain-tragedy, of which this was the theme, touched Shakespeare hardly at all, and then only to be metamorphosed in *Macbeth*. Recognition of the major Shakespearean theme of expiation and reconciliation may prevent such absurdities as the recent arguments that the Elizabethan audience took positive satisfaction in the concept that Othello's suicide damned him to eternal torment. If so, it is the one retributive justice visited on a Shakespearean tragic hero, and *Othello* becomes a villain-tragedy, which manifestly it is not.

The effect of Shakespearean tragedy, as against the Greek, hence, is to emphasize the personal responsibility for action that is necessarily the result of free will, and, thus, strongly to intensify the Aristotelian doctrine of the tragic flaw by a more meaningful emphasis upon motivation. Oedipus, as was his fate, slew in ignorance, and possibly in self-defense. Instead, the personal responsibility laid on the Shakespearean protagonist like Hamlet forces him to choose between good and evil in a moment of crisis. And if he is so blinded by passion that he chooses in ignorance or in willful disregard of the issues involved, the fault is his, personally, and by cause and effect a punishment will follow.

14.   According to this Renaissance ethos, the tragic error of the climax is an act of temporary blindness, a wrong choice by the deceived free will. If the nature of the crime is subsequently understood, and the fatal action reversed by repentance, the necessary punishment is accepted as an expiation, and the tragic hero is reconciled to the vital force that, to the Elizabethans, interpenetrated the universe and alone gave it meaning.

resent the light of self-knowledge breaking through deceptive ignorance, just as in *Samson Agonistes* it is the moment described in
the Argument as "at length persuaded inwardly that this was
from God, he yields to go along with him [the Messenger], who
came now the second time with great threatenings to fetch him."
No greater contrast can be drawn between the Greek and the
Renaissance than the *Prometheus Bound* of Aeschylus, in which
the protagonist is defiant at the start and undergoes no transformation except to grow more defiant by the close after his series
of visitors, this set against Milton's series of visitations in which
the inner light progressively transforms and regenerates the
blinded Samson and from this event reconciles the characters to
the will of God.

Leon Golden has written thus about *Oedipus the King* and the
effects of its catharsis:

> *the particular facts relate to the personal story of Oedipus' at-
> tempt to escape the fate destined for him and his involvement in
> a series of events which force him to commit the very acts he
> sought to escape. These particular pitiful and fearful events have
> been so skillfully arranged and presented by the poet that we are
> led to see that there lies behind them a universal condition of
> human existence that is responsible for these particular pitiful
> and fearful events. This universal condition is the fundamental
> limitation of the human intellect in dealing with unfathomable
> mystery that surrounds divine purpose.*[15]

However, if we draw a parallel between *Hamlet* and *Samson Agonistes* on the one hand and *Oedipus* on the other, both Shakespeare and Milton do indeed penetrate some part of the mystery
that surrounds divine purpose in a way concealed from Sophocles. If divine purpose seems to require an extraordinary restraint
upon Hamlet's action as God's minister of justice in the pursuit
of a non-criminal vengeance on Claudius—so intolerable a re-

15. "Catharsis," *Transactions and Proceedings of the American Philological Association* 93 (1962): 58. Golden then continues: "Through this process of perceiving
that the source of the particular pitiful and fearful events of the play is a universal condition of existence, our understanding of the nature of pity and fear,
as they relate to the human situation, has been 'clarified.'"

straint that his fortitude cracks and he flings himself into a revenge that must involve a crime—yet the purpose of God both in respect to the nature of the revenge, and then to the eventual working-out of the original divine plan, presents no mystery to Shakespeare. Correspondingly, the audience of *Samson Agonistes* is throughout fully aware that Samson remains God's champion; hence the questioning of divine purpose is confined to the characters, exclusively for dramatic effect. Both playwright and audience enjoy the irony shown in the different forms of blindness.

The heart of the matter, surely, is the grand principle of reconciliation. Within the framework of free will, men on earth fulfil divine purpose, especially those like Hamlet and Samson, who have been set apart as ministers of justice. Although both fail, and believe that they have been cast off, God's purpose remains unswerving. Human reason has difficulty in understanding this unfaltering divine purpose, as in *Samson*, because the characters expect the purpose to fulfil itself in the identical terms of the original plan. But the hero's fault changes these terms, though not the essence of the plan. The original victorious end, although it will be fulfilled, will be altered to require the expiatory death of the hero as the willing payment for reconciliation. In *Hamlet*, as in *Samson*, then, the clarification of the minds of the audience by pity and fear suffers a sea-change. The outgoing and generous emotion of pity remains constant, pity that man should fail in a divinely appointed mission through human weakness that might have been avoided. But instead of turning inward, and universalizing the fearful consequences by personal application, a large measure of the Renaissance audience's fear remains generous and attached to the characters by a concern that the hero may not undergo the spiritual insight that will restore him to God's grace in reconciliation and enable him, though in death, to win through to his proposed victory.

Of all Shakespeare's plays *Hamlet* offers us the most perfect example of reconciliation. Again, we may learn something of the peculiar nature of Shakespeare's way by a contrast with the Greek. Just before the catastrophe in Greek tragedy, the protagonist may be given a final chance to escape the fatal consequences of the tragic act that is now on the threshold of retribution. But the logic of character and events is inexorable; the hubris that engendered the original error still blinds the protagonist, and he rejects (or does not recognize) the offered alternative that might, even so late, save his life or prevent the crime that is intended. Ironically, the justice of the catastrophe is prepared for when the audience sees the same lack of self-knowledge repeated as in the original error: evidence that the protagonist, at the brink of disaster, has not learned through experience the significance of his initial misstep. In Sophocles' *Antigone*, for example, if Creon had capitulated to Teiresias immediately and had not re-affirmed his cruel decree, Antigone and his own son would have been saved.[16]

In Shakespeare this moment of final suspense is the augury that Hamlet defies just before the fatal fencing match; the presentiment of evil: "But thou wouldst not think how ill all's here about my heart. But it is no matter." Horatio protests; Hamlet in reply associates the misgiving not with manly caution but with female fears, that is, with an irrational impulse. Horatio continues to take the omen more seriously than this, and he shows his agitation at its import by counselling Hamlet to decline the match if his mind misgives him. Hamlet rejects this counsel with an appeal to the reason of those who, like Horatio and himself, rely not on superstition but on the acceptance of God's overriding Providence, His active care for the world. With this rejection of Horatio's prudent but worldly advice, the tragic die is cast.[17]

The contrast between Shakespeare's use of the device and that in classical drama is clear. Shakespeare has piled up in this episode the characteristic devices of classical tragedy but has fundamentally altered their import and structural purpose. The most causal use of this moment of final suspense by the ancients emphasized the protagonist's blindness in repeating the substance of his original tragic error while Nemesis was poised

16. Another form of this "moment" may appear as an omen, or warning from the gods, that the protagonist in his blindness fails to recognize or chooses to ignore, although his willingness to admit its significance would have saved him. Cassandra's prophetic fit in Seneca containing her veiled warning to Agamemnon that she herself does not understand is an example.

17. See "The Moment of Final Suspense in *Hamlet*: 'We Defy Augury.'"

to strike. One moment of humility, or enlightenment, might have saved the victim, as Creon could have been saved from irreparable crime by a reversal of his original cruelty in instant obedience to the prophet. But, as also with Oedipus, this self-knowledge and understanding do not come: tragic blindness persists, and the protagonist ironically brings about his own downfall.

The difference lies in the fact that Shakespeare has Christianized the ancient pagan device. The Elizabethan audience can only approve Hamlet's rejection of pagan superstition in favor of a Christian reliance on Providence. It follows that the faults that blinded the classical protagonist to his last chance to escape must be taken as virtues in Hamlet that demonstrate the clearing of his understanding as manifested by his refusal to try to evade the required payment for his past error. Only thus can Hamlet be brought to the characteristic Shakespearean final ennoblement of experience that reconciles an audience to accept, even with satisfaction, the tragic end of a sympathetic protagonist fulfilling his original intent though at the expense of his life.

In any Renaissance Christian view of life, nobility equals humility and obedience, the understanding and acceptance of God's will instead of the dictates of one's own. If Hamlet comes to understand the nature of his error in the slaying of Polonius, and if this clarification of his self-knowledge leads to a re-submission of his alienated will to God's, then the line of the play from the climax to the catastrophe must bear on this theme. This is, indeed, the movement of the drama from the moment shortly after the killing when Hamlet acknowledges,

> For this same lord,
> I do repent; but heaven hath pleas'd it so,
> To punish me with this, and this with me,
> That I must be their scourge and minister.
> I will bestow him, and will answer well
> The death I gave him.

Given this acknowledgment of his error, it is idle to query why Hamlet on his return from the English voyage should be so confident that the interim will be his, although obviously he has no plan for action. That is the very point. His confidence derives from his recognition on the voyage that his ministerial function in dealing justice has been restored, that he is once more in the hand of God, Who has promised vengeance for all earthly crimes, and that he will, in God's own time, be the agent of justice on Claudius.

This Christianization of the classical moment of final suspense re-enforces not the protagonist's tragic error and repeated blindness that draw on the doom, as with Oedipus, but instead Hamlet's dearly bought enlightenment that reverses his flaw in the climactic closet scene and so justifies his regeneration. Instead of ironically contributing to his downfall, in the classical manner, the Christian fortitude that Hamlet exhibits in the moment of final suspense leads him with open eyes to choose Providence over pagan augury. His reaction to Horatio's offer of an alternative precisely inverts the classical device, for an escape at this moment would have ruined Hamlet, not have saved him. Shakespeare changes the opportunity to escape to make it, instead, a subtle temptation to flee responsibility for his error by attempting to evade the consequences. When Hamlet resists Horatio's two suggestions that he attempt to alter the events to come, which Hamlet now sees belong to God, not to him, he justifies his catastrophic victory over himself and over Claudius. Flights of angels can, indeed, sing him to his rest.

The tragic experience of *Hamlet*, therefore, exhibits error and then reconciliation through a return to God's plan. As later in *Samson Agonistes*, the audience is clarified as to the unchangeability of God's purposes by seeing them triumphant despite the momentary falling-off of the protagonist. The knowledge that the punishment of death visited on Hamlet and on Samson is just, but that a higher equity stemming from mercy will bring them to their rest, reconciles the audience to the tragic penalty that justice must exact. The victory achieved in death is, then, the visible sign of the final reconciliation of the hero with his God, and of divine acceptance of the results of his mission of justice.

This was *true experience* for Shakespeare's audience, for the ethics of *Hamlet* as revealed in its action re-enforced one of the basic doctrines of religion, and illuminated the blend of justice and mercy that rules the Christian state. In these circumstances the reconciliation of the hero promotes the audience's reconciliation with the penalty that has been paid, and in a catharsis far superior to the Greek, clarifies and fortifies its understanding of the ways of divine equity.

> *All is best, though we oft doubt,*
> *What th'unsearchable dispose*
> *Of highest wisdom brings about,*
> *And ever best found in the close.*
> *Oft he seems to hide his face,*
> *But unexpectedly returns*
> *And to his faithful Champion hath in place*
> *Bore witness gloriously; . . .*
> *His servants he with new acquist*
> *Of true experience from this great event*
> *With peace and consolation hath dismist,*
> *And calm of mind, all passion spent.*

CLIMAX AND PROTAGONIST
IN SHAKESPEARE'S
DRAMATIC STRUCTURE

N O ELIZABETHAN DRAMATIC CRITICISM exists that can correspond to the several early treatises like Puttenham's that
analyze the composition and structure of non-dramatic poetry.
How widely Aristotle's *Poetics* was read in various translations
from the Continent is debatable. For Shakespeare, at least, sufficient evidence has not been adduced that he knew Aristotle;
moreover, his acquaintance with the classical drama, direct,
would have been confined to Seneca in tragedy and to Plautus
and Terence in comedy. When Shakespeare first started writing,
his English models were few and relatively unsophisticated:
chiefly Kyd and Marlowe in tragedy, the slight court comedies of
Lyly, and the sprawling dramas of Peele and Greene, together
with a clutch of elementary history plays, some of them half
comedies or moralities with a semi-historical tinge. The rapidity
with which Shakespeare assimilated what was available to him
and, with an ingenuity that was both original and various, contrived forms of dramatic structure that he could call his own is
not the least manifestation of his extraordinary talent for the
stage.

Aristotle, in fact, was not necessary as a teacher. What Aris-

From *South Atlantic Review* 47 (May 1982); by permission of the publisher,
South Atlantic Modern Language Association.

totle had done was less to codify rules—that was to come later in France—than to observe common as well as uncommon characteristics of the dramas that he knew and to describe their nature, some of their mechanics, and the efficacy of certain devices as dramatic instruments. It is at least partly true that Aristotle as a critic knew no more about the drama than Sophocles, let us say, as a dramatist. Sophocles had been a practicing dramatist, acquainted with his predecessors and contemporaries and building on them a more refined and coherent dramatic structure than he had observed. Just so, a talent like Shakespeare's could vitally modify the drama that he knew, and indeed this is what Shakespeare did without benefit of any more formal or critical rules than were available to Sophocles and with innovations in dramatic art that burst the bounds of Sophocles' achievement.

It is not my purpose to attempt a chronological analysis of Shakespeare's progressive mastery of plot structure. Such a study could be made at leisure, but it would be difficult to dispose the devices and necessities of comedy, tragedy, history, and tragicomedy without being swamped by detail that might lose much of its meaning for one genre if applied to another. Instead, I propose to select two main components of dramatic structure, namely, the treatment of protagonist and of climax, and to endeavor to give a few examples to illustrate their intimate connection and also the variety of the means with which Shakespeare could deal with them, in some part according to genre and perhaps in some part according to his increasing dramatic sophistication.

Well before Bradley, Shakespearean criticism recognized the overwhelming interest of his characters as the main source of his continued appeal without regard for time or place. In more recent years a broader spectrum has been attempted. Shakespeare's poetic expression—always appreciated—has been subjected to closer scrutiny, sometimes at the expense of a recognition that he was writing dramatic, not lyric, poetry. Underlying themes and shadows have had their day, especially that of 'reconciliation' in the tragicomedies or the 'green world' of the golden comedies. In the constant analyses to which Shakespeare is subjected, questions of structure in technical terms have been comparatively neglected. Yet a play is perhaps the most intricately crafted and delicately balanced fictive literary form ever invented. As any current Broadway season will show, before a play is actually presented to a live audience in a regular production even the most experienced man of the theater cannot prophesy its success or failure with any certainty. Of course, as in the making of the filmed drama—one of the theater's spin-offs—the director, stage-designer, and the actors have an appreciable share in a play's success. But stage-history has shown that no one of these elements—except occasionally an outstanding actress in a couturier-made vehicle—can carry a play through to success if the text, the script, is not itself dramatically viable. Form and structure, of course, are not enough, else we should be celebrating either the classical French-derived drama in its leading seventeenth- and eighteenth-century dress, or the more modern French well-made play as adapted by Pinero or Jones, which still has elements of life in it generally in the melodrama or in farce.

Protagonist and the climactic action of a play can scarcely be separated, for in certain respects, either intermediately or through some close relationship, the one involves the other. Let us over-simplify the case and take it that if the main plot concerns the affairs of a protagonist, as ultimately it must, the technical climax or turning point of the action—whether for good or for ill—must necessarily affect that protagonist and his affairs. This is the most neutral statement I can contrive, for it leaves unspecified a question that I shall have to consider in due course: whether the protagonist must participate in his own person in the particular action that forms the climax of the main plot. The answer is of some interest. For example, if as in *As You Like It* a dispute were to arise about the identification of the protagonist of the play, we ought to be able to appeal to the climax for evidence on which a decision could be based. The main climax will most certainly *not* center on the affairs of a non-protagonist, although in some plays there may be a separate climax for the underplot that must be distinguished.

Shakespeare's tragedies are pyramidal in structure. That is, the play begins at some comparative point of rest either before or immediately after the start of the series of complications that is to comprise the main action. In *Romeo and Juliet*, for example, the clash between the two factions of Montague and Capulet, quelled by Prince Escalus, does not directly involve Romeo, who was absent. But the events leading from this clash, particularly the enmity of Tybalt for all Montagues, will shortly draw Romeo into the fatal skein. So in *Hamlet*, the entrance of the Ghost to the watch in the first scene starts a series of events that will lead to the interview with Hamlet and in consequence of that to the complexities of Hamlet's revenge. Once started, the rising action in which the protagonist plays the leading part develops as the forces that have been set in motion gather in complication and intensity. Hamlet finds his path to revenge impeded not only by the significant ethical problem that seems to force him into a murder in the first degree, by the legitimate doubts of the Ghost's veracity (which by a forward action he resolves), but also by the counterplot attempts of Claudius and Gertrude to discover his secret. In a brilliant scene the resolution of Hamlet's doubts by the play-within-a-play triggers the murderous reaction by the now thoroughly alarmed antagonist. It is the height of irony that the exposure of Claudius' secret also involves the exposure of Hamlet's and thereby sets in motion a counteraction that will eventually destroy him in his moment of victory.

On the contrary, in *Othello* the rising action starts immediately with the beginning of Iago's plot against the Moor, an appropriate opening for a tragedy in which the main action will concern more the concealed counterplot of the antagonist directed against Othello than any independent action initiated by the protagonist. Clearly we have here two different plot-lines between *Othello* on the one hand and, say, *Coriolanus* or *Hamlet* on the other. In between, perhaps, comes a play like *King Lear* where once the opening action of the division of the kingdom has been terminated, Lear becomes more the object than the subject of the rising action.[1] *Julius Caesar* and *Macbeth* have some affinities in that the respective protagonists at the start are urged to the

---

1. However, *King Lear* is a special case with a unique plot-structure for Shakespeare. For a discussion, see "The Structure of *King Lear*."

tragic deed by another, although each then takes over control of the action that rises to the climax.[2]

As required by an ethical drama, Shakespeare's tragic climaxes are clearcut and significant. In each case the turning point that will inevitably lead to the retribution in the catastrophe, or finale, is this protagonist's decision followed by the action that clinches this decision and thereupon makes the tragic ending not only inevitable but also acceptable to the audience as an act of justice. In a pyramidal plot structure this climax occurs in the third act, the fourth and fifth then being devoted to the falling action as the play descends to its catastrophic resolution. Two points need brief emphasis. First, the tragic decision is an ethical one in that it is not enforced by external chance, or accident, but by internal, personal impulse or design. That the tragic protagonist betrays a lack of clarity of judgment or insight as to the motivation behind the decision only sharpens the ethical nature of that decision. Admirable men may be led into evil as a seeming good. It is only a villain protagonist who embraces evil with open eyes, and even then a certain amount of self-deception may rule. In this respect the motivation of the tragic climax arises in rough but satisfactory correspondence with Aristotle's description of the tragic flaw in an otherwise good man.[3] Second, the crucial decision is necessarily followed by a corroborating action that removes the decision from the mind and fixes it in the external world of reality where the implementation, and then the conse-

2.   As befits Shakespeare's unique modification of the standard villain-tragedy, Macbeth's urger, his wife, drops out earlier than Cassius. Ironically, however, after the assassination of Caesar, Cassius' role is reversed so that he becomes subject to Brutus and the forces he has unleashed, and Brutus carves his own doom. The same may be said of Macbeth. In *Othello* up to the events just before the catastrophe itself, Iago remains the successful instigator of Othello's actions whereas Cassius loses his influence. To be set against such tragedies where the protagonist falls victim to tempter are plays like *Romeo and Juliet*, *Hamlet*, *Titus Andronicus*, *King Lear*, where the protagonist is alone responsible for his downfall. *Coriolanus* comes chiefly in this latter class since Volumnia's temptation for him to return to the plebs to claim the consulship is not a continued one woven into the fabric as is the relation of Cassius to Brutus.

3.   As a form of villain-tragedy, *Macbeth* differs necessarily. The murder of Duncan that will doom him is not the climax.

quences, make the decision irrevocable. This requirement that an ethical decision to be significant must be followed by action is not only a dramatic necessity, it is also an integral part of popular Elizabethan psychology, which argued, in general, that men are known by their actions, not by their words (which might be hypocritical), and (*pace* St. Paul) no crime is committed in thought if it is not confirmed by a corresponding action. Mere intention can be suppressed or diverted; but from the action that implements the intention, or decision, rise consequences that cannot be suppressed or diverted or aborted, and thus in tragedy these consequences lay out the course of the protagonist's doom.

Hamlet offers the simplest example of a climactic tragic scene. When in his mother's closet Hamlet believes he hears the voice of the king behind the arras, his decision to kill is instantly confirmed by the thrust of his rapier and the quick alibi of madness, "A rat! a rat!" The tragic decision to kill with its simultaneous accompanying action confirms Claudius' suspicions and raises a retributive revenger in Laertes, thus creating the specific counterplot that will cause Hamlet's death. This counterplot occupies most of the descending action, interrupted only momentarily by *Hamlet's* off-stage escape on the English voyage. As I shall discuss later[4] and so will not amplify here, Hamlet's decision attempts to solve an ethical problem and it is tragically flawed in that it enacts what for Shakespeare was the purest and most persistently repeated tragic theme, that of the conquest of reason by passion.

Even in so light a tragedy as *Romeo and Juliet*, which verges on melodrama in its reliance on chance to complicate the descending action, the climactic scene itself involves a tragic decision although one not quite so ethically weighty as Hamlet's. The basic religious and ethical problem is the same in both: the breaking of the commandment "Thou shalt not kill" and also of the divine reservation "Vengeance is mine, I will repay." However, the basic legal situation differs, for by English law Hamlet attempts to kill Claudius behind the arras with malice prepense, a determination held over a long period of time and thus first-

---

4. See the basic "Hamlet as Minister and Scourge," and also "Dramatic Structure and Criticism: Plot in *Hamlet*."

degree murder in cold blood. That it is Polonius who suffers does not alter the legal situation. On the contrary, Romeo's duel to the death with Tybalt is entered upon in hot blood, its cause— the killing of Mercutio—not being separated by a change of place and by enough elapsed time for Romeo's blood to cool. For this reason the killing was pardonable as manslaughter (whereas in first-degree murder no pardon was permitted by English law). For simple manslaughter Romeo is banished, a punishment made harsher than necessary by Escalus' determination to wipe out the feud between Capulet and Montague. Nevertheless, Romeo has shed human blood, and by the strict and invariable tradition of the Elizabethan tragic stage he must pay the corresponding penalty. It follows that after this decision to fight Tybalt and its almost instant implementation by action, the audience of *Romeo and Juliet* was as well aware as that of *Hamlet* that the descending action would mark out the hero's death. The means by which the catastrophe would be brought about still lay in suspense, however, and thus the audience's interest was sustained even though the tragic nature of the end was known.

Lack of appreciation of the convention of climax has caused the structure of *Coriolanus* to be sometimes misunderstood. The tragic action begins in the third act when after the tribunes revoke the consulship the mob apprehends Coriolanus as a traitor although he is able to free himself by force and to escape. To quiet the mutiny, his friends promise his return to answer to the people. The second scene holds the much discussed interview between Coriolanus and his mother in which ambition leads her by arguments of policy to persuade him to submit to the people and thus regain his consulship. Critics have pointed out, quite correctly, the fatal consequence to Coriolanus of the decision to follow his mother's urging and to place himself once more before the people instead of remaining true to his own militarily aristocratic principles. But is this the linchpin of the plot—the tragic decision? If so, what may we make of the final scene of the act in which Coriolanus' attempts to subdue his pride crack under the tribunes' attack and he breaks out in choler, only to be banished by acclamation, a sentence he accepts, in reverse, as his banishing Rome with his curse upon it.

Honest men may indeed differ whether the second or the third scene is the climax. Those in favor of the interview can point to the near impossibility that Coriolanus will subdue himself as he has promised; hence the agreement to return would be the fatal decision. That what would then be the implementing action occurs in another scene would cause no difficulty, for *Antony and Cleopatra* demonstrates that decision and action need not be simultaneous as in *Hamlet*, or substantially so as in *Romeo and Juliet*. Beyond doubt the climax scene is Antony's yielding to Cleopatra's domination and consenting, against all advice and his own conviction, to fight at sea so that Cleopatra may participate in the wars. The defeat at Actium seen through the eyes of Enobarbus and Canidius when she panics and flees the battle, and Antony follows, is only the corroboration, the inevitable action of some fatal sort that must complete his yielding his spirit and judgment to her domination. The defeat is not the climax itself but the implementation.[5] Thus it could be argued that the inevitability of Coriolanus' failure to conquer his pride is as certain as is Antony's loss of military success after he submits to Cleopatra's rule.

There is much that is plausible in this argument, but I think it is mistaken and, instead, that the play hinges on Coriolanus' loss of control in the third scene after he had been well warned to prevent it. I suggest that the certainty of his fatal outbreak is considerably less than the certainty of Antony's failure. No doubts are expressed by Coriolanus' mother, but, more important, none by any of his friends who, after all, agree with Volumnia that the thing is possible and that Coriolanus will temper his pride, contrary to the forebodings of Antony's soldiers at his decision and of Cassius at Brutus' high-minded irrational complacency. In the scene with Cleopatra Antony demonstrates that he has put his private over his public responsibilities. He fails by allowing himself to be dominated in a decision that is to settle the fate of the Roman world. That he makes his decision fully knowing at the moment its irrationality is evidenced by his stub-

5.   This action has been mentioned in "Shakespeare's Tragic Reconciliations" and will be discussed at more length in "Shakespeare's Art: The Point of View."

born insistence "By sea! by sea!" to Enobarbus' protests, and when the common soldier urges him to fight on land, all he can say is "Well, well. Away." This, then, is a full-fledged ethical decision (not merely a military blunder). The world is lost because in the great moment of crisis Antony cannot be his own man. If he is to rule the world he must first rule himself, yet his soldiers go into battle knowing that their leader is led and that they are women's men. After the defeat he can explain to Cleopatra his flight only by "O'er my spirit   Thy full supremacy thou know'st, and that   Thy beck might from the bidding of the gods   Command me." Octavius Caesar, and what he stands for, cannot be defeated thus.

On the contrary, Coriolanus is logically convinced of the rationality of Volumnia's arguments, which are backed by his friends, and with a clear head he goes to meet the tribunes and the plebs. If it was a fatal weakness in him to be dominated by his mother (and his friends) in this scene, the dramatic action—the dramatic motivation as it is called—has not inserted any suggestion of her faulty influence on his actions up to this point except for her wholehearted approval of his military prowess. As a result, the vital tragic preparation for such a crucial turning point based on domination is altogether missing, whereas it has been emphasized in *Antony and Cleopatra*. Moreover, in this scene in *Coriolanus* we should be at some loss to find the overthrow of reason by passion, the motive on which Shakespeare depended for his tragic climaxes.

Thus the clinching argument for *Coriolanus* comes to rest in Shakespeare's customary tragic theme of passion versus reason. This theme moves and explains the climax of *Antony and Cleopatra* but is missing in the parallel interview scene in *Coriolanus*. The argument would be far too subtle that Coriolanus' overweeningly ambitious pride demands the reward of the consulship and so his too ready acceptance of Volumnia's urgings that policy may secure the prize reveals his weakness, his tragic flaw, that he is willing to betray his own convictions by stooping to secure an office that he should not have desired. Again, if this were to be the motive, no dramatic preparation has been made to enable an audience clearly to understand the situation, as is done in *Antony and Cleopatra*. Coriolanus' ambition in the matter of the consulship has not been explored as a fault, nor has it been shown to be in any manner excessive. In fact, he has made no move to secure the prize, and he rather deprecates his mother's earlier confidence that it will be awarded. His preference, he says, is for military glory, which will leave him free (2.2.190–94).[6] Moreover, if he is to stoop now, as a result of the interview, he had already stooped when in the gown of humility he first solicited the votes of the plebeians. It follows that if passion is taken as overcoming reason in the scene with Volumnia, an audience may well be puzzled, whereas there can scarcely be a doubt what happens when in rage he explodes at the accusation that he is a traitor and thus brings on his banishment. Ironically, the fatal violence of his reaction leads him to become in actuality the traitor of which he was then falsely accused; but that is part of the descending action, the linkage between the climactic break with Rome and the catastrophic finale. The structure of *Coriolanus* hinges, I suggest, on Act 3, scene 3, depicting the loss of Coriolanus' control in a crucial event. His earlier outbursts had been remediable, but this final one is irrevocable in the consequences that follow his banishment and his reaction to that decree. Hence whatever the finer strands of meaning in confronting such a son with such a mother, the meeting with

6. After his latest victory over Titus Aufidius and his return as Coriolanus, the general assumption is that he will be offered the reward of the consulship by the Senate. (See Volumnia [2.1.191–92], the Messenger [2.1.250–51], the First Senator [2.1.121–22], and Menenius, who conveys to him the Senate's decision [2.2.130–31].) Although, according to Junius Brutus, Coriolanus had at some previous time considered standing for office (2.1.221–26), he does not appear to be over-eager for the honor. In response to Volumnia's suggestion he says that he would rather "be their servant in my way   Than sway with them [the plebs] in theirs" (2.1.193–94), and when the honor is offered he quietly accepts it as a duty: "I do owe them [the Senate] still   My life and services" (2.2.131–32). In the interview it is Volumnia who is the ambitious one, but her arguments seem to impress themselves upon Coriolanus for reasons other than his own political ambition. His flaw is uncontrolled personal pride, to which any specific ambition to be consul is subsidiary.

Volumnia is structurally little more than a device to provide adequate motivation for Coriolanus' return to the people after the fight with the mob in Scene 1 and thereby to permit the crucial Scene 3 to take place.

One last word may perhaps be said. I suggest that in an authentic tragic climax the audience must feel a sense of doom, of the irrevocability of the action that accompanies or will follow the flawed tragic decision. Othello's frightful acceptance of Iago's insinuations and his vow to kill Desdemona make any return to normality impossible even were Iago to be exposed before the murder was committed, a possibility never dramatically emphasized. Romeo's killing of Tybalt makes irrevocable the already serious breach between the houses of Montague and Capulet, and the audience can recognize that the marriage will be doomed by his shedding of blood. The healing that Escalus enforces at the end could not have been accepted by Capulet or Montague without the shocking cost to both houses of the sacrifice of these young lovers. Antony's capitulation to Cleopatra about the war underlines his inability to fill the imperial role he had assumed. No audience at that moment of personal and political crisis could believe that he deserved to emerge the victor at Actium. In *Julius Caesar* Brutus' insistence in Act 3, scene 1, ignoring the pragmatic arguments of Cassius, that Antony be spared and then that he be allowed to deliver the funeral oration, are too blindly, even proudly or hubristically, highminded for the dangerous reality as any audience can see; and Antony's victorious swaying of the people by his oration only confirms the tragic decision and Cassius' warning against it. Lear's division of the kingdom and his banishment of Cordelia, to adopt the climax of the whole story though not of the play itself (an important distinction, as will be suggested in the essay on *King Lear*),[7]

7. "The Structure of *King Lear.*" The problem of *Titus Andronicus* must be met head-on, for it is the only Shakespearean tragedy in which the hero protagonist does not make the climactic decision in the third act that will enforce the nature of the events in the catastrophe. In this act Titus sees the mutilated Lavinia, he chops off his hand in order to save his sons only to see their heads brought to him, and under these successive blows his mind becomes partly unhinged. It is only in the first scene of the fourth act that the names of his

may well seem irrevocable in its future consequences after the view we are given of Goneril and Regan. On the other hand, although different audiences may no doubt have different reactions, in my view no such sense of future doom is present to one's mind on viewing Coriolanus' decision to accept his mother's politic arguments[8] and the urging of his friends to return to the plebs for one last attempt to confirm the consulship, which, after all, has been awarded by the Senate. A concern may well be felt that, given his past history, he will have serious difficulty in controlling himself but—as suggested above—that the consequences of another outbreak (even if it occurs) will be fatal cannot be seen at the moment. (It is the banishment, not the denial of the consulship, that is the crucial factor in his turning against Rome.) In contrast, no audience can fail to appreciate, and then to dread, the consequences of his irrepressible choler when he cracks under pressure and not only is banished but himself breaks with Rome and casts menacingly foreboding curses on the city to which he will later turn traitor.[9]

At first sight *Macbeth* seems to evade the formula I have sug-

---

enemies being revealed to him by Lavinia, he swears the revenge that is to conclude the play. To the extent that in the third act the events occur that make the tragic ending inevitable, we have the climax there, whereas the decision to revenge implements the events instead of vice versa. This is, in fact, the structure, for in this case the decision to revenge can scarcely be called a tragic flaw, the conquest of passion over reason. The melodramatic cast of the play, thus, reveals its lack of high ethical seriousness in the emphasis, instead, on the event as the climax, a form of structure that we shall see in less serious plays. The most that can be said for an influence of character on the climax is that Titus learns the harsh lesson that his blind loyalty has been misplaced and that he and his family have become victims. This shock brings on his partial madness, which is to be a key element in his revenge. In such terms, I think, the climactic scene in the third act can be defended and the implications of climax as event somewhat softened.

8. No suggestion is made in the scene that he recognizes the shallow basis of the reasons she urges on him. Nor should this obtuseness be his tragic flaw!

9. At the risk of repetition it must be urged that even were an audience to believe, in this scene with Volumnia, that despite his vow he will inevitably be unable to control himself when he once again confronts the tribunes and the people, and hence that his decision to return is the fatal climax, the decision

gested. For instance, if Hamlet's fatal error was the killing of Polonius, why is not Act 2, scene 1, the murder of Duncan, the corresponding flaw, the decision that brings about the tragic end? The difference lies in the tragic genre. Of all Shakespeare's tragedies *Macbeth* is his one attempt at the popular form of drama which had a villain as protagonist, the so-called villain-tragedy. This genre has a different ethical foundation from the hero-as-protagonist tragedy, and as a consequence the structure differs. In the usual villain-play after his initial crime, early presented, the protagonist continues on his murderous course until he is tripped up and retribution follows in the catastrophe. Thus there is no ethical climactic moment of decision such as we find in regular Shakespearean tragedy. The first crime, early in the play, has not only exposed the protagonist as a villain but has also indicated to the audience that he can come to no good end. The crucial difference is that the protagonist's ultimate fate is sealed *before* the climax and does not fall upon him as the result of a flawed climactic decision, which in his case governs not the nature but instead the form of the catastrophe. Hence the climax of a villain-tragedy serves quite a different purpose. Although in this genre a retributive end is inevitable almost from the start, the mistake by which the villain will meet disaster is concealed until the climax. In this crucial episode the villain may overreach himself or make some tactical error in his plots. Occasionally this error consists of a fresh crime,[10] that calls into being the

---

can be considered an ethical flaw, or error, only with some strain. Shakespeare's tragic climaxes are clearcut and without ambiguity, Coriolanus' succumbing to Volumnia's pressure has not been dramatically prepared for and cannot clearly be seen as a definable fault serious enough to warrant expiation by death. His curse on Rome as a reaction to his banishment is quite another matter since it makes for an irrevocable breach and motivates his turning traitor.

10.   Usually this further crime results from the need for self-protection following on the original, but it may also be spurred by mounting ambition generated by the success of the initial crime. A brief discussion of the Senecan-devised villain-play is found in my essay "Classical Antecedents of Elizabethan Drama," *Tennessee Studies in Literature* 7 (1962): 79–85. The genre is explored in depth in my *Elizabethan Revenge Tragedy, 1587–1642* (Princeton: Princeton Univ. Press, 1940), pp. 101 ff.

revenger who will bring about the villain's downfall, although in some plays this necessary retributive agent may not enter until later, with a motivation arising from the descending action and only indirectly from the climax. Whatever the exact nature of the climax, it ordinarily constitutes a decision implemented by the action that will arouse the forces of good, of justice, sufficiently powerful so that the villain's eventual downfall is assured.[11]

By these structural criteria it should be clear that in *Macbeth* the murder of Duncan is not the climax but only the initial crime that sets Macbeth upon his course of attempting to preserve, and in the climax to enhance, its benefits. After Duncan's murder Macbeth might have reigned for years without serious opposition if he had not committed a further crime, a tactical error that eventually proved to be his fatal blunder. In the first scene of the third act, gnawed by the witches' prophecy that not he but Banquo will be the father of a line of kings, Macbeth enters upon the tragic decision by comparing Banquo to himself and admitting that Banquo is the one man he fears. Now he realizes that he has murdered Duncan and damned his soul for a barren sceptre, only to place Banquo's issue on the throne. This thought he cannot endure and he challenges Fate to combat him in the lists, champion against champion. I take this decision concerning his intention to kill Banquo to be the climax, in which he refuses to accept the prophecy and sets himself to reverse Fate. From it flows all the subsequent action. The murder of Banquo is ordered to thwart Fate, but Fleance the son escapes so that the prophecy will be fulfilled.[12] When Banquo's ghost joins the feast, Macbeth's horror that the grave will not hold its dead

11. Occasionally the forces of good are served by the forces of evil, as when another villain (often an accomplice) rises to challenge the protagonist and they destroy each other, or the protagonist is destroyed and the accomplice unmasked and punished.

12. In the commentary notes to the New Arden edition (p. 91), Kenneth Muir calls the escape of Fleance "the turning point of the play," a term that is meaningful only if applied to a climax, but nonsensical here even if used only in a popular sense. The decision to challenge Fate cannot succeed. Fleance's escape is less significant in the play's real action (except as Fate's answer) than

leads to the conclusion that he is so steeped in blood that he has no course other than to continue in crime. "We are young yet in deed," he promises as the scene ends.[13] The deed becomes the slaughter of Macduff's wife and children in retaliation for Macduff's flight to England, an atrocity (part of the descending action) that immediately reinforces the counteraction leading to the catastrophe.

The climax, then, is not the murder of Duncan, which is part of the rising action; nor is it the escape of Fleance, nor the retribution silently foreshadowed by Banquo's ghost that unhinges Macbeth, nor is it the vow made in England to revenge. These are all part of the descending action. Up to the moment that Macbeth challenges Fate by putting into motion the murder of Banquo he has been successful. After that challenge and its first action (made, incidentally, without consultation with his wife), the only question is when and how retribution will overtake him and Fate triumph. We have the climax, then, in a decision, not in an event such as the escape of Fleance. But the decision could be called an ethical one only with some strain: how could a true ethical decision be made by a villain protagonist except to repent

---

is Macduff's flight, the consequences of which shape the exact form of the catastrophe by raising in support of Malcolm a strong opponent who will defeat Macbeth. However, since James I traced his ancestry through Banquo, Fleance's flight had a considerable (non-structural) importance to the Jacobean audience even though Fleance never appears again and the action to overthrow Macbeth has nothing to do with him but is conducted by Malcolm and Macduff.

13. In his Presidential Address "*Macbeth:* King James's Play" at SAMLA on November 6, 1981, now to be read in the *South Atlantic Review* 47 (1982): 12–21, George Walton Williams addressed himself to this scene. I agree with his analysis of the dramatic significance of Banquo's ghost fulfilling the invitation to attend, the effect on Macbeth and on the disorder that follows. That it might be called "the symbolic center of the play, the broken banquet or frustrated feast representing the perversion of brotherhood, order, and peace," seems to me indeed suggestive. My only quarrel is that it cannot be structural in the technical sense of plot-organization that I have been examining in this paper. The turning point must be Macbeth's decision to resume a course of crime by murdering Banquo. The implementation in the actual murder and the further effects of the ghostly visitation are instead a part of the descending action that dramatizes, with much significant detail, the results of that decision.

and expiate his initial crime?[14] Instead, Macbeth's climactic decision is an error of hubris in challenging Fate instead of accepting the prophecy, enjoying the fruits of his own succession to the throne, and letting posterity take care of itself. True, the decision is, in fact, not quite so simplistic, for mixed in with the hubris is a large portion of desperation and of jealousy. Perhaps one may call it a triumph of passion over reason to challenge Fate in mortal terms, for Macbeth is a complex character and the play is the most refined villain-tragedy written in the period, with a character who gains more sympathy from the audience than is usual in the genre. Even so, little sense of ethical expiation comes to Macbeth in the catastrophe, as in Shakespeare's other tragedies, little sense of learning from experience not to repeat the climactic error as in Hamlet's anticlimax, but only a vast sense of tragic despair suited to the stature of the protagonist and to the magnitude of his crimes, self-entrapped.

The Janus faces of tragedy and comedy suggest that drama possesses two aspects but only one genre. It follows that our knowledge of tragedy may be assisted by studying the manner in which comedy deals with its particular structural problems, for both aspects must control the audience's response by structural devices. To make a complete generalization open to numerous objections, let us say that whereas tragedy derives its strength from

14.   As a generalization this statement is of course rather sweeping. If one takes the simplistic view that an ethical decision is one between good and evil, no matter how broadly defined (and not between two degrees of evil), then a protagonist already entered upon an evil course, like Macbeth after the murder of Duncan, can scarcely make an ethical decision to continue in evil unless there were some consideration of the option that exists to confess, expiate, and accept the penalty for his initial misdeeds in order to save his soul, just such an option as Claudius contemplates in the prayer scene in *Hamlet.* In *Macbeth* the element of choice between expiation (good) and evil is not raised in the climax. Macbeth takes it for granted that his soul is damned beyond retrieval and thus his decision is a confirmation of his evil course when he unhesitatingly plans to dispose of Banquo. Whatever ethics are involved, given his acceptance of damnation, concern a choice between the passive enjoyment of the benefits of his throne and the active crimes that must follow his challenge to Fate about the succession.

character, so the peculiar backbone of comedy is plot, rather, or situation. Of course we must not forget the function of wit, both verbal and in situation, but that is not structural, and for the purposes of this discourse very narrow points of focus have been adopted. Since comedy does not plumb the depths of basic human nature but instead is inclined to deal with manners and to treat its people chiefly as the exemplification of these manners—even humours—it follows that the nature of the structural climax differs from tragedy. By its climactic turning point tragedy marks the transfer from the protagonist's good to ill—from the possibility of success to the certainty of failure—by his own decision. Internally generated circumstances force him, and these are more important, or at least more significant, than whatever external circumstance happens to be the immediate occasion. In short, the event in tragedy follows the decision, whereas in comedy a general tendency exists for the situation to bulk larger than the decision, if indeed there is a decision. The turning point of comedy has at least one correspondence, however, in that the complications of the rising action that might have tended to ill, or at least neutrally to lack of success if pursued,[15] receive a new direction by some event, some incident, the effects of which will ultimately lead to the satisfactory ending. Hence the untying of the comic knot, the dénouement that corresponds to the tragic catastrophe,[16] likewise follows as a result of the direction given to the descending action by its turning point or climax. But since the subject of comedy is less fraught with ethical significance, and a marriage dance replaces an expiatory tragic death, the climax decision—in such cases as there is a decision—involves no weightier a problem than the unraveling of the comic action demands. Indeed, for obvious reasons no decision by the protagonist need be concerned at all. It follows that in the usual comic

15.   The tendency to ill success that is reversed is by no means a necessity. The outlook for the action may have been relatively neutral, or at least undecided, until the turning point fixes the natural direction for the descending action. *Love's Labour's Lost* is perhaps a good example.

16.   Actually, in technical terms *catastrophe* and *dénouement* are identical and are not associated either with tragedy or with comedy except in a popular sense.

structure the climax involves an event, not a decision involving character, even though some sort of decision accompanying the event is not unknown.

Much Ado about Nothing contains a striking example of an event forming the climax in which the protagonist takes no part and makes no decision, although this turning-point event is later vitally to affect the dénouement itself and in a nicely complicating comic fashion to influence the course of the descending action up to the dénouement. In the third act Don John's plot against Claudio and Hero ripens. Ocular evidence of Hero's unchastity is promised for that night and is duly produced offstage by a trick. Then in the climactic scene the drunken conversation of Borachio and Conrade reveals the deceit to the overhearing Dogberry and his watch. Thus when Dogberry apprehends these accomplices, the event occurs that will necessarily foil the consequences of Don John's plot and clear Hero. That Dogberry creates problems in getting his message through to Leonatus so that Claudio's mistake continues and the confrontation occurs at the wedding does not portend tragedy (or even tragicomedy) but only more complications before the knot is untied after the accomplices' formal confession. If the audience had not been comfortably assured in this climactic scene that the means existed by which Hero's truth must be revealed, its view of the events would have been vitally affected. Indeed, the play might have hovered on the verge of the seriousness of the tragicomic *Winter's Tale* with such another false accusation and the traumatic consequence of Hermione's supposed death, not recognized by the audience at the time in the absence of any hint that it was feigned.

In *Much Ado* the overheard revelation draws the fangs of possible tragedy before the descending action, and later, in addition, the audience is fully let in on the secret of Hero's supposed death. In *The Winter's Tale* the climactic scene of the oracle's revelation that Hermione is innocent, followed by Leontes' swift repentance, clears the air in one direction but in another obscures the possibility that the ending can be fully healing and satisfactory: in contrast to *Much Ado* the audience sees no way in which the situation can be lightened. Thus even in *The Winter's Tale* the climax is really an event, and the protagonist Leontes' repentance has little to do with the descending action until the time comes for the reconciliation at the end when the lost has been found.

In some comedies the climax may not immediately clarify the course of the future action although an event occurs of which the dramatist will make important use. If we take the turning point of *Two Gentlemen of Verona* to be Proteus' betrayal and the Duke's third-act discovery of Valentine's plan to elope with Silvia which leads him to exile Valentine, only complications without any ray of hope seem about to follow. A significant action has certainly taken place in that Proteus has succeeded in separating Valentine and Silvia so that he can woo her for himself, and to that extent the central plot has taken a decisive turn. All the audience can know, however, is that the course of the future action is now irrevocably set, but in what direction it will go is very much in question except for the recognition that Silvia will remain constant and that Julia's disguise holds latent possibilities for resolving the tangle. Just such another turning point, although slightly clearer in its details, is found in *The Comedy of Errors*, an early play also. I take the climactic scene to be the first time that something of a confrontation or juxtaposition takes place when Antipholus of Syracuse is within the house of Antipholus of Ephesus, who is denied admission by Luce because the master is thought to be at home. But, more important, in this scene Antipholus of Syracuse declares his love for Luciana and denies he is the husband of her sister. This linked event involving both Antipholuses gives some clue that the mistaken identities will eventually be straightened out, the more especially since Balthazar advises Antipholus of Ephesus that there is some cause to him unknown in the refusal of his wife to admit him.

Another turning-point event, but one that more decisively forecasts the dénouement of Falstaff's full exposure and reformation, is the ignominious buck-basket scene in *The Merry Wives of Windsor*. Another but even more decisive event involving the protagonist occurs in *Twelfth Night* when Viola realizes that her brother must be living since Antonio, who has rescued her from the duel, takes her for Sebastian. Once Sebastian is identified and recovered, Viola can doff her disguise as a boy and the love-match with the Duke can be satisfactorily concluded.

Midway between these events and the comic climaxes that involve some sort of decision is the love scene between Ferdinand and Miranda in *The Tempest.* This climax crowns the success of Prospero's schemes since without it a permanent and meaningful reconciliation between the two houses can scarcely be brought about. The structure of *The Tempest's* climax reveals an event that has been formulated by the manipulator protagonist before it occurs and, though part of a decision, in a sense, does not come as a decision taken in the climactic episode itself except incidentally by the two participants. In this respect it differs from the climactic decision by another manipulator, the Duke in *Measure for Measure.* The whole future course of the plot is laid out for the audience when the Duke overhears the interview between Isabella and her brother Claudio, the substance of which causes him to persuade Isabella to join in the suddenly extemporized scheme to entrap Angelo through Mariana. In *As You Like It* Rosalind's disguise permits her to manipulate the future action and to bring it to a satisfactory conclusion. As Ganymede in the climactic scene she introduces herself as Orlando's companion and promises to cure him of his love. By this decision taken at the moment of their meeting in the forest she channels the love-game in the direction that will entertain the audience until the dénouement. Another manipulator is Portia in *The Merchant of Venice,* whose decision to go to Venice in disguise as a lawyer proves to be the key point in turning the tables on Shylock and releasing the protagonist, Antonio.

How large the event bulks in Shakespeare's comic climaxes may be seen by the relation of decision to event in these episodes. In tragedy whatever event it is that triggers the climactic decision is of importance only as the occasion for this decision. But in many of Shakespeare's comedies, as is to be expected, it is the turn of the plot, not the turn of character, that forms the climax and no decision is present. In this respect *Much Ado* and *Twelfth Night* offer the clearest examples, with *The Tempest, The Comedy of Errors,* and *The Winter's Tale* as likely candidates also.

When the plot turns on the intervention of a manipulator, as in *Measure for Measure, As You Like It,* and *The Merchant of Venice (All's Well That Ends Well* is probably to be included despite its mixed nature), it is interesting that the manipulator is in disguise and thus in a position of secret power.[17] Moreover, although in these comedies it is the decision of the manipulator to intervene that turns the plot, this decision is appropriate for comedy as against tragedy in that the course of action proposed is intended to solve a particular problem in a satisfactory manner[18] and character is scarcely involved. Being rationally entered upon, the decision is not forced on the central character by any complicating motive like passion, nor is there any internal struggle since, as concerns the character, no personal ethical situation need be involved. Plot is ordinarily the main condition, not character, and hence the warding off of ill and the triumph of right and of love have no more than conventional ethical significance, and little or no personal application except in such a play as *As You Like It.*

Nevertheless, there are a few comedies in which some form of decision turns the plot with more ethical or personal significance to the person involved than is usually found in the manipulators series. As already remarked, in *The Tempest* it is Prospero's decision to recover his rights by reforming, or amending, his enemies instead of destroying them in punishment that leads to his manipulation that in turn brings Ferdinand and Miranda together. The climactic love scene is therefore partly a scheduled event but, of course, partly personal in that the feelings of the two

17. The omniscience provided by disguise and the consequent ability of the manipulator to control unaware characters insure the direction the plot will take in the descending action once the turning point has been reached in the intervention that will govern what will happen in the dénouement. *The Winter's Tale* has an interesting variant in that there is a joint manipulation by Paulina and Hermione in the Queen's supposed death, but this secret is kept from the audience. It is not a control exercised by the protagonist as in *Measure for Measure,* and only by passive default does it lead to any of the descending action up to the dénouement itself when it is suddenly introduced to complete the reconciliation.

18. Although a tragic climactic action may seem to create a problem, ordinarily it may be said to solve the problem but in the wrong direction, not the right.

participants as they fall in love are intimately involved. A more significant personal involvement because in an unmanipulated decision occurs in *Love's Labour's Lost.* Although in Act 2 the men have begun to show that they are in love, the real breakthrough and hence what I take to be the turning point that begins the action of wooing is Berowne's confession in Act 3 that he is truly in love, followed by his decision to write the love letter to Rosaline. This letter being misdelivered serves as the catalyst to betray the loves of his companions as well.

All's Well That Ends Well has often been called a problem play, but it contains a problem of quite another nature than usually remarked; that is, whether the undoubted seriousness of the play comes close to producing a climax on an ethical plane that for comedy is as high, comparatively, as the climaxes for tragedy or at least for tragicomedy. When Helena receives Bertram's taunting letter from Florence, her decision as communicated to the audience in the soliloquy in Act 3 scene 2 is to remove herself from Rousillon so that Bertram may return to his native country and his own house. In literal terms she is giving up the struggle for possession of Bertram, a theme continued in the letter to the Countess announcing her flight, her pilgrimage to St. Jacques, and her renunciation of her ambitious love.

Two alternative interpretations are possible. In the first, despite the clear statements in the soliloquy and the letter,[19] it could be suggested that she secretly proposes to seek out Bertram in Florence to see what can be done. There is much that is attractive about this proposal, including its coincidence in a major way with Shakespeare's source in Painter's *Palace of Pleasure.*[20] Additionally, it would make Helena's character all of one piece,

19. Since there is no evidence whatever that Helena has changed her mind between the soliloquy and the writing of the letter, it is impossible to argue in dramatic terms that her soliloquy renunciation has given way in the interval to a determination to travel to Bertram in Florence with the intent somehow to meet his terms. Soliloquy and letter must be viewed dramatically as of a piece.

20. In Painter, Giletta hoped that by her good behavior Beltramo would be persuaded to return from Florence to his own estate; but to her message saying that she would leave the country if necessary to draw him back, he returned only the answer about the ring and the child. Giletta communed with herself

with her cleverness as the main theme. The dramatic structure would be well integrated, for action would flow from character (even though an unattractive one to modern sensibilities), and this action would derive its significance not from pure chance but from her taking advantage of an opportunity offered during the carrying-out of a general plan, just as the Duke in *Measure for Measure* seizes on the information he overhears as a means of implementing his own purposes. If from the start, then, Helena sets out for Florence to win back her husband, the climax must be acknowledged as the receipt of Bertram's letter and the decision that she thereupon makes to return to action in an endeavor to meet his terms.

Nevertheless, insuperable difficulties exist that force us to reject any such interpretation. In the scene where Bertram's letter is delivered, Helena's concluding soliloquy gives no hint of such a plan; on the contrary, it is full of remorse for Bertram's situa-

---

how to meet the two conditions, and as a part of her plan she called together the main people of the region and told them "that she was lothe the Counte for her sake, should dwell in perpetuall exile: therefore shee determined, to spende the rest of her time in Pilgrimage and devotion, for preservation of her Soule, prayinge them . . . that they would let the Counte understande, that shee had forsaken his house, and was removed farre from thence" (quoted from the reprint of the third edition of 1575 in the Appendix to the New Arden edition of *AWW*, ed. G. K. Hunter [London: Methuen, 1959]). She then left, telling no man where she was bound, and immediately traveled after Beltramo to Florence in the habit of a pilgrim where she lodged in a widow's house and learned of her husband's love for the daughter of a poor neighbor. The idea of the bed-trick occurred to her and was duly carried out much as in the play. The important point to observe here is that in Painter Giletta's first offer to leave Rousillon so that Beltramo could return is sincere and comes after she has restored his disordered estate to a good economy proper for his return. However, after Beltramo sent back his answer that he does not care what she does, for he will not dwell with her until his two conditions are met, Giletta's second statement, made to the people, is a deliberate ruse to disguise the fact from Beltramo that she is leaving for Florence to discover some means by which she can fulfill the conditions. Shakespeare has transferred Giletta's honest offer to the position of the second on receipt of Beltramo's answer so that Helena's soliloquy (and letter) merge the two incidents of his source but with the motivation of Giletta's sincere initial proposal.

tion, fears for his safety in battle, and it reveals only her determination to encourage his return by her withdrawal. The letter to the Countess merely fills in the details of her resolved course of action to follow the decision taken in the soliloquy. Even though *All's Well* is an intrigue comedy of sorts, it should be conclusive that in no play does Shakespeare ever use a soliloquy as a deliberate means of deceiving his audience. A Shakespearean soliloquy reflects accurately the thinking of the character at the moment of delivery. The character may be mistaken as to the truth of what he is saying—itself a dramatic device to be recognized and evaluated by the audience—but any mistake is an honest one and not consciously intended by the character (or dramatist) to mislead the audience as to the feelings or intentions expressed in the soliloquy. Under this absolute dramatic rule it is impossible to argue that in her soliloquy (and presumably in her letter to the Countess that follows) Helena does not mean what she says: she is leaving Rousillon in all good faith in order to permit her lord to return from Florence in safety.

This is the plain intent of the opening of her soliloquy with its play on Bertram's "'Till I have no wife I have nothing in France," a phrase that determines her "Thou shalt have none, Rousillon, none in France." That is, she will remove herself by pilgrimage to another country so that Bertram on his return will have no wife residing in France.[21] In doing so she will take away the dangers of battle that she so vividly visualizes:

> No! come thou home Rousillion,
> Whence honour but of danger wins a scar,
> As oft it loses all. I will be gone.
> My being here it is that holds thee hence.
> Shall I stay here to do't? . . .
> . . . I will be gone,
> That pitiful rumour may report my flight
> To consolate thine ear.

21. We must not be so subtle as to reflect that in fact Bertram has his wife (consummates his marriage or wives her) not in France but in Italy. This turn could scarcely have been in Helena's mind here.

Her compassion, her renunciation, and her determination to ex-piate her ambitious love by a pilgrimage to another country must be taken at face value.

This perception of the harm she has done, and the self-sacri-ficing means by which she will rectify it, triggers an important decision that opens up new depths in her character. If the in-trigue that secured Bertram were to raise any questions in the audience about her true feelings, the soliloquy reinforces the quiet obedience with which she had followed Bertram's instruc-tions, delivered through Parolles, for her to proceed to Rousillon without a marriage night. In short, in the soliloquy (supported by the letter to the Countess) she shows repentance and a will-ingness to sacrifice herself which attest to her true love. A deci-sion to give up what she had so hardly won certainly represents a turning point in her character, and in a play with a different plot it would certainly have been the climax. But in *All's Well*, as written, it is a false climax, for in what would be the plot's de-scending action only the most tenuous connection can be traced between this soliloquy scene and the dénouement when Bertram shamefacedly is reconciled to her.

One thing is certain. On the evidence we must discard any hypothesis that she goes to Florence planning to recapture Ber-tram. Thus when Shakespeare gives us no hint that she arrives in Florence for any other reason than to join waiting pilgrims to Compostela at a popular staging point,[22] we must take that at face value also. We then have a chain of accident. Because Helena was a good girl in her renunciation of Bertram, in process of her expiatory pilgrimage she finds herself, without ulterior

22. Florence is not precisely on the most direct route from Rousillon to St. James at Compostela, but no need exists to speculate whether or not Shake-speare made an honest mistake in his geography. Compostela was the one Eu-ropean pilgrimage best known in England and hence the most natural place to select as Helena's destination. That she must go through Florence on her way is required by the plot. It is as simple to conjecture that Shakespeare arbitrarily placed Florence on the route (or, rather, Compostela as a natural extension from Florence) purely for convenience as it is to believe that he did not know his geography. If Bohemia can have a convenient sea coast, Florence can lie between France and Spain. Precision for an Elizabethan play laid in foreign parts is scarcely a desideratum.

design,[23] in Florence where by a lucky chance the opportunity to arrange the bed-trick pops up. That she then abandons her sincerely motivated pilgrimage in order to work the bed-trick provides the substance of the succeeding action and the nature of the ending, the untying of the knot at the French court. It must be emphasized that the soliloquy has no effect on the following action except to get her to Florence with good motives. No other line of action flows from the soliloquy, and the bed-trick would have been enacted as it was whether or not the soliloquy had ever been uttered so long as Helena was somehow transported to Florence.

The true climax of the plot, then, would be Scene 5 of Act 3 in which after hearing of Bertram's pursuit of Diana she invites the company to dine at the Widow's house where she proposes to have a conversation with Diana. We must assume that the bed-trick substitution formulates itself in her mind at that moment, and the turning point of the play has arrived.

Important as is the soliloquy, and profound as is its impact, we can see that it is a character device and not a structural turning point in motivated action. Helena's sincerity in the soliloquy encourages the audience's approval for her reversal of course in Florence. After all, she had left Rousillon to free Bertram from danger in the wars, not to give him leisure to seduce the virgins

---

23. It is superfluous to point out that no purpose would be served by deceiving the Countess (and the audience) as to Helena's true destination. The letter appears to be written to prevent a painful parting in which Helena would need to resist the Countess' entreaties to remain; but actually it is an unabashed piece of Shakespearean exposition which supplements the soliloquy by providing the audience with necessary information about the pilgrimage and a further insight into Helena's repentance. Moreover, it is not really a legitimate question to ask whether when she wrote the letter (granting that it was not deceptive as was Giletta's speech to the retainers) Helena could have been aware that she must pass through Florence on her way to Compostela. Since we are not told, and no other information is later given us on the subject, the problem cannot be said to exist in terms of the play, no matter how much in real life (not in a fictive representation) we should like to have known. Shakespeare has given us no hint; hence it is idle speculation to wonder whether at the moment of decision she knew that Florence would lie on her route. The matter simply is not discussible.

of Florence. An audience can scarcely expect that after the news about Diana she would depart Florence, leaving events to take their own course. The way the actress manages the scene will much influence the studied neutrality of the text: that the precepts to Diana will be "worthy the note" is almost a promise of something more than ordinary moral discourse. When the opportunity then comes to take Diana's place, Helena seizes it without blame since it has come unsought, whereas if she had traveled to Florence for no other purpose than to entrap Bertram, as does Giletta in the *Palace of Pleasure* source, her unscrupulousness would have made the dominant impression. That the one important scene of character illumination as found in the soliloquy is divorced from the actual plot-climax, that its sympathetic renunciatory decision is indeed quite contrary to the climactic bed-trick decision,[24] and that the soliloquy does not in itself lead to any of the future action in Florence and then in France, all this reveals a structural weakness in the play not customarily cited, a detraction from its seriousness that Shakespeare was never able to overcome. Helena is a more complex character than a bed-trick intriguer, and her initial success in winning Bertram produces emotional and psychological consequences that she could never have contemplated. But since this problem is not explored except in the soliloquy and letter, it is only fleetingly a part of the play. The false climax, important as it is in influencing the audience in Helena's favor, is not integral in the play's plot

24.   If the structure of the play had focused on the soliloquy as the climax of the plot's action, a considerable amount of its seriousness would have been lost in the abrupt change from a climax scene of self-sacrificing abnegation to a succeeding action of opportunism, a trick to win the match offered by a set of fortuitous external circumstances having little or nothing to do with the climax. In *Measure for Measure*, after all, it is because of the Duke's plan in his disguise to observe the vices of Vienna, and particularly the conduct of Angelo, that he is led to take an interest in Isabella and Claudio and thus to overhear the information he needs to put a general plan into specific action. This association of character and event in *Measure for Measure* would be missing in *All's Well:* if the turning point of the plot's action is to be rooted not in an event but in character, as it certainly must be if the climax is the soliloquy and its decision, then the following action would violate that decision since the intrigue does not flow naturally from the proposed abnegation. Compassion and sacri-

structure and might even be taken as misleading when viewed in the light of the action. Certainly one of the reasons why the play has produced so much puzzlement lies here in this dislocation.

A complicating factor in structural analysis, present in Shakespeare's comedies but largely absent in the tragedies, is the under-plot with its own separate climax. For instance, in *All's Well* the turning point in Bertram's relations with Parolles comes in the sixth scene of Act 3 that separates Helena's invitation to dinner from her securing the approval for the bed-trick in Scene 7. Structurally the two are independent; nevertheless, there is an important dramatic link (as Arthur Kirsch has pointed out to me) in that Bertram's consent to the French Captains' proposals to expose Parolles foreshadows the end of Parolles' influence on him and of an antagonism that has affected Bertram's treatment of Helena. The climactic scene of the Parolles underplot, thus, sandwiched between the two scenes of Helena's climactic decision to win back Bertram and the start of her device, suggests clearly that when she succeeds she will not have to deal with a second opponent.

In *Much Ado* I take it that Hero's gulling of Beatrice so that she admits her love for Benedick is the climax of the underplot. True, it merely completes the gulling of Benedick that has taken place in the second act, but the dénouement of the underplot could scarcely have happened without the corroboration of Beatrice's

---

fice would have given way without warning or explanation or conflict to a complete change of mind, to cleverness and deceit, and thus to a return of the traits that had driven Bertram away in the first place. The action at Rousillon might perhaps seem to correspond roughly to the Duke's banishment of Valentine in *The Two Gentlemen of Verona* in that a turn of the plot has occurred although the implications as affecting the future action are concealed at the moment from the audience. But any attempt at an analogy is too inexact to be useful. In *All's Well* the concealment would be complete (Florence is not mentioned in soliloquy or letter and Helena's arrival there in 3.4 could not have been anticipated by the audience) and even positively misleading, whereas in the *Two Gentlemen* Proteus' proposed action once Valentine is removed is predictable and the betrayal of the friendship between the two gentlemen is sure to provoke both action and counteraction leading to the dénouement.

part in the love affair. It may or may not occur to the audience that Beatrice might be a harder nut to crack than Benedick and that the deception leading to her consent is the more important, especially since it has been made evident that once bit is twice shy. (An indication has been given earlier in veiled terms that Benedick has previously wooed her but had withdrawn for unassigned reasons.)

One further word may be said about *Much Ado*. It has often been remarked that the main plot concerns the Claudio-Hero story but that the Beatrice-Benedick underplot is the more interesting to the audience and is always played by the star actor and actress. Structurally, however, the dénouement can be nothing other than the humbling of Claudio by Leonatus so that he accepts, unwittingly, his true bride Hero. The underplot of Beatrice and Benedick is associated with this dénouement and has its own dénouement in their mutual confession of love which is, in fact, much dependent upon the successful outcome of the central Claudio-Hero plot. But their support of Hero, though helpful, is not essential to the central dénouement, which is out of their hands, and it follows that the climactic scene that insures the happy outcome of the central Claudio-Hero story is the exposure to Dogberry and the watch of Don John's plot. Despite the superior interest to the audience of the underplot characters, the structure shows clearly what we must call the play's main plot.

The structural question of the main versus the subplot could sometimes be open to debate, for it may seem an anomaly that in various of Shakespeare's comedies, like *Much Ado*, what we must call the underplot not only may be more attractive and interesting to an audience than the central action but also may constitute in its concentration of scenes or number of lines (and thus of acting time) a major part of the play. A temptation may exist, as a consequence, to reverse the plots, but this must be resisted. Comedies of this nature have what may be called a framework central plot. The framework governs the total action and attaches to itself the various underplots but it need not usurp the audience's interest more than is required by its overall function. In *Love's Labour's Lost* Shakespeare creates the main action as Navarre's withdrawal for study and his subsequent conquest by the Princess of France which brings him back into the real world. But this action is integrated very closely with the underplot love affairs of his companions and particularly that of Berowne and Rosaline. Indeed, the underplot comes perilously close to a usurpation when the climax is perceived to be Berowne's acknowledgment of his error in following Navarre and his determination to woo Rosaline by letter. But as in *The Merchant of Venice* and certainly in *Much Ado*, the example of climax in tragedy does not at all apply in that the comic climax need not be a decision or an event participated in by the protagonist so long as its purpose is the effect it produces on the affairs of that protagonist as solved in the dénouement. It follows that Claudio in *Much Ado*, Antonio in *The Merchant of Venice*, Navarre in *Love's Labour's Lost* are the structural protagonists without regard for the dramatic interest they generate in comparison to the characters in the important underplots.

Similarly, the affairs of King Cymbeline, especially his revolt and eventual reconciliation with Rome in the person of Lucius, constitute the framework plot within which Posthumus, Imogen, Iachimo, Queen, Cloten, Belarius and the two sons play their respective roles in subplots. The framework climax is certainly Cymbeline's decision to refuse the tribute to Rome. This decision triggers the war in which all the characters are swept up until in the dénouement the dispute is settled by Cymbeline's free action (Britons never shall be slaves), and the stability and peace of the kingdom is confirmed by the revelation of the identities of Guiderius and Arviragus. Because of the powerful underplot involving Posthumus, Imogen, and Iachimo it may seem a little odd to contemplate Cymbeline as the actual protagonist (the title could be only a courtesy as in some history plays), but the structure enforces this conclusion.[25]

The structure of *As You Like It* is unusual in that what might

25. Shakespeare's romantic comedies do not ordinarily agree with the Jonsonian definition that tragedy concerns the fates of characters whose fall can have a broad effect on others, as in national affairs, whereas comedy concerns the affairs of private men. The framework action of *Love's Labour's Lost* must center on the love of the King of Navarre and the Princess of France that will

ordinarily be regarded as the framework plot fails in one important respect in the assignment of the protagonist. At first sight
the life in exile of Duke Senior in the Forest of Arden, the con-
gregation of various characters to him, and the eventual restoration of his rights, might seem to be the framework of the main
plot within which operate the important underplot of the love
story of Orlando and Rosalind as well as the various affairs of
Touchstone and Audrey, Celia, Oliver, Jaques, etc. Moreover, it
does not much matter that—as in *Much Ado* where the framework plot is more integrated and less of a formality—the climax
and happy culmination of Orlando and Rosalind's love action
have no effect on the solution of the main complication of the
framework, the restoration of the Duke. But in *Much Ado* the
main action has its own climax by which the affairs of Claudio
and Hero are vitally affected and the dénouement brought
about, a structural necessity that is wanting in *As You Like It*.
Duke Frederick's decision to raise an army against his brother
Duke Senior in order to kill him is neither acted nor mentioned
before the narrative of Jaques de Boys in the dénouement itself,
which unties the knot by informing Duke Senior of Frederick's
sudden arbitrary conversion and abdication. Without a turning
point or climax that concerns his affairs, Duke Senior can
scarcely be the protagonist of the main plot despite the framework situation: that position and action as protagonist must fall
to Rosalind, who otherwise would have been the main character
in an underplot. If any lingering doubt should persist about
As You Like It, the example of *A Midsummer Night's Dream* should
settle the matter. Here we have a pure framework in the approaching marriage of Theseus and Hippolyta, to which are attached the underplot of the artisans preparing the entertainment
as well as that of the young lovers owing to Theseus' initial judgment, on Egeus' demand, in favor of Demetrius over Lysander to

---

lead to their union. King Cymbeline is the unifying character in the framework,
not Posthumus. Even in *Much Ado* Claudio and Hero are the social superiors of
Benedick and Beatrice. It is slightly unusual to have the Duke in *Much Ado*, the
King in *All's Well*, and (as I shall suggest) Duke Senior in *As You Like It* acting as
subsidiary characters.

be the husband of Hermia. But no action in itself attends the two royal characters and nothing in a climactic action that in any way could be conceived as affecting them. On the contrary, with grace they perform their simple framework function while the main plot of the play devotes itself to the quarrel between Oberon and Titania and its resolution, which provides not only its own climax but also the climax for resolving the mixed affairs of the young lovers.

Underplots in Shakespeare's comedies are widely varied in their structure. Some of them have only a formal relation to the main plot by reason of a social tie between the characters, as in *The Taming of the Shrew* where the Bianca-Lucentio courtship comes into contact with that of Katherine-Petruchio only because the two women are sisters.[26] The Touchstone-Audrey and to a lesser extent the Costard-Jaquinetta-Armado subplots rely on the servant-master or a general household or merely local instead of a familial relationship. These parallel subplots may act as a commentary but ordinarily do not have much of a structural relationship to the main plot in that little or nothing that occurs in them affects the central action. (Costard's misdelivery of Berowne's letter is, of course, an exception.) Although the Beatrice-Benedick subplot is much more sophisticated than usual and these two have a very intimate social tie with the characters of the central action, it still remains essentially parallel to the Hero-Claudio story. Shakespeare has disguised this relationship by the intervention of Claudio in the gulling of Benedick and of Hero in that of Beatrice, an interesting reversal of the usual procedures in that here the characters of the main plot influence the subplot instead of the other way round as Parolles influences the attitudes and action of Bertram in *All's Well* or Sir Toby Belch intensifies the problems of Viola in *Twelfth Night*. Nevertheless, despite the intimate mingling of the characters in *Much Ado*, and Benedick's abortive effort to fight a duel with Claudio to punish him for his treatment of Hero, essentially there is no piece of action

26. Lorenzo and Jessica constitute a sub-subplot in *The Merchant of Venice*, linked on the one part to Shylock by his daughter Jessica and to Antonio by means of Lorenzo's friendship with Bassanio.

in the subplot that affects the development, the climax, or the dénouement of the main plot. Beatrice and Benedick are certainly involved in supportive roles to the central characters and their underplot has certain suggestive contrasts and parallels with the central action; but so far as the development of this central action goes they are without influence on its course and could have been spared.

If Beatrice and Benedick hold the main interest of the play although throughout only attached to the characters of the main framework plot, a few other plays utilize the sophisticated technique of uniting the subplot and the main plot by the transfer of an important character in the subplot to the position of an active and even decisive participant in the main action, usually in a scene that forms the climax. A classic example occurs in *1 Henry IV*, Act 3, scene 2 when Hal makes the decision to forsake the tavern life with Falstaff to join his protagonist father in the war against the rebels. Another such transfer comes in *The Merchant of Venice*. If we take it, as I think we must, that the conflict of the protagonist Antonio with Shylock constitutes the central action, then after Bassanio's futile attempt at intervention with her money it is Portia's decision in Act 3, scene 4, to plead Antonio's cause as a lawyer that marks her shift to become the catalyst of the main plot. It is significant that in both these cases the merging of subplot and main plot forms the climax of the play. Without Hal's assistance King Henry will have serious difficulties with the rebels and will even be defeated. Without Portia's defense Antonio will lose a pound of flesh and his life. The plotting of *1 Henry IV* is tighter since the climax is engineered by the protagonist King in a complex scene in which he insures that Hal will give more than token support and will become personally engaged in the defeat of Hotspur.[27] On the other hand, Portia's decision to engage herself in Antonio's affairs is taken unbeknownst to Antonio, and thus the turning point in the solution

27.   This scene is analyzed at length in "Theme and Structure in *King Henry IV, Part 1*," which from another angle refines the analysis in "Shakespeare's Art: The Point of View."

of his affairs, although involving a decision and not an event, associates itself more closely with such climaxes as in *Much Ado* in which the turning-point event that affects the fate of the protagonist and the outcome of the play is neither instigated by nor taken part in by the unwitting central character. So, it would seem, Berowne's climactic decision to forsake his cloistered compact and openly to avow his love has a vital effect on revealing and encouraging Navarre's similar betrayal of the compact so that he can pursue the love of the Princess of France. It may be remarked that in these comedies the main plot leans more toward a framework action than does the central action of King Henry's struggle to assert his authority over the rebels.

Curiously enough, a variant on this juncture of subplot and main plot may be found in *King Lear.* If we ask who is the catalyst, who brings the catastrophe to a head in the defeat of the forces of evil, the only answer is to point to Edgar. Without his triumph in the duel with Edmund, the throne would have fallen to Edmund and an evil reign would have afflicted England. Instead, the important matter of a good succession is solved by Edgar's action. Edgar has been a figure in the underplot, of course, so that it is a powerful unifying force on the structure of the play to identify the solution of the underplot as creating in the catastrophe the solution of the main action.[28] It is no accident, then, that Edgar joins Lear's party in the third-act climactic storm scene. Although he is in disguise and fleeing for his life, he can be seen as the only hope for the cause of justice if Cordelia's invasion fails as (patriotically) it must.

This unification of main action and underplot in *King Lear,* then, is of a piece with the plotting of *1 Henry IV* and of *The Merchant of Venice.* In both these plays the subsidiary plot forsakes a supportive role and becomes a crucial part of the main plot and its outcome. In each case an independent line of the underplot is essentially concluded in order for the main plot thereafter to take over substantially the entire action. Hal brings the Gadshill

---

28. The importance of the succession to an Elizabethan audience is shown in the entrance of Fortinbras to assert his claim in *Hamlet* so that chaos will not rule as it does in the politically motivated *Gorboduc* after its catastrophe.

jest to its conclusion and at its end prepares for the wars. Portia marries Bassanio after his deserving choice of the proper casket and through Bassanio's concern for Antonio's danger leaves Belmont for Venice to rescue a man she has never met. Obviously, after these merged climaxes the subsidiary characters previously associated with the underplot have little left to do and can only exhibit themselves without affecting the main action. In *1 Henry IV* Shakespeare delicately balances the relationship of Hal and Falstaff in the wars by the splendidly conceived and executed figure of Falstaff the soldier. But though Falstaff prepares for the battle (in a manner of speaking) and partipates even to the extent of an encounter with the Douglas and then with the dead Percy, his actions have no relation to the outcome. In *The Merchant* Lorenzo and Jessica, of a subplot, become housesitters at Belmont, whereas Bassanio, in Venice, fails to buy off Shylock and so dwindles into the role of a mere spectator to Portia's solution of the enigma of the pound of flesh. The business about the ring back at Belmont, and the reaffirmed union in love of Portia and Bassanio, provide a graceful coda but can scarcely be called the dénouement even of a revived underplot.

This is Shakespeare's plotting at its best: the powerful unification of the action by the merging of main and underplot in the climax as a means of turning the play to its necessary and pleasurably anticipated dénouement.[29] Without Hal, King Henry would be killed by the Douglas. Without Portia, Shylock would bloodily carve Antonio. Without Edgar, Lear would die a defeated king, his crown to be snatched by the villain Edmund. The strength of this plotting, then, is to bring forward in the climax a new force which earlier has been only incipiently related to the central framework[30] but which will end by producing a

29. Underplot and central plot may merge in the ending, as in *The Winter's Tale*, but the structure of this play is loose since the characters of the underplot have had no part in the climax.

30. As the son of King Henry, Hal will of course be affected by the rebellion, but he deliberately removes himself from the political action of the main plot and never appears in the central action until the climactic interview with his father. Although a slight connection is established between Portia and Antonio, who by lending Bassanio money to woo her places himself in Shylock's power,

resolution that the protagonist of the main action could not have achieved by his own powers.

In his tragic climaxes Shakespeare generally followed conventional dramaturgy although he gave an ethical weight to the tragically flawed decision that was often wanting in his contemporaries and even more in his Jacobean and Caroline successors. But in comedy his varied use of climax is uniquely his own invention. Sometimes weighted toward an event and sometimes toward a decision; sometimes enacted by the protagonist either as central mover or as participant, but sometimes occurring without his knowledge or responsibility. Sometimes providing only a hint of the possibility of the dénouement solution, sometimes so obviously related that after the turning point no other resolution can be contemplated. In play after play Shakespeare exploited this comic variety according to the needs of the story and the weight of the action. The one binding factor is that the affairs of the protagonist must be altered by the event, or a decision followed by an event, and that the shape of the dénouement, the untying of the knot, must be traceable back to this climax by a line of action stemming from the structural turning point.

---

she remains in Belmont and he in Venice until the time comes to merge the two plots by her intervention.

SHAKESPEARE'S ART:
The Point of View

S HAKESPEARE'S PLAYS were plays, first and foremost. Present-
day critics, in their search for new areas of exploration, do
these plays a disservice by treating them as poems—often as if
they were extended lyric poems. Whether a play is in verse or in
prose, it is primarily a play and must conform to the laws of the
drama, not to criteria that have been set as appropriate for other
literary genres. When dramatic structure is neglected for, say, an
interest in style, criticism ceases to be dramatic criticism.

Moreover, a concern for dramatic structure acts as a check on
another troublesome habit of present-day Shakespearean criticism: the reconstruction of a play—its people and the significance of its action—either in terms of some preconceived
aesthetic theory or in terms of the critic's own ingenious sensibility. Both can be peculiarly misleading. The constant awareness
that drama imposes certain rules on literature written in its form
serves as a check upon mythic theory, or upon quite personal
sensibility, forcibly imposed from without on Shakespeare. Any
critical method that is external and not inductive runs contrary
to the truth that can be sought in Shakespeare from the evidence

From *Literary Views: Critical and Historical Essays*, ed. Carroll Camden, Rice University Semicentennial Publications (Chicago: Univ. of Chicago Press, 1964);
by permission of the publisher, © 1964 by William Marsh Rice University. All
rights reserved.

of his plays as drama. Basically, most laws of drama that are not concerned with simple stagecraft have as their object the manipulation of the audience's point of view. By its nature the drama is perhaps the most highly developed objective literary form in existence, and thus the control of the point of view is a crucial matter. The dramatist must use action as his chief means of working out his story in terms of character. For instance, he can seldom slip into narration, except at the peril of losing the interest of his audience. Even such narrative as may be required to transmit vital facts about the antecedent action—what is technically known as the exposition—cannot be managed in the playwright's own person but must come from the mouth of one or more characters. Yet the audience cannot always be immediately certain that the account these characters give is an accurate one. When dramatic persons are not mere sticks, or automatons, they participate in the nature of all humanity, the chief characteristic of which is to be fallible. Their information may not be wholly accurate; or if it is, their personal reactions may color the interpretation in a manner that should lead an audience to view the account with some caution.

Indeed, when the interpretation of fact is involved, an audience learns to be especially wary of accepting the statement of any dramatic character as infallible truth. When in the opening scene of Shakespeare's *Antony and Cleopatra* Philo and Demetrius discuss Antony's visible subjection to Cleopatra, it is important to recognize that they are Romans. Two Egyptians, like Charmion and Iras, take the opposite position. Which is the audience to believe, or should it believe neither as representing the whole truth?

The peculiar condition of the dramatic form is that the playwright must work exclusively through the words and actions of a series of fallible characters. He can never speak in his own person, else he is breaking the form. Since characters fail if they are simple authorial mouthpieces, and the play is likely to fail with them, the major dramatic problem is to convey to the audience, within the rules of the game, what the dramatist wants it to believe. Moreover, these ideas (in other words, the dramatist's point of view) must be conveyed in such a manner that the audience is unaware that it is being manipulated and directed into certain channels of belief. Today in the experimental theater a dramatist may quite deliberately refuse to impose any point of view upon the play so that the audience is a free agent and can react in whatever unpredictable and various ways it chooses. That indeed may become the very point of the play—the deliberate withdrawal of any attempt at dramatic control over the audience's reactions to, or interpretations of, the events it is watching on the stage.

The Shakespearean drama does not have a twentieth-century soul in this respect. Ordinarily, like every other Elizabethan dramatist, Shakespeare was concerned to control for his own ends the reactions of his audience. He does so, of course, in respect to the audience for which he wrote, and he usually took particular care to control its view of character and of action. Thus if we follow the various ways by which he manipulated his audience in order to maintain his control, we can come upon some useful critical insights, for we shall have clear-cut evidence about Shakespeare's conscious intentions. Surely, before a critic proceeds to unconscious intentions (important as they may be), he had better settle first what the author was consciously trying to impress upon his audience. Such information will offer a factual basis, and for this reason the dramatist's art is singularly important to construe.

The concept of the "touchstone character" is familiar as applying to persons like Enobarbus in *Antony and Cleopatra*, or Horatio in *Hamlet*, whose important function is to act as an intermediary and translator between the audience and the events of the play. For one reason or another, generally because of a belief in the soundness of their judgment, the audience comes to trust the reactions of such persons and to take its cue from them. Hamlet's praise of Horatio's stoic incorruptibility just before the play-within-a-play (3.2.59–79) assists this projection, just as the military bluntness and saltiness of his humor inspire a confidence in Enobarbus as an objective judge of events and persons who is superior to Demetrius and Philo or to Charmion and Iras.

In *Much Ado about Nothing* Don Pedro in some considerable part serves the same purpose, qualifying by virtue of his high rank and the deference he receives as a humane ruler. This being so, his approval of Claudio's public rejection of Hero at the altar should indicate to the modern critic that this exposure is not to be taken as a discreditable action that is intended to besmirch Claudio as a character.[1] That the Duke could be mistaken in believing the circumstantial evidence against Hero is a powerful factor in the audience's acceptance of Claudio's corresponding belief as something other than the reaction of a young cad.

It is a part of Shakespeare's art, and his treatment of point of view, that his most lifelike touchstone characters may be mistaken, as was Don Pedro, at some crucial point in the action, and that the audience is able to see the mistake and to disengage itself from following the touchstone character into error. As just remarked, in *Much Ado* the noble Pedro's error parallels that of Claudio and therefore takes the sting out of the younger man's faulty judgment. But the manipulation of the audience here is elementary compared to that in *Antony and Cleopatra* and in *Hamlet.*

Shakespeare reduces Antony to the lowest depth of fortune before beginning the contrary process of raising him to a generous death and to a height of humanity not previously exhibited. Antony's control over his reason, or judgment, progressively forsakes him under Cleopatra's influence. The different stages are marked by what seems to be the opposite process in Enobarbus, the breaking of his emotional attachment to Antony by the increasing alarm his judgment takes at Antony's irrational behav-

---

1. Modern critics also forget (a) that Claudio (according to his belief) was risking the settlement of his title and the honorable reputation of his family line on a bastard if he pursued the marriage; and (b) if he broke off the marriage without publicly exposing Hero, he would not only ruin his own reputation as an honorable man but also put himself in the position of being an accomplice before the fact to the same deception that Hero would inevitably practice on some other innocent young man. Thus neither Claudio nor Pedro sees anything but disaster in the concealment of Hero's assumed perfidy, and the exposure of her wantonness takes on the aspect of a public duty.

ior. The audience cannot help feeling that Enobarbus' view of Antony's political and moral degeneration is accurate and that unthinking loyalty to such self-destructiveness might indeed be quixotic.

Enobarbus' rational view of Antony's emotional plunge demands, and receives, his desertion according to a defensible code of values. Then occurs a truly amazing dramatic peripeteia, or reversal of the scale of values. Antony in defeat, at the lowest ebb of his fortunes, is personally a greater man than in his triumph; the Roman rationalization that led to Enobarbus' desertion is seen to be an inadequate guide to conduct,[2] like Octavius Caesar and his code set against a larger-souled principle in Antony. Antony the political figure is ruined, but Antony the individual holds to a scale of values that surpasses material success. In this manner he upholds the great human conquest of Fate that has always represented mankind's justification of its rationale of existence. The audience, thus, gladly forsakes the man for the master, the commentator for the true reality; and the contrast—indeed, the actual transfer of the audience's sympathies—is an important technical device in the restoration of Antony to a nobility he has progressively forsaken during the course of the play.

In a less spectacular manner something of the same sort happens in *Hamlet*. When Horatio warns Hamlet to obey the augury represented by the pain about his heart, and to decline the offered fencing match, his lack of understanding of the real issues involved serves to highlight the extraordinary importance of Hamlet's reply that penetrates to the heart of the matter: "Not a whit, we defy augury; there's a special providence in the fall of a sparrow. If it be now, 'tis not to come; if it be not to come, it will be now; if it be not now, yet it will come: the readiness is all."

It can be argued that this is a crucial decision for Hamlet; and that he makes it from a self-knowledge that he had not previ-

---

2. A shrewd audience might receive an early warning that Enobarbus was no longer entirely trustworthy as a touchstone if it recognizes that in the scene that first determines his decision—Cleopatra's reception of Thyreus-Thidias, and her acquiescence, "Mine honour was not yielded. But conquer'd merely"— he was as deceived as was Caesar's messenger about Cleopatra's real intentions.

ously possessed.[3] In short, it represents the healing of the breach between man's will and God's that had opened up in the closet-scene slaying of Polonius in mistake for the King. After this reconciliation, Hamlet can go on to his death-in-victory; and flights of angels can sing him to his rest. He has reversed his previous tragic error and has conquered his fate by reconciliation with divine purpose. This crucial decision in what is technically "the moment of final suspense" in the play is emphasized by Hamlet's rejection of Horatio's limited understanding. The contrast shows all the more the exaltation of perception that has come to him by its being set against the ordinary prudence of Horatio's advice.

The touchstone character is perhaps the most significant of a large variety of dramatic devices in which a playwright can use one character to illuminate another by word of mouth, or by the example of parallelism and contrast. Nevertheless, nothing approaches plot as a means of enforcing the dramatist's point of view. The plot of a play is that series of interconnecting incidents, or actions, by means of which the main story is presented. Plot in Aristotle's phrase is "the structure of the incidents" (*Poetics* 6.9). To Aristotle, "Tragedy is an imitation, not of man, but of an action and of life, and life consists in action, and its end is a mode of action, not a quality . . . character determines men's qualities, but it is by their actions that they are happy or the reverse. Dramatic action, therefore, is not with a view to the representation of character: character comes in as subsidiary to the actions. Hence the incidents of the plot are the end of a tragedy; and the end is the chief thing of all" (6.9–10).

If plot is indeed the end of a tragedy, then we must look to the dramatist to utilize action in contrived episodes to lead the audience to the correct understanding of his theme, or purpose, in the full plot. This view has been stated before and will be emphasized again. It is central to the theme of these essays. The working-out of the plot has various incidents that serve as stations on the way. Of all these, that incident in the plot that one

3. This interpretation is expanded in "The Moment of Final Suspense in *Hamlet:* 'We Defy Augury.'"

calls the climax, or crisis, is the most significant, for in it will reside the main action or decision that in a comedy will eventually lead the ending to come out well for the chief persons, and in a tragedy to come out ill. Since such a turning point must automatically be a significant action—else the play will be trivial, or quite meaningless—it behooves a critic to isolate this episode from the surrounding incidents of the plot. Once this crisis incident can be identified, the major significance of the plot may be determined and an important part of the total meaning of the play thereby assessed.

Long ago Aristotle evolved the doctrine of the tragic flaw in a man of moderate virtue as the central means by which the catharsis, or emotional response of the audience to the tragic outcome, could be controlled. Whether Shakespeare knew Aristotle is not perhaps demonstrable. But the point is unimportant, because Aristotle was merely codifying the dramatic practice he had observed, and such a psychological requirement in the manipulation of the audience is universal. Indeed, the Renaissance drama of Shakespeare and his contemporaries had a strong impulse to intensify the Aristotelian tragic flaw by associating it with the Christian doctrine of personal responsibility for actions, a concept that stems from the belief in the significance of free will,[4] and hence one that sometimes was far removed from the Greek spirit. For instance, if the climax of *Hamlet*—the mistaken slaying of Polonius—were only a piece of bad luck, the sort of joke the gods like to play on mankind, the play means one thing. On the other hand, if it were a morally determinate decision for Hamlet to kill what he thought was the King behind the arras, the whole action of the play, and especially the catharsis at its conclusion, means something quite different. I have already hinted at what I take to be the point of personal responsibility in the climax and its resolution—the setting-up of human will in opposition to divine will, the resulting tragic error, and the

4. By "personal responsibility" I mean the Elizabethan concept that all decisions governing action in this life have a significance for one's fate in the next world; and therefore that mankind's free will places upon him the sole responsibility to choose correctly between good and evil, for more is at stake than the immediate result of the action concerned.

reconciliation at the end when divine will is accepted. But this is a complex matter, and will be best treated at length in another essay.[5]

Instead, let us take another typical Shakespearean climax, that in *Antony and Cleopatra*. If one searches for that incident to which the fatal conclusion by cause and effect inevitably reverts, there is only one answer. The loss of Actium was the loss of Egypt, certainly, but the outcome of Actium could be prophesied, in a meaningful universe, after the scene in which, against the advice of all his followers, Antony was ruled by Cleopatra and decided to fight at sea. The seventh scene of the third act therefore represents the climax, or crisis, since in this scene the fatal decision was reached to fight from weakness rather than from strength.

The question arises immediately: why was not Antony's desertion in pursuit of Cleopatra during Actium the truly decisive action, for we are told that up to that time Antony seemed to have perhaps a slight advantage in the battle? The answer involves the true nature of climax, which in Shakespearean tragedy is usually the episode that shows us the decision. The fatal action may follow immediately, as it does in *Hamlet*, or be somewhat delayed, as in *Antony and Cleopatra*. But the moral responsibility of the decision itself is overriding. It is overriding because, in the Christian terms that Shakespeare perforce utilized, arbitrary action is meaningless without moral determinism. Motivation alone provides the magic significance for actions; otherwise, Christian free will and the personal responsibility for deeds could not exist. Motivation is the reason, or cause, why men behave as they do in specific incidents. When the actions in this world have a crucial bearing on one's actions in the next, a degree of responsibility for choice is felt in Christian literature that is alien to the Greek. If responsibility for action is so weighty, then the causes for action come under scrutiny as being in the highest degree significant. To the Christian, certainly, motivation was the key to action and to its reward or punishment by the rules of the land as well as those of the spirit. Christian tragedy, therefore, put its

5. Especially in "Hamlet as Minister and Scourge," and also in "The Death of Hamlet: A Study in Plot and Character."

weight largely on the effects of premeditation, for conscious choice alone had a major religious meaningfulness. Premeditation means decision, and therefore significant motivation leading to morally determinate action.[6]

These considerations dictate the choice of the seventh scene in Act 3, where the fatal decision is made. The play itself indicates the relative importance. Antony's flight in battle was quickly narrated by an onlooker. But the decision to fight this battle at sea is carefully prepared. Antony's subjection to Cleopatra has led to his desertion of his wife and to an attempt to split the Roman Empire by setting Cleopatra up as Empress of the East with himself as Emperor. That Cleopatra has been urging Antony to fight at sea is clear from her opening words to Enobarbus in this seventh scene, upbraiding him for his remark (apparently in some council) that it was not fit for Cleopatra to be in the wars. She warns him she will not stay behind. Antony, entering, announces they will fight by sea, a statement immediately applauded by Cleopatra. Against the protests of Canidius, Enobarbus, and finally the Soldier, Antony stubbornly adheres to his plan without giving any reasons.[7] Canidius, after Antony's departure, correctly assigns the cause:

> his whole action grows
> Not in the power on't: so our leader's led,
> And we are women's men.

These lines concentrate the various references in the play to Antony's effeminacy in allowing Cleopatra to dictate his course of life while he sinks in pleasure and his political powers melt

6. I draw this most useful phrase from Elder Olson, *Tragedy and the Theory of Drama* (Detroit: Wayne State Univ. Press, 1961), pp. 37–41. Actually, Olson's statement is, "Plot is a system of actions of a morally determinate quality," and he regards the phrase as a generalization of Aristotle's *spoudaios*. I am, perhaps, applying the sense more narrowly than he would approve. The application of moral determinism to tragedy is discussed more fully in "Dramatic Structure and Criticism: Plot in *Hamlet.*"

7. The closest he comes to an explanation is that he can conquer by land if defeated at sea. The wholesale desertion of his forces after Actium exposes the speciousness of this argument.

away. Insofar as this effeminacy in accepting female rule results from the force of his passionate attachment to Cleopatra, the results to the Elizabethans exemplify the conquest of reason by emotion, or passion, what they called the will. To this rich theme is appended the parallelism of the conflict of East and of West, Egypt and Rome, the pleasure versus the rational or governing principle, the male versus the female position in the chain of being, and much else, so that the effect of this personal decision is given a peculiar significance by the vastness of its setting and the complexity of its moral and psychological texture. The emphasis, it is clear, is not really on a mistaken military decision. Shakespeare has made it evident that Antony knows beforehand the decision is a wrong one, and yet he embraces it and persists against all opposition because he has set his will over his reason and is a woman's man who has allowed Cleopatra to have the decisive voice in a matter in which he, not she, was competent. In doing so, he has abnegated the responsibility of his generalship and therefore deserves defeat. The decision itself, viewed externally, is of comparatively small importance. It might have been made for the best of motives, whereupon a defeat would have had no more significance than that inherent in the medieval moralizing of a fall from high to low estate. But when made for faulty motives, as the result of a tragic flaw in character that affects the power of choice, the motivation is everything, the action is morally determinate, and on it hinges the tragedy.

Nevertheless, Actium is not wholly inevitable although its ill success has been abundantly prophesied. We must not forget that *Antony and Cleopatra* is in some sense a double tragedy, and that the fatal decision did not originate with Antony. What leads Cleopatra to demand her part in the wars? It is not enough to aver, as she does, that she is paying for the military preparations and so should have a voice. It is not enough that Octavius has declared war against her personally, and not directly against Antony. The key is that she "will appear there [in the wars] for a man." If Antony is portrayed as increasingly effeminate as his reason is buried under his passions, so Cleopatra is shown as increasingly masculine. It is not entirely a good joke that she swaggers about wearing Antony's sword "Philippan" when he has been drunk to bed and decked in her clothing. She has always used domination as her weapon to keep him in her toils, and she knows no other method.[8] After her experience when Antony was absent in Rome, she will allow him no course of action apart from her. To the Elizabethans brought up to believe in the hierarchical tradition of womanly obedience to male authority, Cleopatra has stepped out of her proper sphere, and her hubris in insisting on acting the male part was so athwart Nature as to demand punishment. Deficiency is the fault of Antony, excess that of Cleopatra. Equal guilt on the part of both protagonists, then, lies in their reversal of the roles intended by Nature to man and woman. Without true experience, Cleopatra is playing at being an Amazon Queen. She is so little prepared for the realities that accompany her play-acting that she turns Egyptian woman in the battle, doffs the masculine responsibilities that she had usurped, and flees in fear, "the breeze upon her, like a cow in June."

In reverse, therefore, Cleopatra repeats Antony's error in allowing her passion, or desires, to overcome her reason, thereby to assume command in a project for which she was not fitted, and finally to turn female coward when her hubris falters. This double error sums up to perfection the whole enveloping relationship of these two people both to each other throughout the play and to the outside world. Each is caught in the tragic point of weakness in his character, and a decision is made that will have its inevitable outcome in defeat. In a tragic universe ruled by law, any decision made for reasons of such levity in the face of an issue of so great momentousness can only be fatal.

In *Antony and Cleopatra* the climax loads the decision with the fullest significant import, and this is suitable, and indeed necessary, for high tragedy. When the outcome is less serious, Shakespeare can direct his audience to the central theme of his play by a curious inversion of significance of the climax. For example, in the comedy *Much Ado about Nothing* the comic spirit plays with

8. See Charmion's advice to humor Antony, and Cleopatra's contemptuous rejection (1.3.6–12).

the ancient inversion of all normally expected values. The two wittiest and most intelligent people in the play—Beatrice and Benedick—have the least self-knowledge of anyone except perhaps Dogberry, and a relatively stupid villain has the most. Thus these two smart people utterly mistake their true emotions both in themselves and in the other.

Nothing in this play works out as it should. What any audience would expect to be the main line of the counteraction, Don John's feeding of Claudio's jealousy of the Duke, dissolves into nothingness and leaves the villain for the moment with no plan in mind until a fresh plot is almost thrust upon him by an underling. The grave Leonato is convinced by the more volatile Antonio that Pedro is going to propose to Hero. This Leonato, as governor of the town and chief magistrate, is too preoccupied with his daughter's approaching marriage to sift Dogberry's information that would have prevented the disaster that falls upon this marriage. Benedick never does manage to fight a duel with Claudio. Nobody gets quite straight what Pedro had said to Claudio about Hero in the garden. The joke on Beatrice and Benedick is planned to culminate in a mirthful exposure of the deceit, this promised in a scene in which each will think the other in love. But no such scene ever takes place, and each falls genuinely in love with the other and reveals it almost instantly, and in private, instead of providing merriment to the onlookers.

These statements are all true, and they add up to an almost Shandyan muddle in which no expectation is ever gratified in the anticipated manner. Nevertheless, if one were to seek for the key to this comedy's inversion of life's normal values, in which wit is used chiefly for self-deception instead of enlightenment, and the more truth is sought the farther removed it is from recognition, one need only seek the climax, which should concern the major theme. Indeed it does. The requirement for a happy ending is the discovery of some concrete evidence that will clear Hero from the deceptive accusations that have been accepted as true. Hence when we search back through the plot for that scene where the vital evidence is found, we see it in Act 3, scene 3, in which the watch under Dogberry overhear the drunken boasts of Borachio. That the simplest and stupidest characters in the play stumble upon the truth[9] and that they fail to secure the hearing of the intelligent characters, who cannot be bothered to attend the narrative of these simpletons, provides us with a key action to the wryly comic theme that is more basic than any other episode in the play.

To my mind, the high point of subtlety in Shakespeare's treatment of the climax as the key to point of view appears in *1 Henry IV.* Truly, if critics had observed the implications of this scene, much misapprehension about the play would have been prevented. In terms of the plot the climax can only be Act 3, scene 2, in which, seemingly, King Henry weans Hal from his dissolute life and sets him on the road to Shrewsbury, the conquest of Hotspur, and the acceptance of his duties as Prince of Wales. By himself, it is implied, King Henry cannot subdue the rebels. By himself, Hal can have no national forces to lead. A scene of high drama can be anticipated in which the father pleads with his son to join him against a common danger: and, on the surface, Shakespeare gives us just that. The King reproves his son for his wild courses and refuses to accept Hal's submission, perhaps because he thinks it too coldly offered. Hal's formal request for pardon receives a quick "God pardon thee!" and sixty-odd lines of further reproof mixed with a lesson on kingship. Hal quietly promises to be himself, that is, to reform. But the King pushes on as if the Prince had not spoken, and delivers the ultimate insult that he really expects Hal, through fear, to join Hotspur's party against him. Stung at last, Hal forsakes his formal protestations and in an emotional speech vows to defeat Percy and reconcile himself to his father by his deeds. Immediately Henry clinches his victory with "A hundred thousand rebels die in this!   Thou shalt have charge and sovereign trust herein."

Every indication points to Henry's having prepared this interview with particular care, as was his way, leaving nothing to chance. The rising tide of his emotion, and finally the obviously

9. As Borachio bitterly recognizes when he taunts Don Pedro and the assembled company: "What your wisdom could not discover, these shallow fools have brought to light."

calculated insult at the right moment, are characteristic of his methods. Are we to believe, then, that the King has truly won over his son by this contrivance, has broken down Hal's indifference, detached him from Falstaff and the idle tavern life that was corrupting him and returned the Prince to the great world of affairs that was to be the training for the hero-king Henry V? If we are to believe so, then we must take it that a real conflict of wills was present and that it was resolved in classic fashion in a turnabout of motive and action, a true peripeteia. The King would have been right, and Hal wrong. Hal would have been convinced of the error of his ways by the force of his father's speech and would have been, in a manner of speaking, converted.

Such a scene might well have been an exciting and significant one; but Shakespeare did not write it so. The true point of this climax is that no peripeteia takes place. Hal makes no decision that he had not previously planned. With or without this scene the play would have had the same ending, for a few hours before, Hal had formally decided to reconcile himself to his father and to join in subduing the rebels.[10] There is no tug of war in which Hal is placed between Falstaff and what he represents, and King Henry and what he represents. The famous "I know you all" soliloquy, at the very beginning of the play, effectively disposes of any dramatic suspense that might have developed from a genuine inability in the Prince to make up his mind about his future. From the start of the play, therefore, Shakespeare has deliberately cast off the legitimate suspense that might have been generated by a lack of Hal's firm commitment. The soliloquy shows Hal to be plain enough. He is amusing himself for the nonce. When an emergency arises he will break through the clouds like the sun and show himself in his true majesty. He is not in the least deceived by Falstaff, nor does he have more than a partial interest in their tavern life.

I pass over the possible moral question that modern sensibility has quite wrongly raised in connection with this soliloquy. Nei-

10.   Hal to Poins at the end of 2.4: "I'll to the court in the morning. We must all to the wars." For an expanded account of this climactic scene, and a slightly modified conclusion, see "Theme and Structure in *King Henry IV, Part 1*."

ther Shakespeare nor his audience were egalitarian, nor was it demeaning to accept the fact that kings were not common men fully responsible to the ordinary law. It was a matter of decorum: kings had their own code of conduct, and the responsibility for their actions was primarily to God. We can be confident that Shakespeare would have been surprised to hear the modern denigration of Hal on the basis of this speech. It is not a character speech at all, as Kittredge has observed. Instead, it is a time-saving plot device, rather on the clumsy side, deliberately to remove from the audience any suspense that Hal was actually committed to his low-life surroundings. A comparison, indeed, may be made with the fifth soliloquy in *Hamlet,*

> 'Tis now the very witching time of night,
> When churchyards yawn, and hell itself breathes out
> Contagion to this world.

This soliloquy has no other purpose than to prevent the audience from feeling an illegitimate suspense in the closet scene that is to follow. When Hamlet promises that the soul of the matricide Nero will not enter his firm bosom, and that he will speak daggers to Gertrude but use none, he is warning the audience that he plans to take a very high line with his mother and, in effect, to frighten her into repentance—a feat that he actually performs. But the audience must not fear for the Queen's life no matter how violently he behaves.[11]

When a playwright deliberately throws away dramatic suspense, one of his main stocks in trade, it is well to look into his motives. In *Hamlet* it is clear that Shakespeare for very good reasons is determined that the audience should not take the wrong point of view about Hamlet's violent actions in the closet scene. So concerned is he with manipulating the audience to guide the reactions he wants in an episode yet to come that he is willing to sacrifice part of the superficial drama of the scene in order to emphasize to the audience the true nature of the conflict between mother and son.

Similarly, the outright manipulation of the audience was a ne-

11. Analyzed in "Hamlet's Fifth Soliloquy."

cessity in *1 Henry IV.* The standard pattern of the plot would have produced a Prince Hal more acted upon than acting himself. Suspense would have developed from his indecision before the three ways of life open to him, each with its separate and conflicting ideals. Then in the climax he would have brought the play to a successful conclusion with his victory at Shrewsbury. This is a possible plot, but it is not Shakespeare's. Recent critics are so occupied with abusing Hal as a cold-blooded prig that they fail to see what Shakespeare was in fact trying to convey in his shaping of the action into a plot. What kind of a play is it in which the Prince from the start reveals to the audience his whole future course of action and therefore destroys the pleasurable uncertainty the audience would feel in the development of the suspense and its resolution? What kind of a play is it in which, faced with three laws of life, Hal chooses all, and none? What kind of a play is it in which the climax goes through all the motions of a decision, but no decision is actually made, for none is needed?[12]

The answer is an obvious one. This is a play about a future hero-king who rose far above ordinary humanity. As in the old fairy tale of the Bear's Son, this future hero had a wild and careless youth, which Shakespeare is concerned to rationalize.[13] We could scarcely expect him to take personally the primitive beef-and-blood picture of Hal in *The Famous Victories.* Hal is to rise superior to the Machiavellian kingship of his father, even though Henry's policy was aimed at a strong central monarchy that any Tudor subject knew was absolutely required for peace and stability. He is to rise superior to Hotspur's narrow chivalric code of honor based on the outmoded feudal ideals that could become a force for evil when used without intelligence. Moreover, the practical value of these ideals was being made obsolete by the nascent central royal authority. He is to rise superior to the chaotic forces of the self-seeking pleasure that denies responsibility in favor of hedonism, as embodied in Falstaff. Three principles of

12. Actually some decision *is* made, for which see "Theme and Structure," which takes a less simplified view.

13. If anything, Shakespeare shows Hal revolting against the principles of his father and dissociating himself from them by his refusal to join in the court life. This is, in brief, the rationalization of Hal's low-life career.

self-seeking are portrayed in this play, each trying to control the future king.[14]

Shakespeare's difficulty in some part resembled that of Milton in *Samson Agonistes* in that his hero can demonstrate superiority for most of the play only by endurance in the rejection of false values offered to tempt him—that is, by a refusal to be acted upon from without—until the time comes for his own positive individual action that cuts the knot and resolves the whole dramatic problem. Once we learn to read the plot, we see what Shakespeare intends to convey to us through the action. Indeed, he was so concerned to insure the audience's point of view that he ventured in the "I know you all" soliloquy to erect the plainest signpost he could contrive. He thereby tried to avoid the confusion that would have lain in any suspense about Hal's future course. In the action he deliberately shows Hal as a committed man biding his time. The time comes, and Hal makes his anticipated move toward the life of superior glory that lay ahead for him. King Henry may think he has converted his erring son, but Shakespeare tells us the contrary in his plot. That the climax is no climax, in respect to any decision not made before, should alert us to Shakespeare's clear intentions. Hal is his own man, and as his own man he chooses his own course of action in his own way. He is not influenced in any manner by the attempts of others to engage him, because from the start he knows the synthesis that lies ahead for him in the ideals of kingship, chivalry, and the proper use of materialism. This is what Shakespeare tells us through the plot, and we should pay attention to its evidence.

These are examples from three plays of Shakespeare's methods of guiding the audience to a specific point of view when, in his opinion, an exactness of response is necessary, and he cannot trust to the normal trial-and-error dramatic method in which an audience evaluates the dozens of small pieces of conflicting evi-

14. In this sense Falstaff and his crew represent in concentrated form the commons, which are antigovernment, since their duty is to be governed, generally contrary to their true desires. Thus they avoid responsibility as much as possible and concentrate on their private concerns. Hotspur allows his feudal ideals to overcome his patriotism; the commons are, in their own self-seeking way, equally unpatriotic.

dence and comes to a generally anticipated collective judgment. It is obvious that something important is at stake when Shakespeare uses extraordinary methods to manipulate the audience's point of view, and that critics need to inquire into these circumstances. By evidence of such nature we can demonstrate Shakespeare's conscious intentions and in some part pull back the veil from the concealed figure of the dramatist, who is the despair of the critic seeking after a certainty that the dramatic form must usually hide.

SHAKESPEARE'S
DRAMATIC
VAGUENESS

A S EVERY DRAMATIST MUST, Shakespeare ordinarily is careful
to guide his audience to the point of view that should be
taken by any audience about his action and characters. We are
well aware that Iago is not the hero of *Othello*, and we come to
see that Richard II fails in his kingly duties. In *The Winter's Tale*
Leontes is not a long-suffering abused husband. In *Much Ado
about Nothing* wit may conceal a comic lack of self-knowledge. Yet
at the opposite pole, Shakespeare may refuse to provide the normal guideposts to assist an audience in its interpretation of the
action. This occasional Shakespearean vagueness, as it may be
called, is calculated, we may be sure; and it is a strength, not a
weakness, when its purpose is understood. If, then, Shakespeare
consciously employs dramatic vagueness in order to secure a special effect not obtainable by normal means, as critics we should
be aware of the device and be prepared to evaluate its purposes.

I do not wish to suggest that vagueness can be more interesting than precision because it leaves room for an argument that
can never be entirely resolved. But I certainly do suggest that in
some special circumstances there is a danger in over-precision.
Immediately, we come bolt against the quite proper concept that

From *The Virginia Quarterly Review* 39 (Summer 1963); by permission of the
editor.

life in art is not life in the world. The function of art, however, is not to put order into chaos; on the contrary, in a meaningful universe (which art must assume) the problem is, instead, to discern and to grasp the order that actually exists in life concealed under the specious appearance of lack of order or, at the best, of neutrality. Whatever artistic validity may inhere to present theories of naturalism or existentialism, they do not apply to Shakespeare and the world of the Renaissance, which had a passion for order and a universally credited system for its structure and maintenance. In all essential matters, therefore, we must never expect Shakespeare suddenly to withdraw from the dramatic responsibility of imposing artistic order on the raw and seemingly disorderly materials of actual life. In *Macbeth*, or in *Othello* he does not obscure the issues or falsify the sentiments we may justly feel in respect to the action and the characters who embody it. And even in *King Lear*—the greatest portrayal of the unleashed forces of evil that he ever attempted—the universe eventually rights itself from the staggering impact of the powers of darkness, and the play can legitimately end in a hard-won peace (though close to exhaustion) and even in the reconciliation of men to the unseen but orderly purposes of the universe.

Nevertheless, the overall world of order that Shakespeare understands and portrays is not without its mysteries, chief of which is the human heart. By common consent, Shakespeare observed and conveyed his understanding of a larger part of the varied human condition than any other writer who has come down to us. It is amazing the extent to which his observation presented with accuracy various psychological aberrancies to which only recently we have been able to assign analytic names after clinical case-history study. But his comprehensiveness does not mean that in any matter he was so omniscient that he could have offered a detailed and precise analysis if closely questioned by a present-day critic. Milton's Adam, in the opinion of God, correctly analyzed the nature of the various beasts by assigning to them their correct names. However, there comes a point for each writer when observation outstrips not the emotional understanding but that analytic understanding that can place a name to an experience and thereby categorize it. The ability to name, or to assign to categories, often evinces a comprehension of a phenomenon that results only from an analysis that may sometimes be highly technical.

For some parts of *Hamlet*, in various respects the most mysterious and perpetually intriguing of all his plays, Shakespeare's observation and emotional comprehension were sufficient. We may be sure that he had never heard of the Oedipus complex; on the other hand, it is clear according to present-day knowledge that Shakespeare deliberately portrayed a Hamlet whose feeling about his mother was not cast in an everyday mold. Yet I find objectionable the sexual symbolism in the closet scene that Laurence Olivier in the film directed to Gertrude's bed. Partly my feeling is based on the distortion that results from pouring the new wine of sophistication into old bottles; partly because in Shakespeare's day a closet was not a bedroom, and it is evident from the text that Gertrude should be sitting in a chair during this scene.

The mystery of Hamlet goes deeper than an Oedipus complex, however. Analysis in dramatic terms shows us that the much-remarked delay is not actually integral in the plot. Very likely Aristotle would not have admitted it (except for the prayer scene) among the incidents making up the plot. Although delay in the revenge, for specific reasons, is built into the primitive source, Shakespeare does not utilize the source motivation. Indeed, it is interesting to contemplate that the question of Hamlet's delay seldom arose as a critical problem until the nineteenth century. Shakespeare never gives us an objective clue to this delay. Hamlet assigns various reasons for his inaction, but no audience can take them seriously as representing a correct analysis of his true motives. He is not a coward, or a peasant slave. Most of his questioning about the delay is not, in fact, analytic at all, but dramatic; that is, he gives himself the worst of motives in order, by rejecting them, to spur himself on to some positive action. Indeed, he never ends by taking such self-recrimination seriously, but casts it off.

Before we attempt a partial answer to this puzzle, let us look at another play in which the facts of human motive are also concealed in part. When we come to judge certain key episodes in

Cleopatra's conduct, it becomes evident that Shakespeare has left many questions open to surmise. Was the exposure of the withheld treasure by Seleucis a put-up job between the Queen and her loyal servant, aimed at convincing Caesar she wanted to live, whereas, in fact, she was seeking only such relaxation in surveillance as would enable her to choose her death? Or was the treasure hoarded by a guilty woman intent on living under almost any circumstances, according to the odds of the moment? Or was it the action of a woman so accustomed to trickery and playing both ends against the middle that it was a simple reflex impulse without significance for ultimate motivation? Shakespeare gives us no evidence by which one point of view can be demonstrated; nor does Plutarch, whose mention that Caesar was deceived may perhaps refer to Cleopatra's excuses but more likely to her actions after Dolabella had secretly informed her of Caesar's plans to remove her from Egypt. It is possible to hold any one of the three as part of a consistent view of Cleopatra's character.

Again, when the Egyptians deliver their ships to Caesar after pretending to row out to fight, Plutarch records the action and Antony's accusation—all of which Shakespeare dramatizes—but Shakespeare does not tell us what he did not know, whether the accusation was true. These two incidents are important to the audience's comprehension of Cleopatra's precise motives as they affect certain specific actions; but Shakespeare makes little or no attempt to direct the audience to any conclusion.

If we ask why he was content to leave these matters wide open for variable points of view, it is not enough to answer that he was merely following Plutarch. Elsewhere he is not so chary of assigning motives when Plutarch was silent: the very important explanation from Ventidius why he did not follow up his victory over the Parthians is an example. Nor was Shakespeare averse to suppressing motives that Plutarch had assigned. One illustration is Plutarch's speculation that the Soothsayer in an attempt to please Cleopatra may have warned Antony to leave Rome, although quite possibly his art had led him, instead, to the conclusion. In the play we do not see behind the action.

What we are led to believe is that as a conscious dramatic

theory Shakespeare was at times unwilling to over-simplify a complex character by assigning only a single motive for action since at best any such specification could be only limited and partial and therefore was as likely to obscure as to reveal the truth. In *Antony and Cleopatra*, I take it, the matter goes no deeper than that. Shakespeare could easily have seen some loss and no positive gain in specifying Cleopatra's innocence (or guilt) in the surrender of the fleet, an incident on which history did not rule and one in which an audience will generally incline to give her the benefit of the doubt since she makes no attempt to capitalize on the surrender.

The question of her motives and her hidden plans in the scene about the treasure is a more subtle one, and indeed at this point the calculated vagueness, or ambiguity, that Shakespeare allows to the scene is as good an indication as any that she likely did not know her own mind and had no precisely delimited objectives that could be indicated to the audience without distorting the true state of her mental ambiguity. It seems to be evident that Shakespeare felt he was creating in Cleopatra a character who was consistent to herself, and therefore believable, without the necessity of dotting every *i* and crossing every *t* that would, in the end, have resulted in a too limited view of human motive, which is seldom wholly clearcut and specific. The orderliness and complete clarity that Dryden brought to the characters of this story marked a drop in rich complexity and in trueness to life and experience, an example of art over-ordering the material of life and thereby reducing its dimensions.

We should be idolators, of course, if we did not consider the hard fact that Shakespeare was a practicing dramatist to whom aesthetic considerations were not always paramount when the whole was unaffected by his treatment of details. It will sometimes happen that he wants a particular effect but does not dare allow the audience to question it, as would inevitably happen if a precise motivation were provided, since in fact the motivation might not be equal to the demands put upon it by the effect of the scene. The exact reason why Hamlet shifts his ground and treats the ghost under the stage with remarkable levity is subject to varying interpretations that do not interfere with the highly dramatic staging of this incident. Viewed scrupulously, Hamlet's pretense of madness does not protect him, as in the old story when the murder was a public one; instead, the pretense of madness invites a most uncomfortable attention to the causes, because if these are once guessed, then Hamlet's life is in danger. The danger, indeed, is so acute that Hamlet spends much of his time preserving his safety by encouraging a multiplicity of answers to the problem. Yet Claudius' dissatisfaction with all the answers provided represents a positive danger to Hamlet. Various rationalizations have been suggested, chief among them the safety-valve hypothesis, but Shakespeare gives no hint whatsoever to motivate Hamlet's device, and Hamlet himself is silent in respect to his reasons. The oath that Horatio and Marcellus swear under conditions of great solemnity is concerned chiefly with the preservation of their secrecy about Hamlet's future mad pretenses; but so far as the plot is concerned Hamlet gains nothing by assumed madness except for the concealment of the fact of murder in the slaying of Polonius. This the plot tells us, but little else. Perhaps it is enough; and certainly few audiences are inclined to puzzle about the motivation. In such cases the proof is in the pudding: Shakespeare is willing to risk much if his gains are correspondingly great. *Hamlet* the play is the best demonstration in the whole canon that Shakespeare's art succeeded.

In *Hamlet* the question, I take it, is slightly different from that in *Antony and Cleopatra* in that Shakespeare seems deliberately to have used vagueness as a dramatic device to maintain interest, and even realism, in a complex character whose every motive he could scarcely be expected to clarify by precise explication. If it is not *lèse-majesté*, I might even suggest that though Shakespeare seems himself to have comprehended Hamlet in the large as a character, since the result certainly gives us satisfaction, nevertheless such total general comprehension need not imply Shakespeare's own ability to write an expository essay that in detail would "explain" in a manner that would end all further curiosity the puzzling features that have been found in the play and its central character.

If, as some critics have asserted, Hamlet honestly does not know why he cannot bring himself to revenge before the quick action of the closet scene, Shakespeare had the choice of objectively presenting his character and his bewilderment, quite without comment, or of assigning such specific reasons as the audience would accept. I suggest that in some respects Hamlet as a character was as much a surprise to Shakespeare as he still is to us today, and that it is a fallacy to suppose that an author can ever be completely omniscient about the characters whom he creates. This fallacy is behind the theory—generally held by impatient pragmatists accustomed to dealing with tangible evidence—that all one has to do to determine the meaning of a book is to ask the author. It is true that not all authors are so elusive in explicating their works as Mr. T. S. Eliot, who has raised the cat-and-mouse technique of answering to a fine art. Yet his principle is sound, even though he carries its practice to extreme lengths. That is, human motive can seldom be reduced to a formula that can be neatly wrapped up and packaged as definitive explication. It is quite possible, and even probable, that in the creation of complex literature an author's observation—his intuitions and instincts, even—can outstrip his analytical understanding. In such cases any author's attempt to satisfy the public demand to explain what his work really means, in detail, will not only be unsatisfying as literary criticism but often truly destructive of the implicit meanings, the half-lights, the contrasts, the intuitions, whether recognized or not, that he has put into the creation of the work. An author does not necessarily see a character or a situation in the white glare of the clinical arc-light that reveals every detail in stark outline. He is not writing case-histories, but is recreating life as he has seen and felt it with what understanding is possible for mortal man. The act of creation is the act of giving some tangible form to a mystery without losing its essential nature. Half-lights and shadows, much feeling rather than all thought, are inevitable, or the mystery comes apart like a corpse dissected as a demonstration in the operating-theater.

Quite evidently, Shakespeare found the precise and limited motivation for Hamlet's delay as offered in Belleforest unsuited not only to his more complex situation but indeed impossible once the murder of the elder Hamlet was changed to a secret crime. Quite evidently, Shakespeare himself must have had more of an idea than Hamlet reveals in his several attempts at self-analysis, why a man like Hamlet found difficulty in committing a premeditated and cold-blooded murder. There are, of course, numerous technical dramatic reasons, divorced from all considerations of character, why an instant revenge cannot be taken, including the prime fact that there would have been no problem and no play. Yet over and above all knowledge that analysis can recover—and critics in their analyses have gone a considerable way into certain areas of truth—there is still a mystery in the human heart that defies exact analysis except in clinical, not in dramatic, terms. Any critic who thinks he has found the whole answer to Hamlet's madness or to his delay—the ultimate truth about the play—knows more than Shakespeare did, I am sure. Nevertheless, I have suggested that although Hamlet never gives any reason for his delay that we can trust, it would be an anomaly if Shakespeare had not had some private notions about the matter, even though—in the nature of the case—we cannot expect them to have been either wholly explicit, comprehensive, or exhaustive. That he never allowed these to come out, except implicitly in certain features of the plot where motivation could not be concealed, shows his dramatic wisdom. Any reason that could satisfy an inquirer would be so limited as to be basically untruthful.

It would have a further danger, however. So long as a mystery holds—if it is an authentic, living, breathing mystery—critics, readers, and playgoers will remain interested in its presence. Here we have Shakespeare's calculated policy of dramatic vagueness: the complete refusal to attempt to manipulate the audience's point of view about Hamlet's delay beyond establishing the obvious fact that he is neither knave nor fool. Any answer that suggested a reason could in the nature of the case be a limited and imperfect answer; but it would be seized on, in lieu of a better, as affording the satisfaction of normal curiosity about motive. (This is what happens in *Der Bestrafte Brudermord*, which completely rationalizes the situation.) When curiosity is satiated, the mystery appears to be solved and the matter can be dismissed from one's mind. It is no longer a problem. We *know* why Hamlet delayed. There were too many guards about the King, or Hamlet was so congenitally a man of thought that action was impossible, or any other basically nonsensical, because incomplete, interpretation. When any explanation that might be offered in concrete terms would be only partially true but would serve to quench the audience's curiosity about human motives, a dramatist is well advised to refuse to specify. Shakespeare did not confine his dramatic vagueness to *Hamlet*. It will be found in every one of his tragedies in greater or lesser degree once one recognizes it for what it is, as, for instance, in Edmund's unmotivated delay in disclosing his order to kill Lear and Cordelia although he is repentant and designs to save them. Had Othello seduced Bianca, or is the suspicion only a product of Iago's tainted imagination?

Isolation of Shakespeare's deliberate vagueness when treating large issues of human conduct will not spoil the game of speculation, necessarily, but it may in some part narrow the rules by emphasizing that there is no magical formula that—if we could only once grasp it—would in some miraculous manner really "explain" Hamlet, or Lear, or Othello, or Iago, or Cleopatra, and so satisfy us as to what Shakespeare really meant. We know, indeed what Shakespeare meant us to know in every play. When it is important to him to control our reactions and to confine us to a definite if limited point of view about an episode or a character, on the evidence he does so. Of this there can be no doubt. The evidence is too profuse, and often too obvious, to question. Indeed, his usual practice is to exercise a constant control over the audience's point of view. But when the complexity rises, so will the dramatic vagueness as Shakespeare enters into areas where his observation and imaginative intuition can form coherent patterns that have remained permanently satisfying by the very reason that they are not subject to the stultifying results of limited explanations. It is a sentimental view that thoughts exist too deep for words. But it is not sentimental to assert that some thoughts exist too deep for what may be called exposition. Imaginative recreations and factual completeness capable of detailed explication are not necessarily antagonistic but they are not natural bedfellows. There still remains more mystery in heaven and in earth than Philosophy, natural or divine, can pinpoint.

HAMLET AS MINISTER
AND SCOURGE

W HEN HAMLET is first preparing to leave his mother's chamber after harrowing her to repentance, he turns to the dead body of Polonius:

> For this same lord,
> I do repent; but heaven hath pleas'd it so,
> To punish me with this, and this with me,
> That I must be their scourge and minister.
> I will bestow him, and will answer well
> The death I gave him.   (3.4.172–77)

These provocative, if not enigmatic, lines have received comparatively small attention. In my opinion they contain perhaps the clearest analysis Hamlet makes of his own predicament, and are therefore worth a scrupulous enquiry.

The Furness Variorum quotes Malone's paraphrase, "To punish me by making me the instrument of this man's death, and to punish this man by my hand." This is surely the literal meaning of the first lines. Going beyond Malone by seeking the nature of Hamlet's punishment, both Dover Wilson and Kittredge agree

From *PMLA* 70 (1955): 740-49.

that "To punish me with this" means, substantially, that Hamlet perceives his secret will be revealed to Claudius, with serious consequences to himself. Kittredge writes, "the King will at once perceive that he killed Polonius by mistake for him, and will take measures accordingly." And Dover Wilson (quoting "This man shall set me packing"): "The death of Polonius has placed Hamlet within the power of the King."

This view is only superficially plausible, and it should not satisfy as offering the complete, or even the true, interpretation. The reason for Heaven's punishment is left unexamined, and no account is taken of the close syntactical relationship between the first statement about the double punishment, and the second, "That I must be their [i.e., Heaven's] scourge and minister."

For a moment let us look at this second statement. Kittredge comes near to the meaning: "heaven's scourge (of punishment) and heaven's agent—minister of divine retribution." This implies a difference between a scourge and a minister, that is, between an instrument of punishment and one of divine retribution; but how retribution differs from punishment is not indicated, nor is the question considered why Hamlet describes himself in both capacities.

In cases of doubt it is always well to work back through the text. "For this same lord, I do repent." In spite of whatever callousness Hamlet exhibits in "Thou wretched, rash, intruding fool, farewell!" and in "I'll lug the guts into the neighbour room," or in "Safely, stow'd," his stated repentance must be based on more than merely practical considerations that now the hunt will be up. Although Polonius' folly has been punished by Hamlet, yet an innocent man has been killed, and Hamlet has stained his hands in blood, without attaining his main objective. His attempt at revenge has led him to commit a murder which he had never contemplated. A modern audience is less likely to feel the horror of Polonius' death than an Elizabethan, which would have known from the moment the rapier flashed through the arras that Hamlet was thereafter a doomed man. On the Elizabethan stage, blood demanded blood; and at the most only two or three tragic characters who draw blood for private motives survive the dénouement, and then only at the expense of a retirement to the cloister for the rest of their lives.[1]

Hamlet, no bloody madman, may well repent that he has killed an innocent person. This mistake does not excuse him. Elizabethan law, like ours, was very clear that if by premeditation one kills, but accidentally mistakes the object and slays the wrong man, the case was still premeditated murder in the first degree, not manslaughter.[2]

Hamlet repents at the personal level, yet adds, "but heaven hath pleas'd it so,   to punish me with this." There are two implications here. First, Hamlet recognizes that his repentance cannot wash the blood from his hands, and that he must accept whatever penalty is in store for him. Second, the "this" with which he is punished is certainly the body of Polonius, and thus the fact of murder, carrying with it the inevitable penalty for blood. To view heaven's punishment as no more than the exposure of Hamlet's intents to Claudius, so that the revenge will thereafter be made more difficult, is a shallow concept which ignores the blood that has just been shed in defiance of divine law. I am concerned that the primary implication be made clear: Hamlet feels that it has pleased Heaven to punish him with the central fact of murder and one that bore no relation to his mission of justice; moreover, that he has killed the wrong man is an essential part of this punishment.

If Heaven's punishment is taken merely as the revelation of Hamlet's secret to Claudius, with all the consequences that are sure to follow, the punishment would have been comparatively mild, for the play-within-a-play had already effectively revealed Hamlet to Claudius, as well as Claudius to Hamlet. If we carefully follow the implications of the action within the setting of the time-scheme, it is clear that immediately following the mousetrap, and before the killing of Polonius, Claudius has seen Hamlet's murderous intents and has set on foot a plot to kill him.

1. As in Marston's *Antonio's Revenge* and Fletcher's *Bloody Brother.* See also my *Elizabethan Revenge Tragedy* (Princeton: Princeton Univ. Press, 1940), pp. 11–12, 39–40.

2. *Elizabethan Revenge Tragedy*, p. 9.

When first conceived after the eavesdropping on Hamlet and Ophelia in the nunnery scene, the English voyage was an innocent expedient to get a peculiarly behaving Hamlet out of the country, perhaps to his cure. However, it becomes a murderous scheme immediately after the play-within-a-play when Claudius changes the ceremonious details and plans to send Hamlet away in the same ship with Rosencrantz and Guildenstern, a necessary factor for the altered commission ordering Hamlet's execution in England. No hint is given that Claudius has altered the original commission in the short interval between the Queen's announcement of Polonius' death and the appearance of Hamlet before him for questioning, nor would there have been time. We learn only that Polonius' death must expedite Hamlet's departure; and hence we are required to assume that the discussion of the commission immediately following the mousetrap play involved what we later learn to have been the important change commanding Hamlet's death. Viewed in this light, the dead body of Polonius cannot punish Hamlet by revealing his secret to Claudius, for that has previously been revealed, and Claudius has already set on foot a lethal plot to dispose of his stepson.

Of course, Hamlet does not know of the change in the purport of the commission, it might be argued. But it would be most difficult to argue that Hamlet was not quite aware that in stripping the truth from Claudius by the doctored-up *Murder of Gonzago*, he had simultaneously revealed himself. The circumstances and language of the play were too damning for him to think that more than the facade of pretense could stand between him and Claudius after that episode. Hence I take it that the conventional interpretation of Hamlet's words ignores their deeper religious significance, and offers only a meaningless redundancy as a substitute.

> *but heaven hath pleas'd it so,*
> *To punish me with this, and this with me,*
> *That I must be their scourge and minister.*

We may paraphrase thus: Heaven has contrived this killing as a means of punishing us both and as a means of indicating to me that I must be its scourge and minister.

One need only dig down to this bare meaning to reveal how little the basic ideas have really been explained. Three difficult questions immediately assert themselves. Why was Heaven punishing Hamlet by making him the instrument of Polonius' death? Why does this punishment place him in the position of scourge and minister? What is the difference, if any, between scourge and minister. These are best answered, perhaps, in inverse order. The standard religious concept of the time was that God intervened in human affairs in two ways, internally and externally. Internally, God could punish sin by arousing the conscience of an individual to a sense of grief and remorse, which might in extraordinary cases grow so acute as to lead to madness. Externally, God worked through inanimate, or at least subhuman objects, through the forces of Nature, and through the agency of human beings. God's vengeance might strike a criminal by causing a sudden and abnormal mortal sickness, by sinking him in a squall at sea, by hitting him over the head with a falling timber, by leading him accidentally into a deep quicksand or unseen pool. The Elizabethans, if there was any suspected reason, were inclined to see God's hand in most such accidents. But sometimes Heaven punished crime by human agents, and it was standard belief that for this purpose God chose for His instruments those who were already so steeped in crime as to be past salvation. This was not only a principle of economy, but a means of freeing God from the impossible assumption that He would deliberately corrupt innocence. When a human agent was selected to be the instrument of God's vengeance, and the act of vengeance on the guilty necessitated the performance by the agent of a crime, like murder, only a man already damned for his sins was selected, and he was called a scourge.[3]

Any man who knew himself to be such a scourge knew both his function and his fate: his powers were not his own. Taking the long view, no matter how much he could glory in the triumphs of the present, his position was not an enviable one. Any human agent used by God to visit wrath and to scourge evil

---

3. Roy Battenhouse, *Marlowe's "Tamburlaine"* (Nashville: Vanderbilt Univ. Press, 1941), pp. 13–15, 108–13.

by evil was already condemned. This idea is clearly stated at the end of John Fletcher's *Maid's Tragedy*:

> *on lustful kings*
> *Unlook'd-for sudden deaths from God are sent;*
> *But curs'd is he that is their instrument.*

When Hamlet called himself a scourge of Heaven, it is inconceivable that the Elizabethan audience did not know what he meant, and that Hamlet did not realize to the full what he was saying.

Although some writers, as in Fortescue's translation *The Forest*,[4] used scourge and minister interchangeably, there was a general tendency to distinguish them. The references in the concordance show, for our purposes, that Shakespeare always means minister in a good sense unless he specifies that the minister is of hell. A minister of God, in contrast to a scourge, is an agent who directly performs some good. In this sense, heavenly spirits are ministers of grace, as Hamlet calls them. The good performed by a human minister, however, may be some positive good in neutral or in good circumstances, or it may be some good which acts as a direct retribution for evil by overthrowing it and setting up a positive good in its place. The distinction between minister and scourge, thus, lies in two respects. First, a retributive minister may visit God's wrath on sin but only as the necessary final act to the overthrow of evil, whereas a scourge visits wrath alone, the delayed good to rest in another's hands. To take a rough and ready example, the hunchbacked Richard III was thought of as a scourge for England, the final agent of God's vengeance for the deposition and murder of the anointed Richard II; but the good wishes of the ghosts before the final battle make young Henry Richmond—the future King Henry VII—in Raleigh's description, "the immediate instrument of God's justice," that is, a minister who will bring to a close God's wrath by exacting public justice in battle on the tyrant Richard, this triumph to be followed by a reign of peace and glory under the Tudor dynasty. In the second respect, as a contrast to the evil and damned scourge, if a minister's duty is to exact God's punishment or retribution

---

4. See Battenhouse, p. 13, for a typical quotation.

as an act of good, his hands will not be stained with crime. If in some sense he is the cause of the criminal's death, the means provided him by Heaven will lie in some act of public justice, or of vengeance, rather than in criminal private revenge.

We are now in a position to examine Hamlet's "scourge and minister." We must recognize that the Ghost's command, though not explicit, was at first interpreted by Hamlet as a call to an act of private blood-revenge. Yet there is no getting around the fact that to an Elizabethan audience this was a criminal act of blood, not to be condoned by God, and therefore it represented a particularly agonizing position for a tragic hero to be placed in. If Hamlet hopes to right the wrong done him and his father, and to ascend the throne of Denmark with honor, he must contrive a public vengeance which will demonstrate him to be a minister of Heaven's justice. Yet the secret murder of his father, so far as he can see, prevents all hope of public justice; and therefore the circumstances appear to him to enforce a criminal private revenge even after he realizes that he has been supernaturally appointed as a minister. The enormous contrast between Hamlet's first promise to sweep to his revenge and his concluding, "The time is out of joint.   O cursed spite,   That ever I was born to set it right," has often been remarked, but not sufficiently against this background. Moreover, it has not been well considered that if the Ghost is a spirit of health, it could not escape from purgatory under its own volition in order to influence affairs on earth. Since divine permission alone could free the Ghost to revisit the earth, the Ghost's demand for the external punishment of Claudius, and its prophecy of the internal punishment of Gertrude, is not alone a personal call but in effect the transmission of a divine command, appointing Hamlet as God's agent to punish the specific criminal, Claudius, but to save Gertrude.

With the final line of *The Maid's Tragedy* in our ears—"But curs'd is he that is their instrument"—we may see with full force the anomalous position Hamlet conceives for himself: is he to be the private-revenger scourge *or* the public-revenger minister? If scourge, he will make his own opportunities, will revenge murder with murder, and by this means visit God's wrath on corruption. If minister, God will see to it that a proper opportunity is offered in some way that will keep him clear from crime, one that will preserve him to initiate a good rule over Denmark. This crux for Hamlet has not been really pointed up, in part because Shakespeare had no need to make it explicit for his own audience.

As a consequence, Hamlet at the start finds himself in this peculiarly depressing position. He has been set aside from other human beings as an agent of God to set right the disjointed times, and he may reasonably assume from the circumstances of the ghostly visitation that he is a minister. Every private emotion urges him to a personal revenge of blood as the only means of solving his problem, and this revenge seems enforced by the secrecy of the original crime. But if he acts thus, he will be anticipating God's will, which in its good time will provide the just opportunity. If he anticipates and revenges, he risks damnation. If he does not revenge, he must torture himself with his seeming incompetence. In moments of the deepest depression, it could be natural for doubts to arise as to his role, and whether because of his "too too sullied flesh" he may not in fact have been appointed as a scourge, in which case his delay is indeed cowardly. Finally, there arises the important doubt whether the Ghost has been a demon to delude him into damning his soul by the murder of an innocent man, or indeed an agent of Heaven appointing him to an act of justice.

With these considerations in mind, the two months' delay between the Ghost's visitation and the next appearance of Hamlet in Act 2 may seem to have more validity than certain rather bloodthirsty critics will allow. I suggest that this delay, which Shakespeare never explicitly motivates, was caused not alone by rising doubts of the Ghost, or by the physical difficulties of getting at Claudius, or by the repugnance of a sensitive young man to commit an act of murder, or by his examining the circumstances so over-scrupulously as to become lost in the mazes of thought, motive, and doubt; but instead as much as anything by Hamlet as minister waiting on the expected opportunity which should be provided him, and not finding it.[5] The strain is, of

5. Strongly corroborative is the evidence of Tourneur's *Atheist's Tragedy*, a play manifestly influenced by *Hamlet* and one that carries this situation to its logical conclusion.

course, tremendous, and it gives rise not only to his depressed musing on life and death in "To be or not to be" but also to the self-castigation of "O what a rogue and peasant slave." The corruption of the world, of men and women, and of Denmark with its interfering Polonius, its complaisant Ophelia, its traitorous Rosencrantz and Guildenstern whose loyalty has been bought away from their schoolfellow—but especially of Denmark's source of corruption, its murderer-King and lustful, incestuous Queen—seem to cry out for scourging. To satisfy at least one question, he contrives the mousetrap and secures his answer, in the process revealing himself. And immediately an opportunity is given him for private revenge in the prayer scene, but one so far different from divinely appointed public vengeance that Heaven would never have provided it for its minister, a sign that the time is not yet. He passes on, racking himself with bloodthirsty promises, and—no longer trusting to Heaven's delays—impulsively takes the next action upon himself. He kills Polonius, thinking him the King. He repents, but does not expect his repentance to alter the scales of justice. Heaven, it is clear, has punished him for anticipating by his own deed the opportunity that was designed for the future. The precise form of the punishment consists in the fact that in killing, he has slain the wrong man; and the fact that it was Polonius and not the King behind the arras is the evidence for Heaven's punishment. He has irretrievably stained his hands with innocent blood by his usurping action, and foreseeing Heaven withheld his proper victim as its punishment.[6]

As I interpret it, therefore, Hamlet is not only punished *for* the murder of Polonius but *with* his murder, since Polonius was not his assigned victim; hence this fact is the evidence for Heaven's displeasure at his private revenge. The punishment *for* the murder will come, as indeed it does: it is this incident which for the Elizabethan audience motivated the justice of the tragic catas-

6. That Heaven was behind all acts of reward or punishment is so much an article of Elizabethan tragic doctrine as to be instantly accepted at its face value by Shakespeare's audience without scrupulous inquiry into the hidden workings by which Heaven produced the results. Nor is it likely that Shakespeare

trophe and makes the closet scene the climax of the play.[7] Hamlet's words show his own recognition that he has in part made himself a scourge by the mistaken murder; and I suggest that it is his acceptance of this part of his total role that leads him to send Rosencrantz and Guildenstern so cheerfully, at least on the surface, to their doom. In his mind they are of the essence of the court's corruption under Claudius. They are adders fanged.

When next we see Hamlet, after the interlude of the graveyard scene, a manifest change has taken place. When he left for England, as shown by his "How all occasions do inform against me" soliloquy, he was still torn by his earlier dilemma of somehow reconciling the combat of his private emotions for revengeful action against the restraint of waiting on divine will. But it appears to him that very shortly Heaven reversed its course and actively demonstrated its guidance by preserving his life from the King's plot and returning him to Denmark, short-circuiting the delay of an English adventure. The conflict has certainly been resolved, and it is a different Hamlet indeed who tells Horatio that "There's a divinity that shapes our ends,   Rough-hew them how we will." He directly imputes his unsealing of the commission to heavenly prompting, and Heaven was even ordinant in providing him with his father's signet to reseal the papers. The

---

worried much about the exact method or implications of this working in the situation in question. Heaven could readily order the ironic accident which, as a punishment, placed Polonius rather than Claudius behind the arras. However, with the proviso that there is no need to believe that Shakespeare or his audience sought out the implications in full detail, it may be remarked that the action of Heaven was theologically explicable. The crucial point is the distinction between foreknowledge and foreordination. It cannot be taken that Heaven foreordained that Hamlet should disobey and impulsively attempt revenge before Heaven had provided the opportunity and means for exhibiting the act as one of justice. On the other hand, one cannot limit the knowledge of God; and thus Heaven could foresee that Hamlet would perform this action. Conditional upon this foreknowledge, therefore, Heaven orders it so that Polonius substitutes for Claudius. The actions of Heaven conditional upon God's knowledge of the future are theologically quite different from Heaven's preordination, which wills certain events to take place.

7. For an extended discussion of the climax in *Hamlet* see "Dramatic Structure and Criticism: Plot in *Hamlet*."

pirates, it is clear, were only the natural culmination of Heaven's intervention on his side to bring him back to Denmark for the long-withheld justice.

When he recapitulates his wrongs, a new and quite different item is appended. It is true that Claudius, as he says, has killed his father, whored his mother, popped in between the election and his hopes, and has even attempted Hamlet's life by treacherous device. He demands for these, "Is't not perfect conscience To quit him with this arm?" And then, significantly, he adds, "And is't not to be damn'd   To let this canker of our nature come   To further evil?" This is a note not heard before, an argument from Elizabethan common law which would be used not by a private revenger but by one seeking public vengeance and justice. It says in effect: knowing what I know now, especially in this attempt on my life, I should be an accessory before the fact, and thus equally guilty with Claudius, if by further delay I permit him to enact more crimes. I should be directly responsible for further evil effects, and therefore I must see that his crimes are stopped.

Shakespeare here, as elsewhere, gives Hamlet no precise plan. But the note of confidence, not hitherto heard, is of the utmost importance. Before, when the ways of God were not at all apparent to his mind, we had "what a rogue and peasant slave," or "How all occasions do inform against me." Now he says to Horatio, "The interim is mine," serene in trust that divine providence will guide him. Critics have noted this end to self-recrimination and conflict but have thought it odd that his confidence was based on no definite plan of action. Properly viewed, that is the precise point and it is one of supreme importance. His lack of plan and thus his insistence on providence arises from his confidence in Heaven. This is not lip-service or religious commonplace, but the very heart of the matter.

Immediately, Claudius' counterplot begins and the fencing match is arranged. Hamlet's assured feeling that he is only an instrument in the hands of God sustains him against the ominous portent of disaster that seizes on his heart. For he has learned his lesson from the results of killing Polonius. "There's a special providence in the fall of a sparrow," he says to Horatio;

"if it be not now, yet it will come"; and, finally, the summation, "The readiness is all." He is in God's hands.

From the Elizabethan point of view, divine providence works out the catastrophe with justice. The plotters are hoist by their own villainous schemes; and then, triumphantly, the opportunity is given Hamlet to kill Claudius in circumstances which relieve him from immortal penalty for blood. By stage doctrine he must die for the slaying of Polonius, and, more doubtfully, for that of Rosencrantz and Guildenstern perhaps, the first in which he was inadvertently and the second consciously a scourge; and that penalty is being exacted Since he cannot now ascend the throne over Claudius' body, all possible self-interest is removed. He has not plotted Claudius' death in cold blood, but seized an opportunity which under no circumstances he could have contrived by blood-revenge, to kill as a dying act of public justice a manifest and open murderer, exposed by the death of Gertrude, while himself suffering the pangs of death as Claudius' victim. The restitution of right lies only in him. Despite the terrible action of his forcing the poisoned cup between the King's teeth, Shakespeare takes great pains to remove the blood guilt from Hamlet by the expiation of his own death, and to indicate that the open killing was a ministerial act of public justice accomplished under the only possible circumstances.[8] Hamlet's death is sufficient to expiate that of Polonius in the past and of Laertes in the present. With Christian charity Hamlet accepts Laertes' repentance and forgiveness accompanied by the prayer that "Mine and my father's death come not upon thee" in the future life; and in turn he prays that Heaven will make Laertes free from the guilt of his own. Finally, Horatio's blessing, "Flights of angels sing thee to thy rest," are words of benediction for a minister of providence who died through anticipating heavenly justice but, like Samson, was never wholly cast off for his tragic fault and in the end was honored by fulfilling divine plan in expiatory death. In more ways than one, but not necessarily more than he meant by his prophecy, Hamlet kept his promise for Polonius, "I will answer well the death I gave him."

8.   The ethical and legal implications of this scene are surveyed in "The Death of Hamlet: A Study in Plot and Character."

HAMLET'S
FIFTH
SOLILOQUY

O F THE SOLILOQUIES IN *Hamlet*, the twelve lines at the end
of Act 3, scene 2, beginning "'Tis now the very witching
time of night" seem, on the surface, to be the least interesting.
In this brief fifth soliloquy no "philosophy" is being propounded,
no consideration of the world and its ways or of Hamlet's internal anguish is forthcoming. In the hurried action that follows on
the success of the Mousetrap stratagem, these lines (3.2.406–17)
bridge the gap between, on the one hand, Hamlet's excited dis-
missal of Rosencrantz and Guildenstern followed by his exasper-
ating encounter with Polonius and, on the other, the prayer
scene (3.3) that is prelude to the climactic closet scene (3.4).

All of the immediately preceding action has anticipated this
closet scene in which Gertrude is primed to sift her son to discover his dangerous secret. The scheme for the interview has
been set on foot before the play-within-a-play. and it is one of
the many ironies that this strand of the counter-action that is to
lead to the play's climax has automatically followed its prescribed
course as earlier planned between the Queen and Polonius,
though to Claudius the information they hopefully looked for

Reprinted from *Essays on Shakespeare and Elizabethan Drama in Honor of Hardin
Craig*, ed. Richard Horsley, by permission of the University of Missouri Press.
Copyright 1962 by the Curators of the University of Missouri.

from the interview is no longer necessary. Hamlet's secret is not now an enigma to the King.

But Claudius is the only one who has recognized the significance of *The Murder of Gonzago*. In the disorder following his retreat he has either forgotten to cancel the projected meeting between Hamlet and Gertrude or he has chosen not to expose himself to questioning by the issue of such an order. Thus the plans for what would be an essentially futile meeting go forward as originally proposed. At Gertrude's instance Rosencrantz and Guildenstern summon Hamlet, Polonius seconds them to make sure that the son will obey, and Hamlet starts toward the Queen's apartments after his short soliloquy at the end of 3.2. In the meantime Claudius has made his own plans to dispose of Hamlet. Rosencrantz and Guildenstern are commissioned for England and dismissed; and only then, when the matter is unimportant to him, is Claudius told by Polonius that Hamlet is on his way to his mother. At this crucial moment, when the slayer of the father has set in motion a plan to destroy the son, Claudius makes his last attempt to escape the consequences of his initial crime; but he fails. And, ignorant that Claudius' heart has not been softened by grace, Hamlet spares him and moves on to the interview.

In this sequence the fifth soliloquy looks both backwards and forwards. Hamlet's "Now could I drink hot blood" sums up the effect on his resolution of his success with the Mousetrap and the certainty that this has brought. These opening lines are the serious counterpart to the feverish jests with Horatio: "For if the King like not the comedy,   Why then, belike he likes it not, perdy." His bloody resolution is clearly directed against Claudius, for the interjection "Soft! now to my mother" introduces another line of thought. But his new resolution carries over into the next part of the soliloquy when he must caution himself against allowing his bloody frame of mind to influence his actions against his mother. He intends no harm to her, and only in words will he pierce her with daggers.

The first part of the soliloquy corresponds roughly to the general use made of the other soliloquies in that it opens a window into Hamlet's mind. The audience can interpret his preceding jocularity in the light of what is now revealed to be his inner seriousness, and this revealed determination will help to interpret his subsequent action in the prayer scene. In this particular respect the soliloquy looks two ways.

The remainder is of a different order, however. In a relatively crude manner the second part acts as a signpost to direct the audience to what the dramatist wants them to understand in a scene that is to follow. Such obvious manipulation is unique in the soliloquies of this play and is not characteristic of Shakespeare elsewhere, though the "I know you all" soliloquy in *1 Henry IV* is an even more egregious example of the same kind. The shift in the dramatic technique is manifest. Ordinarily the audience is given two sorts of evidence: Hamlet's words and actions in relation to other people, and (in the soliloquies) his verbalized moods and thoughts. The connection between these, the way in which they interrelate, and their significance, are left up to the audience to determine for themselves from the evidence thus dramatically presented.

On the contrary, in the second part of this soliloquy, under the palpably thin pretext of talking to himself about his future intentions, Hamlet steps out of the dramatic framework to warn the audience not to misinterpret his actions in the scene that is being anticipated. The crudeness of the device must reflect what Shakespeare felt to be an unusually urgent need to guide the audience's reactions in what was about to be presented. When a dramatist so patently refuses to allow an audience to judge a scene without special direction, he makes us curious about the danger he anticipates. Hence an investigation of the alternative may give us a valuable insight into Shakespeare's general as well as his specific intention.

For the moment let us pass by the kneeling Claudius and come to the closet scene (3.4). Mother and son are immediately embroiled in a bitter contest for domination, in which Hamlet's high words are so startling to Gertrude, accustomed to his filial respect, that she does not know how to deal with his unnatural metamorphosis. In obvious anger at his blunt attack, which operates as a refusal to hear her and thus to recognize her authority, she threatens him, "Nay, then I'll set those to you that can speak." Since she herself has been unable to "speak" to Hamlet, the "those" must be persons who will have the power to force Hamlet to hear them. We have every reason to believe that Gertrude is proposing to call in a guard which will arrest him. (That imprisonment as a public danger is a risk Hamlet runs has been emphasized shortly before, at 3.2.194–95, where Polonius in proposing the interview to Claudius has remarked casually that if Gertrude does not discover the cause of Hamlet's melancholy the King may send him to England, "or confine him where your wisdom best shall think.")

It seems evident that Gertrude has received Hamlet seated, that she has risen to her feet at his threat and taken a step towards the door, and that Hamlet has forced her back into her chair. (There is no authority for the bed that has become traditional in modern productions, nor would a bed be present in her 'closet,' or private sitting-room.) This unexpected physical violence must be made so extreme in the action as to cause her to fear for her life at the hands of an insanely antagonistic son. In her bewilderment, turning to panic, she interprets his violence as a murderous attempt on her, and abandoning all pretense of reasoning she calls wildly for help.

It is a profound irony that she is not in danger of her life. (The audience knows this secret because they have overheard Hamlet's intentions in the fifth soliloquy.) Her mistake therefore reveals the hidden presence of Polonius whom, in a final irony, Hamlet mistakes for the King. The impulsive murder seals Hamlet's own doom.[1]

It is clear that Shakespeare felt that this scene posed a real danger if the audience were permitted to be in any doubt about the outcome of the action. Obviously, the difficulty was that an unwarned audience would be as alarmed as Gertrude and would take it that Hamlet was, in fact, assaulting his mother in such a frenzy that her life was endangered; in other words, that Hamlet's control had become so shattered that an initial violent act (his thrusting her back into the chair) had opened the door to a murderous impulse.

---

1. The question of the choice that Hamlet made in killing the eavesdropper, and its tragic consequences, is worked out in "Hamlet as Minister and Scourge."

In retrospect it is easy for us to see that an audience might readily make such a mistake if Hamlet had not previously revealed that he planned to be violent in his actions, but that he had no intention of becoming a matricide and that though he would "speak daggers to her" he would "use none." Without this vital information the audience might well take it that the reaction from the success of the Mousetrap, the exasperation of dealing at this critical time with Rosencrantz, Guildenstern, and Polonius, the fixed bloody resolve, the tension from sparing the life of Claudius at prayer—all these, it might be feared, had culminated in an emotional unhinging when his mother rose from her seat to betray him to prison in his moment of triumph. The pent-up hatred for his father's murderers (for Gertrude is an accomplice, he seems to think, at least for the moment) might easily under these conditions lead him to retaliatory violence that in its consequences would go beyond his conscious intention.

If this is so, it is proper to inquire what is so wrong with such a conception that Shakespeare could not permit his audience to entertain it even for the moment that the swift action was in progress. It is, after all, inherently a situation of enormous suspense, and when a dramatist (for whom suspense is a stock in trade) deliberately keeps the audience from enjoying this uncertainty, and feels he must cut the ground out from under any such possible interpretation, he must have some powerful reason.[2] It is not enough to point out that Shakespeare scorns the sort of titillation that Beaumont and Fletcher would have enjoyed extracting from the scene. The overwrought son in frustration turning against his guilty mother is a sound enough dramatic concept. True, one part of the irony would be lost if Polonius were slain protecting a Gertrude who was in authentic peril; but

2. Just so, in the "I know you all" soliloquy, Shakespeare deliberately removes the suspense the audience would have enjoyed throughout the play if they had been permitted to feel that Prince Hal was actually uncommitted. This device should lead the critic of 1 *Henry IV* to discover what greater benefit Shakespeare had in mind for such an expensive sacrifice, as is remarked in "Shakespeare's Art" and is more minutely examined in "Theme and Structure in *King Henry IV, Part 1.*

this irony could be spared, perhaps, in the interest of the heightened drama of the scene.

The fact is that the grand design of *Hamlet* was too important to endanger by allowing the audience the normal leeway here in the interpretation of action dramatically (which is to say, objectively) presented. The Ghost lays upon Hamlet two injunctions: (1) revenge the murder; but (2) in the pursuit of this revenge do not contrive any plot against your mother (1.5.84–88). In itself the latter injunction need not have led Hamlet to a conviction of Gertrude's innocence in the murder. The Ghost could have been sparing his son the crime of matricide by reminding him of Heaven's promise to revenge all crime ("Leave her to heaven"; that is, "Vengeance is mine saith the Lord, I will repay").[3]

However, a very important statement remains. The Ghost forbids Hamlet to "taint" his mind, and he must not plan harm to his mother. The syntax is just loose enough to admit a query, but there can be little doubt that "Taint not thy mind" refers to Gertrude and not to the method of pursuing "this act" of destroying the marriage. Thus the command about Gertrude is in two parts: (1) do not allow your mind to become tainted in respect to your mother; (2) do not punish her. In conjunction with the total lack of evidence for Gertrude's complicity in the

---

3. In fact, it is not altogether certain that the Ghost is calling for blood-revenge on Claudius, even though Hamlet so interprets the injunction. *Revenge* need not be equated exactly with *blood-revenge*: for example, the English were accustomed to calling a legal suit for murder a revenge, and the public revenge against a tyrant or usurper was accounted meritorious. (See *Elizabethan Revenge Tragedy*, pp. 7–8, 36–37.) When the Ghost finally gets down to business and lays his solemn commands on Hamlet, he urges him not to allow the royal bed of Denmark to be a place for lasciviousness and incest: "But howsoever thou pursuest this act" (i.e., the cleansing of the royal couch by the separation of Claudius and Gertrude), do not harm thy mother. By implication, Claudius is not to be left to Heaven, and thus may be punished by earthly justice; but this is still a long way from any literal command to murder. That Hamlet cannot see how else to take revenge on Claudius, given the secrecy of the murder, is another matter. There is nothing in the Ghost's orders that would not be satisfied by Hamlet's exposing Claudius to legal justice or leading an armed national uprising against a murdering usurper. Private blood-revenge becomes a necessity only if these two alternatives remain blocked by the lack of demonstrable evidence.

Ghost's detailed narrative of his death, the warning not to taint his mind seemingly was intended to convey to Hamlet that his mother was not an accomplice to the murder either before or after the fact, and that he must not corrupt his mind by thinking her so.[4] Yet from 3.4.27–30 it seems possible but not certain that Hamlet had indeed gnawingly suspected his mother of prior knowledge of his father's murder.[5]

Nevertheless, at no time do Hamlet's thoughts run to matricide, and from the conduct of the action it is evident that he scrupulously tries to adhere to the Ghost's distinction between earthly justice for Claudius and heavenly for Gertrude.

The Ghost had ordered that Gertrude be left to Heaven, "And to those thorns that in her bosom lodge   To prick and sting her." Patently, the thorns represent her conscience. It follows that if these thorns rankle enough, she will be led to a repentance and a change in her life that will allow Heaven to temper justice with mercy.

Adultery was a mortal sin, and deliberate incest (even of Gertrude's form) more than its equal. If Gertrude does not repent (and repentance involves action as well as thought), her soul will be damned for eternity. The Ghost has forecast the possibility (perhaps even the start) of repentance that will enable Gertrude to throw herself on heavenly mercy instead of suffering earthly

---

4.   In this context, "Leave her to heaven" signifies that her sins of adultery and incest will be dealt with there and are not to be Hamlet's concern to punish.

5.   The lines "A bloody deed—almost as bad, good mother,   As kill a king, and marry with his brother.... Ay, lady, it was my word" are the sole evidence for Hamlet's suspicion, and it is remarkable that this is the first time the audience has been told that he has associated his mother with knowledge of the murder. The oddity of Shakespeare's withholding this information, and the fact that so little is made of it in the closet scene (even if Gertrude's reply shows Hamlet he was mistaken), leads to the query whether this accusation is not a spur-of-the-moment trial—a sort of fishing expedition. If so, then the weight of believing that his mother has guilty knowledge of the murder has not been a contributing cause to Hamlet's melancholia. On the whole, however, the traditional explanation of these lines may seem to be justified, even though one cannot be certain that the accusation did not flash into his mind just at the moment. Such a view is certainly plausible.

justice. Yet by the time of the interview, Hamlet has seen no evidence whatever of Gertrude's thorns of conscience. It is of the utmost importance that after Polonius' murder he devote the minutes of freedom left him to breaking down his mother's stubborn will and forcing her to repentance by his passionate eloquence. In this act he is indeed following the Ghost's instructions. For a son to be oblivious of the fate of his mother's soul under the weight of mortal sin would be unnatural, and it is clear that Hamlet recognizes the paramount importance of assuring Gertrude some degree of mercy by "converting" her to a repentant way of life in which her deeds will match her new thoughts. So far as he can know at the time, this is the last gift he can make his mother. Although we cannot wholly ignore the very real sexual disgust in his rhetoric, and indeed perhaps even the jealousy, the force of this disgust is aimed at awakening her to a sense of sin and shame: "I must be cruel, only to be kind."[6]

It is of singular importance for us to recognize that this breaking-down of Gertrude's stubborn will and her restoration to a state of grace is not a fortuitous accident resulting from the slaying of Polonius and a seized opportunity to assail her in a moment of weakness. The Queen is not in the least softened by the shock of Polonius's death, for when Hamlet immediately returns to the attack on her, she answers with a contemptuous stubbornness equal to that at the beginning of the scene: "What have I done that thou dar'st wag thy tongue   In noise so rude against me? ... Ay me, what act   That roars so loud and thunders in the index?" And it takes a long and disgustingly detailed speech from Hamlet before she is beaten down and overcome with a conviction of her sin. Only then, softened at last, she moans, "O Hamlet, speak no more!"

The plain fact is that the murder of Polonius only momentarily interrupts an interview that Hamlet has controlled from the start and that has had from the start only one purpose—the separation of Gertrude from Claudius by awakening shame and

6. This scene is greatly vulgarized in Q1 (1603), where the Queen vows she knew nothing about the murder and Hamlet swears her to assist him in the revenge as a means of wiping out her infamy. This is obvious stuff that a hack would invent.

repentance in her. This we know in part from the very beginning of the scene when Hamlet thrusts his mother back into her chair:

> *Come, come, and sit you down. You shall not budge!*
> *You go not till I set you up a glass*
> *Where you may see the inmost part of you.*

The exordium he later delivers would then have followed even if the Queen had not mistaken his abrupt violence and called for help.

The soliloquy ending 3.2 shows clearly that when he obeyed his mother's summons Hamlet had planned on forcing her to repentance, through fear if necessary:

> *Let me be cruel, not unnatural;*
> *I will speak daggers to her, but use none. . . .*
> *How in my words somever she be shent,*
> *To give them seals never, my soul, consent!*

It follows that the violence of his action that provoked the Queen's outcry was part of this plan. Gertrude had summoned no wearily passive son who happened to seize a sudden and un-expected chance to force his will into domination over hers. There is no evidence that Hamlet has been alone with his mother since the audience saw the assembled court in Act 1. Thus when her summons afforded him the opportunity for a private meeting, a determined Hamlet went to his mother's closet with a fixed end in view, which he fulfilled despite, rather than because of, the murder of Polonius. That he succeeds here means, in effect, that he has successfully concluded one part of the Ghost's injunctions. In separating Gertrude from Claudius and bringing her to repentance in thought and action,[7] he has accomplished the first of the two revenges allotted him.

In our interest in following the conflict between Hamlet and his mighty opposite Claudius, we must not lose our awareness of

---

7. It is clear that her partly sacrificial death in Act 5 and her warning to Hamlet of the cup confirms her repentance in Act 3. Modern sentimentalism forgets the Elizabethan insistence that words must be accompanied by deeds if they are to be taken as valid.

the fact that Gertrude and her fate are included in the Ghost's commands for the revenge, and that they form an important balance in the play.[8] It is a significant irony that Hamlet's fatal misstep that later requires his death-in-victory for his second revenge is made in the very scene in which he succeeds in his first revenge. It is also an irony that Hamlet's misinterpretation of Claudius' attempt at repentance balances his success with Gertrude.

Hamlet tells the audience two things in the fifth soliloquy: in respect to Claudius I am prepared for blood; on the other hand, I must first put into effect my plan to force my mother to repent by separating her from her husband.

The first lines have an obvious bearing on the prayer scene (3.3) that immediately follows. It is part of the rich density of *Hamlet* that Shakespeare consistently refuses to permit us to pin the characters down to a single precise motive for action: by this means he prevents us from supplying a limited answer that would too easily serve to satisfy our curiosity by "explaining" Hamlet. Thus Hamlet's refusal to kill the kneeling King may be partly the honest revulsion of a civilized man when faced with blood. Although his bloodthirsty explanation is in some part a face-saving device,[9] we must not discount its partial validity and its considerable value in enabling him to rationalize his withdrawal.[10]

To the various explanations for Hamlet's action in sparing Claudius at prayer we may perhaps add one more: the pending

8. We may not interpret "Leave her to heaven" as an order to leave Gertrude alone. Instead, in his action Hamlet is not to plot against her or to enforce retributive justice on her, as on Claudius. It is the ultimate judgment resulting from Heaven's own retribution that Hamlet must leave to a great power that will, in this case, repay. Hamlet in no manner has been forbidden to "convert" his mother in the process of cleansing the royal bed; instead, he has been forbidden to punish her.

9. That the killing of one's victim's soul as well as his body was an Elizabethan shocker type of story associated with the vilest depths of Italian treachery (as in Nashe's *Unfortunate Traveller*) undoubtedly helped Shakespeare's audience to recognize its face-saving function in *Hamlet*.

10. In his acting version of *Hamlet* with commentary, John Gielgud has suggested that Hamlet's decision to spare Claudius might be partly clarified if Hamlet played his scene on the upper stage, with Claudius at prayer below.

interview with his mother and the importance of its purpose. That the interview is coming has been adduced previously as one of the complex of reasons for his failure to act, but critics have tended to misinterpret the motive, taking it that Hamlet weakly clung to his previous engagement (in a manner of speaking) as an excuse for avoiding action. But the soliloquy indicates the contrary. The time has come to carry out an important part of the revenge as it applies to Gertrude. In the soliloquy (before the prayer scene) this is given precedence over the part that applies to Claudius. The following action thereupon confirms the soliloquy and the order of the revenge. It is not, I think, fantastic to suggest that, to Hamlet, Gertrude's fate is at least as important as his revenge on Claudius, and that her fate depends wholly (so far as he can see) upon his forcing her to a recognition of her sin.[11] This he has determined on, as Shakespeare takes some pains to inform us. We should take this hint from the playwright and accept the order of events that Hamlet proposes for his double revenge, especially in view of the less-than-perfect circumstance for meting out justice to Claudius that chance thrusts upon him and that he rejects.

When we at last return to the original query suggested by this soliloquy, the answer is reasonably clearcut. The grand plan for *Hamlet* comprised a double action for the Ghost-directed protagonist: justice for Claudius; and the separation of his mother from her incestuous marriage, an act that was to include the awakening of her conscience as a means of saving her from the consequences of her mortal sin. The redemption of Gertrude is firmly

11.   Whether too fine-spun or not, the point must be made, also, that the circumstances of repentance had, for the Elizabethan, much to do with the grace that might follow. That is, Gertrude sorrowing over the death of Claudius could repent her sin with greater facility when the opportunity to enjoy its perquisites was no longer in existence. On the other hand, the sincerity of her repentance can be vouched for when, expecting herself and Claudius to continue living, she removes herself from the royal bed, which obviously she has enjoyed. We need not suppose that such limited considerations governed Hamlet's sparing of Claudius for the moment, in so far as we can supply a motivation for it. The strength of his purpose to reform and thereby to save his mother is sufficient on general grounds when added to the other reasonable suggestions that critics have offered.

planned. We hear of it in the soliloquy at the end of 3.2, we follow its course in Hamlet's rejection of an opportunity to murder Claudius while supposedly in a state of grace as yet denied to Gertrude, and we see it crowned with success despite Gertrude's initial violent opposition and the resulting murder of Polonius. Its importance is attested by the arrangement of the events leading up to Gertrude's death in Act. 5.[12]

Any exploitation of the sensational in the closet scene would necessarily detract from the audience's understanding of Hamlet's purpose and the firm manner in which he carried it out under the gravest difficulties. Indeed, it was so important for the audience to recognize that Hamlet was acting a part for a fixed purpose in his violence to his mother that Shakespeare could not permit any question on this score lest the audience lose sight of or else misinterpret the mainspring of Hamlet's actions. This rigorous control of the audience's reactions to a scene could not be managed by normal dramatic means. Hence the special quality of the fifth soliloquy, which points forward to the order of the succeeding events and unmistakably enforces the desired interpretation. When the Queen sobs, "O Hamlet, speak no more," Hamlet's purpose has been achieved and the soliloquy has been justified.

12. I discuss Shakespeare's concern with the fates of his characters in "The Death of Hamlet: A Study in Plot and Character."

THE MOMENT OF FINAL
SUSPENSE IN *HAMLET:*
"We Defy Augury"

JUST BEFORE THE CATASTROPHE IN Greek tragedy, the protagonist may be given a last chance to escape the fatal consequences of the tragic act that is now on the threshold of
retribution. But the logic of character and events is inexorable:
the hubris that engendered the original error still blinds the protagonist, and he rejects (or does not recognize) the offered alternative that might, even so late, save his life or prevent the crime
that is intended. One element of this device is certainly suspense
for its own dramatic effect. But, simultaneously, the audience is
doubly assured of the justice of the catastrophe when it sees,
ironically presented, the same lack of self-knowledge repeated as
in the original error: evidence that the protagonist, at the brink
of disaster, has not learned through experience the significance
of his initial misstep.

An example may be found in Sophocles' *Oedipus the King.* The
Messenger's narrative, in destroying the accepted picture of Oedipus' paternity, reveals the truth to Jocasta, who tries to dissuade
Oedipus from demanding the fatal revelation that she knows will
follow on the summons to the herdsman. Oedipus' blind pride

From *Shakespeare 1564–1964*, ed. Edward A. Bloom (Providence: Brown
Univ. Press, 1964).

leads him to misunderstand her motives. Thinking that Jocasta is ashamed of what appears to be his base origin, he avows that his deeds mark him as Fortune's child—therefore of worth—and despite her repeated pleas he orders in the herdsman who brings the light that will make him blind in fact. This device is sometimes known as "the moment of final suspense."

Another form of this "moment" may appear as an omen that the protagonist in his hubris fails to understand or chooses to ignore, although his awareness of its significance, or (better) his willingness to admit its significance, would have saved him. This is the augury that Hamlet defies. Cassandra's prophetic fit in Seneca's *Agamemnon*, containing her veiled warning to Agamemnon that she herself does not understand, is an example, in the classical drama.

The events leading directly into the catastrophe of Hamlet move with exceptional speed. Hamlet has returned from the abortive English voyage to come most unexpectedly upon Ophelia's funeral. Immediately thereafter he recounts his adventures to Horatio, accepts Laertes' challenge, and the fatal match is on.

In this action Shakespeare has built up a moment of final suspense that is of some complexity. The acceptance of the fencing match is the key action leading to the catastrophe, for the agreement to meet Laertes means that Hamlet has walked into Claudius' trap and is doomed. Characteristically, Shakespeare treats the episode itself in a comic light that serves by his habitual principle of contrast and parallelism to intensify the underlying serious purport of the action which the audience knows but which is not seen by any of the characters directly involved.

In the disparity between the agent and the action, between Osric and the King's plot, lies just such contrast as is found in the Clown bringing the asps to Cleopatra, the Fool counselling Lear, and even the Porter in *Macbeth*. We do not know whether the choice of such an innocent lapwing[1] was intended by Shake-

---

1. That Osric is innocent is demonstrated by his surviving the catastrophe. Elizabethan tragic justice would have disposed of him if he had been one of Claudius' accomplices.

speare to be a manifestation of Claudius' Machiavellism to conceal the deadly purpose, or whether Shakespeare merely seized on the occasion to show Hamlet in an innocent fencing match of words, which he wins while losing, as contrast to the oncoming match which he loses though truly winning—and not just at the odds. It is a characteristic feature of the density of Shakespeare's dramatic writing that even this simplest of actions, the delivery and acceptance of a wager, is not huddled through in bald terms but becomes a part of the human complex.

Is Hamlet's unsuspicious acceptance a fault, like the blindness of Agamemnon or the egoistic obstinacy of Oedipus? In a sense it is, but not in any deep sense—certainly not one that involves the audience's acceptance of the catastrophic justice of Hamlet's death-in-victory.

Hamlet's defense that the deaths of Rosencrantz and Guildenstern do not lie on his conscience leads naturally to his recapitulation of the justice of his retaliation on Claudius. Respectfully, Horatio intimates that Hamlet can expect Claudius' next crime to be directed against himself in repayment for the deaths of Rosencrantz and Guildenstern, a fact that must soon be known. This speech, of course, implicitly warns Hamlet that he must act without delay.[2] Both men seem to assume that Claudius will be quiescent until he is stirred to further action by the revelation that Hamlet discovered the plot against his life and may have evidence to present in the matter. In this belief they are mistaken, as the audience knows, for Claudius has not waited to mount his counteraction, which therefore strikes a Hamlet who is unprepared.

Is the mistake a culpable one? It is worthy of note that Horatio

2.   Kittredge would seem to overrefine the meaning by reading into the two lines "It must be shortly known to him from England   What is the issue of the business there" a tacit comment that Hamlet's action will be in self-defense. On the contrary, since self-defense can scarcely be defined in any legal (or in any ethical) manner as anticipatory, or preventative of the actual fact, Horatio is only suggesting, quietly, that time is of the essence: Hamlet must act for himself during the short interval that he will be a free agent before the counteraction is mounted against him.

shares in it, and as a result the audience has no clear lead from a touchstone character. Hence the assumption must be that in itself the error is not a tragically characterizing or justifying one wherein the audience is invited to sit in judgment on the decision. Claudius is not helpless, nor do Hamlet and Horatio assume that he is. What seems to be contained in Hamlet's confident pronouncement "the interim is mine" is a belief that the balking of Claudius' plot has robbed the King of the initiative until a new one can be contrived. The new plot will evidently rest on using the Rosencrantz and Guildenstern execution to Hamlet's disadvantage. Until this new plot will be started by the receipt of the evidence, Hamlet takes it that he himself is in command.

In fact, this diagnosis might well have been correct if a complementary mistake had not followed. Hamlet's generous nature cannot conceive that Laertes will turn villain. Hence there is extreme irony in his regret that he had lost his temper with Laertes at Ophelia's grave, "For by the image of my cause I see   The portraiture' of his." Laertes has legitimate grievances, which Hamlet can understand; they are two young men who have been wronged; Hamlet's wrong has sat for the portrait of Laertes'. He feels pity for Laertes and proposes to "court his favours." That Laertes may be feeling toward him as he feels toward Claudius— and is proposing to act upon the feeling—does not, apparently, cross Hamlet's mind, so strong is his assumption that they have a common bond. It may be that Hamlet believes he is secure in his alibi of madness, the theme of his attempted reconciliation with Laertes before the fencing match. It may be that his recognition of his own innocence of intent, corresponding to the innocence of unhinged madness, which cannot act from premeditation, makes him too self-confident and unsuspicious. It is clear that he does not envisage Laertes as a revenger of blood, and thus he cannot suspect that Claudius will immediately have formulated a counteraction utilizing Laertes as a tool.

If this error in estimating Laertes is to correspond to the classical use of the moment of final suspense, a fault in character or in attitude as evidenced by a want of a proper self-knowledge must be shown. Moreover, this generosity of mind (which at least evokes no warning comment from Horatio) is repeated in the indifferent choice of the rapiers at the duel, another error at the final moment, and so is of a piece. A lack of due suspicion of the world; an innocence, or generosity, that can be a luxury in time of peace but is criminally careless in time of danger—if this is to sum up the view of Hamlet that Shakespeare wanted the audience to hold at such a crucial moment (in the manner of Sophocles portraying with intensity the willfully blind Oedipus driving himself to destruction), then we should have had good evidence earlier in the play of such motivation. Also, earlier in the play, we should have been introduced to a characterization that emphasized what Milton was to call unwariness, or levity, a serious charge in context. Moreover, we must suppose that the moment of final suspense as logically used by the Greeks should confirm the original tragic error.

Here, at least, we are on safe ground in rejecting any such view: if Hamlet's tragic error were his generosity of mind—his incapacity to deal with a barbaric duty—we should find the play's climax centering on this tragic flaw. But the climax of the play centers not on his incapacity but on his capacity for killing. The murder of Polonius, mistaken for the King, when Hamlet gives way to a moment of unbearable temptation,[3] has nothing to do with this part of Hamlet's characterization, his generosity of mind. We must conclude, therefore, that the events immediately antecedent to the delivery of Osric's message are not structural, in the sense that they have not been designed in the classical manner to illuminate or to exemplify the initial tragic error. That they illustrate an element in Hamlet's characterization is undeniable; but that this strand, through the illustration, is structurally involved in the tragic web itself—this we may deny.[4]

3. Explored in "Hamlet as Minister and Scourge."

4. It may follow logically what is apparent to any student of dramatic structure, that the famed temperamental hesitation and inability to act have, actually, nothing to do with the essential plot of the play insofar as this comprises the tragic action. For an elaboration of this point, see "Dramatic Structure and Criticism: Plot in *Hamlet*."

Let us, then, pass on to the last of the possible escapes before the start of the fatal action of the fencing match. This episode involves the presentiment of evil that Hamlet feels after his acceptance of the wager. "But thou wouldst not think how ill all's here about my heart. But it is no matter." Horatio protests; Hamlet in reply associates the misgiving not with manly caution but with female fears, that is, with an irrational impulse. Horatio continues to take the omen—for that is what it is—more seriously than this, and he shows his agitation at its import by giving Hamlet the second direct piece of advice he allows himself in the play (the first having been his attempt to restrain the prince from following the Ghost). Hamlet rejects the counsel with an appeal to the reason of men who, like Horatio and himself, rely not on superstition but on the acceptance of God's overriding Providence, His active care for the world. With this rejection of Horatio's prudent advice, the tragic die is cast.

Omen and augury, which are interchangeable, were favorite devices in classical drama to lend dignity and inevitability to the tragic action of the conflict of the wills of men and gods. Sometimes the augury chastens human will that has broken divine law, as Creon has done with his cruel decree in Sophocles' *Antigone*. Ironically, in this play, the import of the augury is first rejected, and then accepted too late to prevent the tragic disaster.[5] On the contrary, in Seneca's *Agamemnon* the simple understanding of the augury would have saved the protagonist.

The contrast in Shakespeare's use of the device as against that in classical drama is clear. The Elizabethan audience can only approve Hamlet's rejection of pagan superstition in favor of a Christian reliance on Providence. One can scarcely discover here the final irony of lack of insight as in Greek tragedy.

At this point it should be evident that Shakespeare has piled up in the episode the characteristic devices of classical tragedy (whether found in the Greeks or in Seneca) but that he has fun-

5. The intention seems to be present to suggest to the audience that the delay in Creon's acceptance, accompanied by his accusations against Teiresias, uses up valuable time. If he had humbled himself immediately, instead of too late, Antigone might have been saved.

damentally altered their import and structural purpose. The most causal use of this moment of final suspense by the ancients[6] emphasized the protagonist's tragic blindness in repeating the substance of his original tragic error while Nemesis was poised to strike. One moment of humility, or enlightenment, might have saved the victim, as Creon could have been saved from irreparable crime by instant obedience to the chosen of the gods. But this self-knowledge and understanding do not come; tragic hubris persists, and the protagonist ironically brings about his own downfall.

The difference lies in the fact that Shakespeare has Christianized the ancient pagan device. Indeed, Hamlet's opposition of Providence to pagan augury is intended to emphasize the change. Little doubt can exist that Shakespeare intended a close equation between Hamlet's serene "the interim is mine   And a man's life's no more than to say 'one,'" and the biblical overtones of "we defy augury; there's a special providence in the fall of a sparrow. . . the readiness is all."

The point of the catastrophe is Hamlet's death-in-victory with its reconciliation and Divine acceptance of the penalty he must pay for his tragic error. It follows that the faults that blinded the classical protagonist to his last chance to escape must be taken as virtues in Hamlet that demonstrate the clearing of his understanding as manifested by his refusal to evade the required payment for his past error. Only thus can he be brought to the characteristic Shakespearean final ennoblement of experience that persuades an audience to accept, even with satisfaction, the tragic end of a sympathetic protagonist.[7] In any Christian view of life, nobility equals humility, the understanding and acceptance of God's will instead of the dictates of one's own. If Hamlet comes to understand the nature of his error in the slaying of Polonius, and if this clarification of his self-knowledge leads to a

6.   Augury and the consequences of a too late recognition appear less causally in Sophocles' *Ajax*, where they are seemingly divorced from characterization.

7.   Something of this ennoblement may be faintly seen in classical tragedy, as perhaps in Creon's final religious fear, or in Ajax' last soliloquy, but it is elementary compared to the Shakespearean apotheosis.

resubmission of his will to God's, then the line of the play from the climax to the catastrophe must bear on this theme. It is my contention that this is, indeed, the movement of the play. If so, it is idle to query why Hamlet should be so confident that the interim will be his, although obviously he has no plan for action. This confidence derives from his recognition on the English voyage that his ministerial function in dealing justice has been restored, and that he is once more in the hand of God, Who has promised vengeance for all earthly crimes.[8]

It would be equally idle to accuse Hamlet of weakness in failing to suspect Laertes of villainously revengeful motives, or of tragically unwary inaction in supposing Claudius to be checkmated for the moment. Last, it would indeed be folly to accuse Hamlet either of hubris or of weakness in linking his own fate to the fall of a sparrow.

The Christianization of the classical moment of final suspense reinforces not the protagonist's tragic error and continued blindness that draw on his doom, but (on the contrary) his dearly bought enlightenment that justifies his regeneration. Instead of ironically contributing to his downfall, the Christian fortitude that Hamlet exhibits in the moment of final suspense leads him to choose Providence over pagan augury. The offer of an alternative precisely reverses the classical device, for an escape at this moment would have ruined, not saved, him. Shakespeare

8. It is tempting to connect the practical advice that Horatio gives here with Hamlet's "There are more things in heaven and earth, Horatio,   Than are dreamt of in your philosophy" (1.5.166–67). Kittredge glosses *your philosophy* as "this philosophy that people make so much of." The unemphatic and generalized use of "you" is well known, as in *Hamlet* 4.3.21 ff., cited by Kittredge. Nevertheless, the early emphasis in 1.1, on Horatio as a skeptic, and the hint at 1.5.166–67 that he is at least acquainted with the skepticism of natural science, may join with his prudent superstition here to suggest a contrast between him and Hamlet in some ultimate matters of belief. Certainly Horatio's secularism (if that is a proper word) mistakes the point of the augury and it is clear that—though acquainted with all the facts—he fails to interpret them as does Hamlet. The final worldly contrast occurs in his mistaken attempt to commit suicide from which Hamlet saves him. Horatio is a sympathetic character, but all the contrasts favor Hamlet.

changes the opportunity to escape, making it instead a subtle temptation to evade responsibility. When Hamlet resists Horatio's two suggestions that he attempt to alter the events to come, which belong to God, not to him, he justifies his catastrophic victory.[9]

9.   If, as I have suggested, the tragic error creating the play's climax was Hamlet's killing of Polonius, an act performed in his own instead of in God's time and therefore an alienation, the defiance of augury restores him to a trust in Providence that he had rejected in the closet scene. In this manner Hamlet refuses to repeat his initial tragic error and therefore merits his victory in the catastrophe, even at the price of death. To illustrate: if the classical protagonist had taken the right advice or had correctly understood the omen, he could have altered his course of action and escaped the threatened consequences. In Shakespeare's Christianization of the device, Hamlet understands the omen and—by choice—accepts the consequences. If he had moved to avoid them (as Horatio urges) he would have been repeating his initial tragic error. Hence the classical protagonist repeats his initial fault and dooms himself by blindly failing to heed the omen, whereas Hamlet saves himself by ignoring the omen with open eyes.

THE DEATH OF HAMLET:
A Study in
Plot and Character

IN THE DEATH SCENE OF *Hamlet* Shakespeare includes a rather extraordinary number of approving statements about the hero and seems to have been at some pains to order the final action to justify these sentiments. The causes for this emphasis on Hamlet's "good end" and the conducting of his soul to heaven by an angelic guard are intimately bound up with the play as revenge tragedy a form that often posed ethical problems. The extra number of signposts that Shakespeare erects in the final scene to direct the audience toward the view of Hamlet he wants it to hold indicates the nature of the central problem. With the exception of the protagonist of Tourneur's *Atheist's Tragedy* and of Chapman's *Revenge of Bussy D'Ambois*, Hamlet is perhaps the least criminal of all Elizabethan tragic revengers; and it is clear that Shakespeare throughout the play took considerable pains to keep Hamlet on the weather side of the audience's approval. This good will is secured in large part through the shaping of the plot and the analogous shaping of character.

An important problem for the revenge-play dramatist was

From *Studies in the English Renaissance Drama: In Memory of Karl Julius Holz-knecht*, ed. Josephine W. Bennett et al. (New York: New York Univ. Press, 1959); by permission of the publisher.

where to begin.[1] Two major varieties of plot were available: that in which the crime that calls forth the revenge is enacted on the stage; and that in which the crime is antecedent to the play's own action and the plot concerns only the revenge. *The Spanish Tragedy* is representative of the first; *Hamlet*, of the second. The first plot method places less strain on the dramatist's ability to invent appropriate incident; but if the dramatist can avoid the various pitfalls, the second method is likely to make a superior play in its fifth-act intensity of concentration on a single powerful action.

The classic formula for the revenge play calls for revealing the fact of the crime to the revenger by a medium in which he cannot place his immediate or his whole trust. Action is generated by his endeavors to confirm the truth of this suspect information. Once the facts are ascertained, this line of action is exhausted and the dramatist faces the problem of further delaying the revenge. According to the formula, the antagonists are thereupon apprised that the crime is no longer secret, as a consequence of which their counteraction against the threatening revenger becomes an important strand in the plot. Accompanying this difficulty imposed from without on his successful operations is an internal difficulty that saps the protagonist's will to action. This internal difficulty may be formed by ethical or religious scruples, or by a partial disintegration of the will caused by sporadic fits of madness brought on by discouragement and an overwhelming consciousness of the burden of the revenge, or by both. The tragedy is ordinarily then brought to a close in the clash of plot and counterplot, causing the destruction of the antagonists and the death-in-victory of the protagonist revenger.

Obviously the plot structure that involves the maximum stretching out of the revenge action for an antecedent crime is more difficult to manage than the structure in which a considerable portion of the rising action may be taken up with the initial conflict that produced the crime to be revenged. The difficulty is only in part due to the strain placed on the dramatist's

---

1. I am depending in part on conclusions reached some time ago in my *Elizabethan Revenge Tragedy* (1940); use has also been made of my "Hamlet as Minister and Scourge," of which this present essay may be considered an extension.

mere inventiveness of illustrative incident, though this strain is not to be ignored. How to maintain an audience's interest for three or four acts in a revenger who may not revenge is a serious problem. If the protagonist-revenger were a villain, the problem was readily solved; but otherwise really major difficulty occurred—and one that in large part governed the form of the necessary illustrative incident—in the maintenance of the audience's estimate of a revenger of blood as a sympathetic hero. The paradox was, of course, that the Elizabethan audience could sympathize with the need for the revenge but could not sympathize with the revenge itself when its consummation involved the crime of murder. In short, the Elizabethan tragic revenger could remain a blameless hero only so long as he proposed to revenge but did not succeed.

This paradox was solved in three different ways. First, and least popular, the revenger is brought into conflict with the antagonist, but the antagonist's death, which revenges the crime, is caused by some agency other than the revenger. Tourneur's *Atheist's Tragedy* illustrates this solution. The revenger's religious scruples force him to refuse to revenge. Unimpeded by the revenger's action, therefore, the counter-action gathers speed and the play ends only when the original criminal knocks out his own brains in the very act of attempting to execute the revenger. The relieved hero correctly imputes his survival and the enactment of justice to the direct intervention of Heaven.

The most marked characteristic of this type of play is the change in the method for creating suspense. The audience's attention is caught and held not by a series of forward actions on the revenger's part. Instead, the emphasis is shifted from plot to character. Whether under the strongest provocation the psychological frustration created by the religio-ethical barrier to his action will destroy him, or whether to escape such destruction he will break through his scruples so that action will be taken in opposition to his moral or religious doctrines—it is this conflict within his own mind that creates the suspense. Threat of action substitutes for the suspense created by action itself.

This art of titillating the audience by the threat of action is well illustrated also in Beaumont and Fletcher's *Maid's Tragedy*.

Whether Amintor will crack under the strain created by his self-imposed inaction is the suspenseful element. The paradox is apparent that if the hero yields to the strain, the result is not inaction (as in the release by madness of Hieronimo's revengefulness in *The Spanish Tragedy*), but instead, action. That this action is at once desired and not desired by the audience is the point. The essential conflict therefore moves from the external field of action and counteraction into the mind of the hero. Since he can offer simply the threat of action, a static character can be avoided only by the application of ever-stronger incitements to action, increasing the chance that his self-control will be overcome. These stimuli are ordinarily furnished by an increase in the importance of the counteraction directed against the protagonist. Thus at one stroke the dramatist achieves suspense in whether the hero's control will be broken and also whether the inaction caused by this control will lead to the protagonist's destruction by the antagonist's counteraction. Since drama is action, mental action is furnished by the protagonist; and external, or stage action, by the antagonist.

The second form that tragedy took in search of a solution to the problem was that exemplified by Chettle's *Hoffman*. Here the protagonist's action is the central one and the counteraction relatively feeble in its interest. A bold solution has been made to the problem of illustrative action. Instead of there being only one revenge which can be consummated on a single individual, or on a coherent group, at one time, the central revenge is worked out by a continuous series of separate revenges against a staggered group of antagonists. By this string-of-beads method of plotting, the forward action can be carried on as long as the dramatist wishes merely by adding another antagonist on whom the protagonist may revenge.

Whereas the essence of the first sort of plot is the protagonist's inaction, the essence of the *Hoffman* type is his excessive action. And because this action must by necessity pass speedily from a state *in posse* to *in esse*, the penalty attendant on successful revenge action is imposed. Since a series of killings accompanies Hoffman's various revenges, the protagonist cannot be maintained as a hero whose survival can be permitted or whose death-in-triumph can be accepted as adequate expiation for his fault. In Chettle's hands the revenger Hoffman becomes a villain protagonist as the penalty for his action. Hence the tragic conflict has been resolved in favor of action at the expense of sympathetic character. Consequently, in the dénouement the central death required is that of the protagonist; it is an act of justice administered by a surviving antagonist; and the ethics of the stage demand that it represent the retributive punishment of the protagonist.[2]

Historically the third, or *Hamlet*, type of plot appears to have been the one initially contrived,[3] whereas the other two developed from it as later variants. At the risk of some confusion, therefore, I place it last since it attempts to resolve the dilemma by a middle course. On the one hand, although the protagonist's mental conflict is preserved, the religio-ethical scruples or the psychological disabilities of frustration and madness are not strong enough to repress all action; instead, he struggles through to a partial series of actions even if with serious internal difficulty. On the other hand, because the protagonist's line is insufficient to provide enough illustrative suspenseful action for the play, the deficiency is made up by an increase in the interest normally expected from a counteraction.

The compromise results in a mixed character for the protagonist. Since he is allowed to kill the antagonist in the dénouement, he is given enough action to justify that killing. However, the action is sufficiently confined to the one justified premeditated killing (and its offshoot in *Hamlet*, the unpremeditated killing of Polonius) so that the audience's sympathy is retained, not alienated as by Hoffman's series of brutal murders. Moreover, by an increase in the value of the counteraction, the dénouement is brought about, in *Hamlet* at least, more by the protagonist's reaction to the deadly success of the counterplot than as the result of any chain of cause and effect in his own line of action.

2. Corresponding, in short, to the required death as punishment (not as expiation) promised for the villain Iago. Othello's suicide, I should urge, is expiatory.

3. In my view in the *Ur-Hamlet*, very likely preceding *The Spanish Tragedy*.

In this respect the plot of *Hamlet* is better calculated than that of *The Spanish Tragedy*. Since Kyd's villain Lorenzo appears to have no further counterplot against Hieronimo once he has quashed Hieronimo's attempts to secure justice from the king, he is brought low without conflict by Hieronimo's unimpeded action.[4] As a consequence, the expected death-in-triumph is morally obscured by suicide. Clermont in *The Revenge of Bussy* is also a suicide, but Chapman succeeds in philosophizing the deed as admirable stoicism. This escape is denied Kyd, who seems to confuse the requirements of an expiatory death with those for a death in punishment of crime. I can find no other explanation (save mere sensationalism) for Hieronimo's arbitrary continuation of the murders except that Kyd felt the need to persuade the audience to accept the justice of Hieronimo's death by removing any doubt that in the play-within-a-play he had committed a punishable crime.

Kyd's problem arose from the fact that his protagonist's death was not in expiation for some past deed embedded earlier in the plot, and therefore a part of the dramatic action leading to the dénouement. Rather, Hieronimo's death is expiatory only of the killing of Lorenzo and Balthazar, which the audience has just witnessed in the dénouement. To make sure that its justice would be accepted, Kyd seemingly felt the need to pile on additional and less defensible murders. In doing so he crudely obscured the issue by mixing punishment with expiation.

No moral obscuration is found in the plot of *Hamlet*. The means by which Shakespeare[5] secured the remarkable balance of plot, character, and ethics are worth some particular analysis. The most prominent device is to confine the forward action of the protagonist, with one crucial exception, not to a revengeful and therefore murderous intrigue against the life of the antagonist but instead to a determination of the antagonist's guilt. No

4. That is, unimpeded by any counterplot. The main threat to Hieronimo's success is internal, the dissipation of his will to action by extreme melancholia created by grief.

5. I write "Shakespeare" although it is likely the major incidents of the plot itself had been contrived from Belleforest by the author of the *Ur-Hamlet*. What Shakespeare did with them was undoubtedly another matter.

moral taint can inhere to this investigation. Thus Hamlet has an action to perform that moves him from his initial point of rest, yet one in which success will not require a moral judgment from the audience. The crux of the matter is, the action does not involve the commission of a crime. Its successful outcome can therefore be anticipated with unmixed pleasure. That this success will immediately present a further problem in requiring the initiation of another course of action that cannot be so wholeheartedly approved on an ethical basis—that is, an intrigue against Claudius' life—does not affect the anticipatory pleasure. However, the audience is kept mindful of this later possibility by two means: by Hamlet's own promises of dire action if the Ghost's word proves true; and by his constant urge to revenge (even though this is held down by frustration) preceding and then accompanying the plot of the mousetrap.

For a time the counteraction somewhat resembles that in *The Spanish Tragedy* following the death of Pedringano. Claudius seems to be invulnerable to detection, and the secrecy and success of the crime have prevented any need for further criminal action. Hence the counteraction is also at a point of rest when the play opens; and it is set in motion only when Hamlet's madness calls for explanation. Until the start of the play-within-a-play scheme the action is occupied largely by Hamlet's resistance to the attempts of various antagonists to penetrate his secret. He is only incipiently in danger, however; just as Claudius is only incipiently in danger from him until the success of the mousetrap. The most forward action finally resulting from the counteraction is the plan according to which Hamlet is first ordered on embassy to England. It is worthy of note that at the start this plan is completely innocent. It results, however, from the most overt of the antagonist's line of action, the overhearing of Hamlet's nunnery-scene interview with Ophelia and the consequent dissatisfaction that Claudius feels with any of the explanations yet produced for Hamlet's madness. This English voyage, the culmination of Claudius' pre-mousetrap counterplot, is economically used to link with the post-mousetrap murderous counteraction when it is altered to become an attempt on Hamlet's life.

The counteraction having paused with its first decision about the embassy, the protagonist's line of action takes over by an implementation of the mousetrap scheme, which had first been conceived before the nunnery scene. In this case, therefore, no interplay exists between plot and counterplot. The success of the mousetrap does not create a corresponding pause in the main action, which hurries on to a second stage of completion before the retaliatory counteraction is engendered. This forward push takes two forms: the ironic relinquishment of opportunity in the prayer scene, followed by the apparent success of the sudden unpremeditated action at the start of the closet scene. This moment is the high point of Hamlet's success as a free agent. But it rapidly reveals itself as a failure when, ironically, the wrong man slumps into view from behind the arras. To date in the play Hamlet has taken one innocent action against Claudius, the mousetrap; and one strictly revengeful action, which results in the murder of Polonius. The paradox that a stage revenger cannot revenge without penalty is well exemplified by this climax of the play. Hamlet's tragic error that will inevitably lead to his own death is enacted here in this morally determinate scene.[6]

From now on the counteraction takes over and wholly guides the working out of the plot. The interlinking of action is interesting. The early innocently conceived English voyage is turned into a deadly instrument; but this, the sole unaided scheme of Claudius against Hamlet, proves abortive and is dropped when Hamlet escapes with the pirates. Here, then, the two enemies have reached a point of temporary balance. Hamlet has survived Claudius' secret counteraction but has no definite plan of his own to secure revenge. Claudius has, so far as we know, exhausted the possibilities of secret intrigue against Hamlet. Then to break this stalemate come the first consequences of Hamlet's climactic killing of Polonius and Ophelia's resulting suicide: Claudius receives Laertes as an ally, and Hamlet has a second enemy who is destined to be his death. Following immediately on Hamlet's return to Denmark the counterplot is formulated.

6. For my effort to place this climax not as mere accident but as true tragic error, see "Hamlet as Minister and Scourge."

Hamlet has scarcely time to witness Ophelia's funeral and to report his adventures to Horatio before he is caught up in its events and is killed by the envenomed rapier.

That Hamlet from the climax to the dénouement is not a static figure while the counterrevenge churns ahead is due to two devices. First, he is allowed some positive innocent actions such as his opposition to Laertes in the grave; the reflection of his masterful handling of Rosencrantz and Guildenstern, and the pirates; and even the mastery of intellect shown in his superiority over Osric at the game of obfuscation. Second, I should urge that the quiet assurance he shows as the agent of a Heaven which has at last begun to move in vengeance gives him the confidence of the audience as a dynamic character still. His will, which in the closet scene had opposed Heaven, is now reconciled, and he is prepared to take his proper place in the scale of Heaven's designs. No other explanation can be evolved on any evidence for his firm confidence after the return to Denmark despite the lack of any plan of his own.[7] The audience is led to share this infectious confidence even though specification is lacking.

The events of the dénouement itself now need attention. That the events culminate according to a divine plan is the necessary assumption of the Elizabethan audience. That the divine plan will deal out perfect justice is also a necessary assumption.[8] Shakespeare has brought up to this point in the play the char-

---

7. Ibid., for more detailed argument on this point.

8. The critical assessment of justice in Elizabethan tragedy has been impeded on occasion by failure to see this fundamental tragic distinction. Results of the rising, and even the falling, action may well represent injustice. It would be idle to attempt to argue that Ophelia merits her death because she was obedient to her father, that Polonius' nosiness was justly penalized by death, or even that Rosencrantz and Guildenstern were justly sent to execution because they had behaved as provocative agents to Hamlet. The only desideratum in Elizabethan tragedy is the righting of injustice by justice in the final results as seen in the punishment of crime. The injustice for which penalty must be exacted may continue to the very dénouement, as in the death of Desdemona, but even more remarkably as in the death of Cordelia. (The operation of the law of retributive justice may be seen in one useful small respect in *Hamlet*, in that we may be *positive* that Osric knew nothing of the unbated foil on the evidence that no comment is made or punishment dealt him.)

acter of a revenger who is as guiltless as he could well be save for a single tragic error.[9]

In terms of the three basic possibilities for plotting, Shakespeare has solved the problem of illustrative action in large part by emphasizing the importance of the counteraction and the protagonist's reaction to it. The internal struggle of the protagonist, frustrating his action, has not been neglected but its mixture of nature and art has not been so inhibiting as to prevent some positive action. This positive action successfully passed its first stage in its demonstration of the justice of the revenge. In the process, however, Hamlet was forced to reveal himself and thus to bear the brunt of the renewed counteraction. Yet the counteraction immediately deriving from the mousetrap exposé is abortive. What does finally lead to Hamlet's destruction is that counteraction depending upon his *second* forward action, the attempted killing of Claudius, a less innocent matter than the

9. This is, of course, the killing of Polonius instead of Claudius. Whether the defense of his execution of Rosencrantz and Guildenstern is to be accepted literally I hold in some question. Shakespeare, as usual in this play, has deliberately (and wisely) avoided assigning too limited and precise motives for every action. There is no way that Hamlet could *know* that Rosencrantz and Guildenstern were not aware of the contents of the sealed papers: it might seem to him a natural assumption that they were aware. If so, in his view they receive justice for their intention to assist in his death. If it is argued that Hamlet does not say this to Horatio but instead assigns other reasons, I should remark that such a course represents Shakespeare's method elsewhere in the play. Scrupulously viewed, the case might be argued that if they knew the contents, they would scarcely continue to England to present a useless, and to them a deadly, document. However, Shakespeare is by no means always capable of bearing up under such a scrupulous inquiry. Indeed, we might presume (if Shakespeare troubled to think about the matter) that the papers would include the original demand for tribute and other business planned for the first embassy before the change was made in its purpose by ordering the death of the bearer. It may be that in this action Shakespeare is chiefly concerned to show Hamlet as an efficient, even a stern, man of action who is not held back from death by sentimental reasons. It is unlikely, however, that he is also concerned to strengthen the killing of Polonius as a sufficient act to require Hamlet's own death in justice: Hamlet's action is not a much watered-down parallel to Hieronimo's continued slaughter following on the masque-play. The exact, limited intention here is not to be demonstrated, perhaps, but it may be loosely associated with Hamlet in his role as scourge.

mousetrap test for truth. Ironically, the death of Polonius occurs from a kind of coda to the initial counteraction, for Claudius' first decision to send Hamlet out of the country in large part superseded the plan of Polonius to eavesdrop a second time on Hamlet's private conversation. In this ironic interplay of action and counteraction Shakespeare has preserved the essentially sympathetic nature of Hamlet's character, yet provided him with an error in his own action that will, by all stage ethics, call for his expiatory death.

In the dénouement Hamlet kills two more men, Claudius and Laertes. It is interesting to see that Shakespeare in fact contrives it so that the deaths would not be legally classifiable as murder.[10] The way the fencing match is arranged, we have no certain means of knowing whether Hamlet intended to kill Laertes with the unbated foil or only to wound him seriously in retaliation (he does not yet know of the poison). Thus when Laertes receives his death wound from Hamlet, we may disregard for the moment all questions of poetic justice and emphasize only that an audience would have a difficult time proving motive on Hamlet's part. And even if it could be demonstrated (which it cannot be) that Hamlet in the scuffle after the change of foils was proposing to kill Laertes, or even when a moment later he shouted

10. Murder, i.e., death by premeditation, differs from manslaughter, or death in hot blood. It is worth remark that by strict legal doctrine the killing of Polonius, in mistake for Claudius, was first-degree murder since Hamlet's motives, being revengeful, presupposed malice prepensed. That the occasion scarcely gave time for the formulation of a premeditated act is of no legal account, since the general premeditation to kill Claudius had long since been formulated and awaited only the proper opportunity. On the other hand, sentimentally (and such factors are not to be neglected), the instantaneous decision would seem in a sense to be made in hot blood. Moreover, an Elizabethan barrister for the defense might well have argued that in the short interval between the end of the mousetrap play and the beginning of the closet scene, Hamlet's blood had not had time to cool. There could be drawn a certain analogy between a duel fought still in hot blood so long as the disputants went directly to the dueling ground without delay, thus permitting a shift of place from that where the insult had been given. (Ordinarily such a change of ground would be taken as allowing the blood to cool and thus rating the duel as murder.) In this case, however, the lawyer would need to prove that Hamlet had not actually determined to kill Claudius until after the mousetrap.

"Nay come! again!" at the least the death was only one by manslaughter. If Hamlet had not intended to kill Laertes (and he
certainly had no intention of killing him by the poison), the accidental death by poison was simple manslaughter. If Hamlet in
wounding Laertes in the scuffle had in fact intended to kill him,
the accident of the poisoned tip that actually caused his death
would not have been the legalism to free him, but instead the
plain fact that in his instant retaliation when wounded he was
acting in hot blood. In either case, therefore, his deed would
have been legally pardonable and he is not stained with murder.

Shakespeare draws a clear distinction between what is perhaps
something of an inadvertent killing of Laertes and the meditated
killing of Claudius. Moreover, for Claudius the clear intent is
most dramatically emphasized by Hamlet's forcing the poisoned
drink between his lips even after wounding him with Laertes'
envenomed weapon.[11] If this killing had no other ground than
the revenge for Hamlet's father, it would have been first-degree
murder since the fact had long been premeditated. (Premeditation of the precise means of executing the fact is of no legal
importance.) In some part we must assume it is so, and that
Hamlet has achieved a successful revenge for his father. On the
other hand, Shakespeare has so ordered the action as to introduce other legal factors. Although Laertes does not actually so
specify, we must assume that when he ends "The King, the King's
to blame," Hamlet recognizes the part Claudius must have taken
in the unbated rapier plot against his life. Claudius' responsibility for the death of Gertrude is quite clear cut. Thus when Hamlet wounds Claudius and forces him to drink poison, he is
symbolically retaliating with the rapier for his own death and
with the cup for that of his mother. In either case he could have

11. Kittredge, among others, recoils from the implications and would like to
make 5.2.337, 339 figurative: "anything," he declares, "is better than to make
Hamlet force the dying King to drink." It would have to be "anything" indeed
to interpret these lines figuratively, especially l.339, "It is a poison tempered by
himself." If one must be concrete as to motive, one could suggest that Hamlet
wanted to make sure that all of the venom had not been expended in the
wounding of himself and of Laertes. But poetic justice and one-for-one are
sufficient explanation.

pleaded manslaughter on the grounds of hot blood. If we regard the fact that Hamlet would necessarily have acted as he did here even if his father had not been murdered, we can see that the actual killing of the King would come under the head of manslaughter since the fruition of the revenge was at this point in fact only secondary.[12]

Shakespeare, then, has so manipulated the final slaughter as to free Hamlet from any guilt of murder. Hence his death must rest on his mistaken slaying of Polonius for the King; and Laertes pleads that Heaven may free him even from this. When, as we may suppose, Heaven hears Laertes, there can be no question of Hamlet's death in continuing sin or crime. His death can be only expiatory, and thus a death-in-victory quite different from the clouded death of Hieronimo in punishment for the dénouement crime he has committed. In consequence, the fate of Hamlet's soul is elaborately prepared. The mutual forgiveness of Hamlet and Laertes demonstrates his lack of wrath and the propriety of his state of mind for the reception of mercy himself. He saves Horatio from the sin of suicide and like a careful prince places his successor in nomination. Fortinbras speaks most admiringly of him. If ever a tragic hero died peacefully, sung to his rest, it is Hamlet.

The extraordinary effort that Shakespeare makes in this death scene to prompt the audience toward a charitable view of Hamlet's end as one of expiatory justice certain to be tempered with mercy is remarkable both in the construction of the death action itself and in the variety of the commentary by the attending characters. Whatever deliberate haziness there has been earlier in the play about Hamlet's motives for delay, or ambiguity in his

12. This distinction between primary and secondary causes for the killing of Claudius seems to be maintained in the text. Hamlet nowhere specifies that he has killed Claudius to satisfy his revenge; and his words, "Here, thou incestuous, murderous damned Dane" (though I take it that they at least refer to the death of his father as well as his own), could be satisfactorily explained as applying only to himself. When shortly he begs Horatio to "report me and my cause aright," he is clearly referring to his revenge, which may be utilized as additional evidence to "the unsatisfied" who want more facts than the demonstration of Claudius' guilt has just revealed. But this line has no bearing on his motives for killing Claudius.

sparing of Claudius in the prayer scene, in the dénouement Shakespeare somewhat uncharacteristically is not willing to leave the facts to the interpretation of the audience. He must interpret these facts for his audience. This unusual interposition, combined with the exact arrangement of the final action to remove guilt, must have seemed to him both warranted and necessary. It is critically significant, therefore, and must be considered in any whole view of the tragedy and of Shakespeare's conscious intentions in shaping its fable and its characters.

DRAMATIC STRUCTURE
AND CRITICISM:
Plot in HAMLET

IF WE ARE TO BASE AESTHETIC CRITICISM of the drama on any kind of evidence that may seem tangible, we must start with the plot. The chief fault of most searchers for tangible evidence is their treatment of a play as if it were a transcript of real life, a view that Stoll and his followers have effectively exploded. Characters in a play do not have secret lives off-stage that are subject to guesswork as if actions, thoughts, and emotions not portrayed, or even mentioned, in the play can nevertheless be reconstructed. Speculation cannot piece together a full continuum of detail that will weld what we see and hear on-stage to what we do not see and hear off-stage.

Aristotle defined plot as follows: "the Plot is the imitation of the action:—for by plot I here mean the arrangement of the incidents" (*Poetics* 6.6), and he remarks shortly (6.9), "the most important of all is the structure of the incidents"; and again, "the incidents and the plot are the end of tragedy, and the end is the chief thing of all" (6.10). Butcher (p. 347) paraphrases in this manner: "It is the plot . . . which gives to the play inner meaning and reality as the soul does to the body. To the plot we look in order to learn what the play means; here lies its essence, its true

From *Shakespeare Quarterly* 15 (1964).

significance. Lastly, the plot is 'the end of a tragedy' as well as the beginning. Through the plot the intention of the play is realised."

Modern critics have tended to overlook the uses of plot analysis in the service of aesthetic criticism, a form that should be aimed at the determination and evaluation of the meaning of a work of art, insofar as this end is possible within the framework of an artistic production. "Meaning" is a slippery term, of course. At one end of the scale we have authorial conscious intention deliberately worked out in a play; at the other, we have unconscious meaning penetrating and shaping any great work of art well beyond an author's precise conceptions. Let us leave the unconscious to other critics and concern ourselves, more humbly, with what must be the starting-point for accurate criticism, of whatever kind: an attempt to utilize the evidence of plot to determine at least some elements of an author's conscious intention. In doing so we shall be escaping the older-fashioned method of seeking meaning through character analysis in the Bradley manner, for Aristotle places character in a tragedy as secondary to plot. We shall also be escaping the analysis of Shakespeare's imagery as the key to his true meaning. Aristotle again disagrees, and assigns to diction a place behind plot and character. Certainly, the complaint is true that criticism of a play as a poem involves an analytical method suitable for lyric or narrative but not necessarily appropriate for dramatic poetry on the stage.

Since *Hamlet* has been more than ordinarily subject to critical speculation, we may take this difficult example and see what the analysis of plot in one or two respects can show about problems that lie at the heart of the play.

In every developed play there is one incident, or action, on which the main plot turns. The plot may be said to turn on this episode because, when the whole play is viewed in retrospect, the audience can see that the end (whether for good or for ill) was the direct result of a chain of causality linked to this one episode which, in effect, directed the action into a particular path that determined the outcome of the plot. Aristotle seized on this incident as the determinant whether a plot would be, as he phrased it, single or complex, according to the means by which "the change of fortune" took place (9.2) That a tragedy must have an incident in which a change took place that determined the conclusion, however, he never doubted.

The modern term for this incident is the climax, or crisis. In popular thinking, climax is confused with catastrophe or dénouement, and is thought to be the high point of the action in the sense that it is the most exciting incident, usually that episode at the end when the decisive conflict takes place that settles the fates of the characters. The true climax is, indeed, an incident in which the fate of the protagonist is irrevocably decided; but the popular identification of the climax as the untying of the knot obscures the important objection that the tragedy (if we may talk only of this form) would scarcely be inevitable if at the last moment its course might be altered. The nature of this catastrophe or outcome has been decided long before in the true climax, the key scene of the play which causes the action to turn against the tragic protagonist. After this point, the details by which his unhappy end will be brought about may be subject to variation, but not the outcome itself.

If we are to attempt to discover what significance the action of a tragedy possesses, we must first determine what is the true turning-point of the action, for that incident will give us the clue to the essential tragic meaning of the play. In truth, if the tragedy itself has any significance, its climactic incident that determines the ultimate fate of the chief character must be the key to unlock this meaning: a climax cannot itself be without meaning in a truly meaningful play.

In the usual tragedy the action in the early stages favors the protagonist; in the last stage of the catastrophe, the action goes contrary to his interests, and usually the chain of events leads to his defeat or death. The incident responsible for the alteration of the course of the action will be the climax. It can be discovered in two ways. First, the turn of the action against the protagonist must be traced to this point and to this point alone. Second, if the tragic action is to have a significance, a significant decision by the hero must be contained in this episode, a decision that is in some way mistaken or unfortunate, and usually one that will justify the tragic fate that as a result overtakes him. When these two criteria join, the critic has isolated the climax.

In the action of *Hamlet* three scenes are commonly suggested: the play-within-a-play, the prayer scene, and the closet scene. The play-within-a-play, it is asserted, is crucial because only after the test is Hamlet positive that Claudius is the murderer of his father and that the revenge can proceed with justice. We must admit that if Hamlet throughout the antecedent action had been tormented by doubts of the Ghost, and if as result of the mousetrap his mind was so clarified that he engaged himself to a course of revengeful action that succeeded, and, at the end, he survived, then the play-within-a-play would certainly be the climax in a very different drama called *Hamlet*. In such a plot the incident that changes paralyzing uncertainty and delay to certainty and action, and thus leads to the successful conclusion, must be the turning-point.

But if we take *Hamlet* as it is, we may ask, first, was Hamlet's doubt of the Ghost the major reason for his failure to revenge between the time of the Ghost's revelation and the acting of *The Murder of Gonzago*? If so, Shakespeare has neglected to inform us. The hard truth is that no concrete reason for delay in this interval is ever given us by narrative or by action up to the moment, the night before the play-within-a-play, that Hamlet decides to test whether the Ghost be demon or spirit and in the process to secure "grounds more relative" than the mere word of an apparition. If doubt of the Ghost has been a deterrent to action, we do not know it. A climax is very odd indeed that clarifies the hero's mind on a problem that the audience has not known existed until two scenes before.[1]

Secondly, we may enquire what is the significant issue of this scene, what the fateful decision that thereupon makes the tragic catastrophe inevitable. Might not the identical scene serve as the climax for a dénouement in which Hamlet succeeds in a well-planned revenge and ascends the throne of Denmark?

There is, however, another argument in favor of the mousetrap scene as crisis that might be advanced: the play-within-a-

1. I am taking the soliloquy that ends 2.2 substantially at its face value and thus not concerning myself with the view that this doubt of the Ghost is Hamlet's sudden rationalizing of his congenital inability to act.

play warns Claudius that Hamlet knows his secret and thus turns the King from an ostensible benefactor to Hamlet's mortal enemy. It is perfectly clear that Claudius' first action after his exposure is to alter the innocent commission for the English voyage to a command to execute Hamlet on arrival. The catastrophe, moreover, is directly brought about by another plot of Claudius against Hamlet's life that succeeds where the initial one had failed. Thus it is true, in one sense, that the plot line alters after the play-within-a-play, and that the change in Claudius' attitude to Hamlet that brings about the catastrophe can be traced back directly to the mousetrap scene.

Is this, then, the turning-point, the incident in the plot in which the action veers from prosperity to defeat as a consequence? The answer would be yes were Claudius the protagonist. Yet the enmity of Claudius, as an antagonist, need not be successful, even though it is admittedly aroused in this scene. Moreover, the second test for the climax will not work. If the play-within-a-play is the turning-point, then a fateful decision by Hamlet must be involved that arises in some sort from character. A subtle critic might argue that Hamlet made a fatal blunder in staging *The Murder of Gonzago*, since the clarification of his mind was achieved, ironically, only at the expense of warning his foe that the murderer of Old Hamlet was known and that a revenger was in being. Hence the gain was ironically accompanied by inevitable loss, and Hamlet sealed his doom by alerting his victim to the danger of his position.

Such an argument might suit melodrama but not Shakespearean tragedy, for it omits not only the role of character in the decision but also the ethical issue. What Elder Olson calls a morally determinate action (closely related to the requirements of Aristotle's tragic law) would be inoperative.[2] I do not wish to argue that all tragic heroes must conform to the Aristotelian formula, no matter how psychologically sound it may be. But the linking of a fateful decision to some principle of action is essential if a tragedy is to be a meaningful criticism of life. If Hamlet

2. See the reference to Olson in "Shakespeare's Art: The Point of View," note 6.

is damned if he does, and damned if he doesn't—which is the crux of the ironic argument just sketched—then no decision can be right or wrong, and therefore no significance can inhere to whatever choice is made. This dilemma might suit a naturalistic or existentialist drama, or a Theater of the Absurd, but it would not suit Shakespeare and the Elizabethans.

Let us revert for a moment to the meaning of the phrase "a morally determinate action" as a requirement for tragic drama. The heart of the matter is that a decision that triggers the climax cannot be one dictated by chance or accident, for such a choice has no personal significance, whatever its philosophic import may be in respect to the human condition for those to whom the world and human life possess no significant pattern. Even in such a semi-tragedy as *Romeo and Juliet* in which the ending seems removed from any rigorous application of the doctrine of tragic flaw, the climax following Romeo's decision to fight with Tybalt involves a personal choice that carries moral responsibility and is therefore morally determinate.[3]

Thus a morally determinate action means not only that the character is aware of the issue and nevertheless makes a choice that is inherently fatal, but also that the audience is aware of the significance of the choice on a plane higher than simple expediency and can approve or disapprove accordingly. That is, if the hero is to suffer death as a result of his choice, the audience must acknowledge the justice of the outcome. This recognition can be achieved only if the audience sees the violation of some impor-

3. I refer to attempts to equate a tragic flaw with Romeo and Juliet's precipitate falling in love and immediate marriage. If every elopement were to be condemned by death—a view that is the logical extension—we should need to alter our beliefs about romantic love. Although Aristotle's doctrine of the tragic flaw does not explain very much of the tragic situation, nevertheless Shakespeare does succeed in portraying life in this play according to some sort of significant pattern. The theme of the "star-crossed lovers"—that is, Fate—seems to be the answer. If so, the tragic plot concerns two lovers caught up in an action that draws its rationale from the logic of externally motivated events and less from character flowering into (and ultimately responsible for) the consequences of the action. In these circumstances Shakespeare is in serious danger of arousing, as Aristotle remarks, the audience's resentment at a lack of

tant moral principle in the choice and agrees that the decisive action had significance and was not entered upon by accident, or blindly selected without a recognition of the issues involved. This is only to re-state the Aristotelian doctrine of the tragic flaw in a man who is neither a devil nor an angel, and the cathartic effect that results from contemplating his fall.

Under these circumstances it is proper to inquire whether Hamlet's choice to prove Claudius' guilt at the expense of alerting his opponent to the mortal danger in which he stood was a morally determinate action—anything that could qualify as an action springing from a tragic flaw. The answer can be only a strong denial. Hamlet's choice in setting the mousetrap may be existentially tragic, but it is not tragic in any sense known to Shakespeare or his contemporaries. No ethical issue is raised by the choice, only one of expediency. The play-within-a-play cannot be the climax to a meaningful tragedy.

However, it is argued that the information received in this scene gives Hamlet the readiness to kill Claudius, as he thinks, in the closet scene. This may well be, depending upon the seriousness with which one takes the final soliloquy in 2.2, with its statement of need to test the Ghost's revelations. The play-within-a-play followed by the prayer scene, it is true, offers a rising sequence of strain; but this is only to say that the decision to kill made in the closet scene was more important than the motivation, such as it was, offered by the success of the mousetrap in respect to that decision. Indeed, that the closet scene

---

justice. He avoids this danger, it would seem, by finding his climax in a morally determinate action, even though it is so strongly shaped by external events as to constitute less than a real tragic flaw. Moreover, the emphasis on Fate as a positive force lends in this early work a dignity and a pattern to the action that might not otherwise be felt as significant. Finally, Shakespeare chooses to emphasize the pity of the cathartic reaction rather than the fear, perhaps, although fear is not entirely absent. However, the fear is not created by the identification of the audience with the lovers—the feeling, "There but for the grace of God go I." Instead, the fear is generated by the identification of the audience with parental blindness: "But for the grace of God I might behave like this to my children."

follows the play-within-a-play is largely adventitious, and the sequence is deliberately emphasized as not an effect of a cause.

Instead, Shakespeare has very carefully arranged the cause-and-effect linkage of the incidents to show that the interview with Gertrude and the concealment of Polonius were planned before the play-within-a-play, and that Hamlet went to his mother's apartment not because of the success of the mousetrap but as the result of a plan laid much earlier. Indeed, it is an irony that the scheme for Gertrude to worm the secret of his melancholy from her son is no longer necessary after the play-within-a-play, for Claudius has learned the secret but is not in a position to countermand the orders for the original plan to go into effect. Polonius and Gertrude, the audience knows, are engaged to a plan that has no longer any rationale. If, in the plot, there is no necessary connection between the play-within-a-play and the closet scene (indeed, quite the reverse), then the argument fails that the closet-scene killing of Polonius is only the working-out of the climax decision made as a result of Claudius' self-betrayal at the play. The climax, thus, is still to seek.

The prayer scene is also a candidate, and superficially there is something to be said for it. Certainly, if Hamlet had not spared the King here, Claudius would not have lived to fight another day and to lay the plot that finally caused Hamlet's death in the catastrophe. Yet analysis shows that all evidence in favor of the prayer scene is superficial. In relation to the plot line, no definite action from Claudius directly depends upon his being spared. It is only his determination to conceal his initial crime at all costs that leads him to the specific practice against Hamlet's life that causes the catastrophe. For example, Claudius alters the commission for the English embassy to order Hamlet's execution, as the first result of the play-within-a-play revelation. But this counteraction proves abortive. Hamlet escapes the danger, and thus the altered commission has nothing to do with the terms of the catastrophe. Another, and later, intrigue causes Hamlet's death.

Correspondingly, the failure to dispose of Claudius in the prayer scene merely enables him to continue with the same plan for the English voyage that is later to prove useless. At this point no action has been taken that will necessarily prove to have a tragic outcome. There is no reason why Hamlet cannot still outwit Claudius and take his revenge in safety. That Claudius could not rise from the grave to kill Hamlet in the catastrophe if he had been slain at his prayers is obvious enough, but the action of a dramatic plot requires more of a chain of cause and effect between specific incidents, one leading to another, than this very general connection. No specific action derives from Claudius as a direct result of his having been spared, unwittingly, in the prayer scene, but only a continuation of an action decided upon after the play-within-a-play. Whatever the significance of the prayer scene, therefore, it cannot be defended in terms of the dramatic plot as the turning-point of the action in which the advantage, previously in Hamlet's favor, shifts to Claudius' side.

Indeed, to revert for a moment, it would be a poor matching of wits if the revelation of Hamlet's revengeful purpose were actually the turning-point. If Hamlet is so weak that he must kill an unsuspecting victim instead of an opponent on guard, he would have been a puny tragic hero. We must agree that Claudius' recognition of his own danger does not mark the crisis of the drama, for the baring of his secret only makes the two men equally matched in their knowledge of each other. Shakespeare emphasizes this point by showing us Claudius' first retaliatory action after the mousetrap as a failure. The crucial incident that decides the issue between them is yet to come.

Within these terms the prayer scene cannot be that incident, for no new line of the plot leads from it that has not already had its origin in the play-within-a-play, to which the prayer scene is only an appendage. This is to speak technically. In terms of the plot, it is the joining of Laertes to Claudius that directly leads to Hamlet's death. What the action of the play would have been like if Laertes had not had the occasion to revenge his father's death, we cannot tell. In itself, this point is enough to remove the prayer scene from consideration as the climax.

But other and even more important considerations appear: the ethical implications of the climax that are part and parcel of the Aristotelian doctrine of the tragic flaw as it appears in English Renaissance drama.[4] If Hamlet's sparing of Claudius at prayer is to be a tragic error of such magnitude that the audience will accept his death in the catastrophe as an act of justice, we must take it that he should have killed Claudius at this moment. If so, the audience must believe that Hamlet's decision to spare him was not only ill-advised but even culpable despite his belief that Claudius was then in a state of grace. It is difficult to see how such a bloodthirsty and morally obtuse theory could be defended on the grounds of heroic action. If a tragic flaw in a sympathetic character is to be pinpointed as his refusal to kill a defenseless man at prayer, then the English dramatic hero was modelled on the tradition of the Renaissance Italian villain, a patently absurd proposition. Hamlet's refusal to slaughter Claudius when he is presumably at peace with his Maker is a morally determinate action, right enough, but it does not result from an inner weakness, a character flaw.[5] If it were a fault requiring death in the dénouement, Christian docrine would have no influence on an audience's moral judgment. Let us move on.

The direct means by which Claudius kills Hamlet is the poisoned rapier in the hand of Laertes. This is the only counteraction we see except for the abortive attempt to have Hamlet

4. The English Renaissance drama had a strong impulse to intensify the Aristotelian tragic flaw by associating it with the Christian doctrine of personal responsibility for actions, a concept that stems from a belief in the significance of free will, and hence one that sometimes was far removed from the Greek spirit.

5. The point, actually, is not whether Hamlet would have been culpable if he had known the truth about Claudius' lack of repentance but not culpable if he had acted on the assumption that Claudius was in a state of grace. Critics are in general agreement that Hamlet's bloodthirsty reasons are a rationalization of (or a recompense for) his unwillingness to kill at this moment. If the drawing back from the commission of a murder when the opportunity is first offered is a weakness in character that will enable catharsis to operate in the consequences, then an argument for the climactic nature of this scene can be made. But, it should be noted, not in a civilized Christian society, whatever would have been the reaction of Hrothgar's subjects. One simply cannot argue that an Elizabethan, or a modern, audience would take the refusal to commit a cold-blooded murder as a moral weakness rather than a moral strength.

executed in England. If Laertes had not joined with Claudius against Hamlet, we have no means of knowing how the play's catastrophe would have been brought about and whether its action would have been for or against Hamlet. But Laertes, a noble young gentleman, could not have been suborned like Rosencrantz and Guildenstern to join Claudius' party. The one cause that leads him to seek Hamlet's death is the murder of Polonius. Since it is the revenge of Laertes that tips the scales against Hamlet and directly brings about the catastrophe, whatever scene it is that shows the origin of his revenge on Hamlet will meet one part of the plot requirements for the climax. This scene is, of course, the interview with Hamlet's mother in the course of which Polonius is slain by mistake for the King. If, as I have suggested, Claudius and Hamlet are two evenly matched opponents, the turning-point of the plot must be this mistake of Hamlet that causes Laertes to intervene and to ally himself with Claudius against Hamlet's life. By a chain of cause and effect, the events of the catastrophe are firmly bound to the closet scene.

The closet scene must next pass the second test, that of being a morally determinate action resulting from a tragic flaw. I suggest that this ethical climax does indeed coincide with the climax of the action. Greek tragedy might have made of this scene a study of simple fatal error, something like the hotheaded bad luck by which Oedipus slew his father; and in this manner it might have drawn a moral of the ways in which supernal fate interferes, with a force too strong for mortals to triumph over. But the Elizabethan is not the Greek drama, and the English tragic writers would necessarily have agreed with Milton's God, Who pronounces, "What I will is Fate." The general framework of Elizabethan tragic ethics, which depend upon the Christian doctrine of free will and personal responsibility, demands that the slaying of Polonius be more than an unlucky accident.

We now come to a view of the closet scene that may be briefly summarized, since it has been considered elsewhere in some detail.[6] Shakespeare's *Hamlet* is not a play glorifying pagan ethics; it

---

6. "Hamlet as Minister and Scourge" and "Hamlet's Fifth Soliloquy."

cannot help being addressed to an audience that takes the Christian point of view for granted. Blood-revenge is a pagan, or at least an anti-Christian, duty, since it requires a man to place his will above that of God and to violate the commandment, "Thou shalt not kill." The premeditated murder sought by a revenger of blood endangered his immortal soul. Elizabethan law joined with Christian doctrine to exclude private blood-revenge as a way of justice. When public justice was not practicable, men must rely on the biblical promise, "Vengeance is mine; I will repay, saith the Lord." Generally interpreted, this punishment for crime might be delayed until the after-life; but, obviously, a more concrete manifestation was desirable, and thus the Elizabethans were inclined to see God's justice-dealing hand in the downfall or death of all evil-doers. Sometimes God might work through natural forces, as a storm; sometimes through brute creation. But often He used human agents as ministers of His justice. In doing so, however, He reserved those actions that repaid a crime by a crime for men called scourges who by their fixed rejection of divine grace had damned themselves irremediably in this life. Justice that required no crime for its administration was performed by good men, called ministers.

When we apply this ethos to *Hamlet*, we see the absurdity of taking it that God would release the Ghost from Purgatory to corrupt his son by urging Hamlet to a murder that would condemn his immortal soul to hell fire. In fact, the Ghost never suggests to Hamlet that Claudius should be killed, even though that is Hamlet's assumption. As we may see from a very important object lesson, Cyril Tourneur's play *The Atheists's Tragedy* put the Christian revenger into God's hands, confident that Providence would offer the means, ultimately, for a revenge that would not be criminal.

Thus it may be argued that it was a real error for Hamlet to attempt his private revenge in the closet scene since this action ran contrary to his position as a minister of Heaven, for whom public justice would be arranged at Heaven's own pleasure. The tragic error consists in the fact that Hamlet's emotional drive is too strong, or compulsive, to permit him to wait upon what appears to be Heaven's quite exorbitant delay.[7] After the mounting pressure of his success in the play-within-a-play and then the frustration of the prayer scene, the opportunity offered for an ostensible madman to slice up a rat proves more than he can resist. Hamlet rejects the biblical command against private blood-revenge, and instantly finds his error when he discovers he has slain an innocent man. This decision to cast off Heavenly guidance may fairly be called a morally determinate action suitable for tragic dignity, and the inability to endure the cumulative strain of inaction may fairly be called the tragic flaw. Without question we have here the true climax.

It rests briefly to assess the value of this analysis for a critical view of the play, even while we keep in mind that this has been only one episode under scrutiny and that there are others that need similar analysis before any total criticism can be attempted.

Tourneur's *Atheist's Tragedy* must be cited once more, with its protagonist who is in the same dilemma as Hamlet but who successfully overcomes the temptation to anticipate Heaven, and who therefore survives when Heavenly vengeance strikes down his antagonist at the very moment of his anticipated triumph. The lesson to be drawn is—paradoxically—that the tragic fact is not Hamlet's inaction, except for its effect on his cumulative impatience. One cannot emphasize too strongly that the critical identification of the climax reveals this truth: the catastrophe occurs not as a direct consequence of Hamlet's delay but instead as a direct consequence of his rash and overhasty action. This is what the plot tells us. There is no other choice.

The long history of discussion about Hamlet's delay, as if its complex causes were the central fact of the drama, and indeed as if the tragedy were the outcome of this delay, is quite unsupported by the evidence of the plot. The only episode of delay that is shown us in the action (and Aristotle admits as part of

7.   This is also the reason for the tragic decision made by Hieronimo in Kyd's *Spanish Tragedy.* See Bowers, "A Note on *The Spanish Tragedy,*" *MLN* 53 (1938): 590–91.

the plot only what is shown in action) is the sparing of Claudius at prayer. If under the peculiar circumstances of this scene any audience believes that Hamlet was so culpable in neglecting the opportunity that his catastrophic death is a just return for an egregious error of delay, then there is no ethical relation between art and life, and we have reverted to savagery. The plot tells us that it was Hamlet's ill-advised action, not his inaction, that led by consequence to his death-in-victory.

The critical analysis of Hamlet's delay, therefore, as if it were an error, a weakness, is itself wrong-headed. By its climax the plot tells us that it was the breaking of the inaction that was the fatal error, indeed the tragic flaw that justified his final death and made it acceptable, in Aristotelian as well as in Christian terms, to the audience of his own and of our day, for Hamlet must expiate the murder he has committed. The elevation of psychological delay as the central theme of *Hamlet*, and its main interest, is the result of placing character above plot as the chief end of tragedy, an error that Aristotle warned against.[8] The fault lies in analyzing character in isolation, or in relation only to individual incident, not in relation to the great chain of cause-and-effect incidents forming the coherent plot in Aristotelian terms. In this case much critical theory about Hamlet's character runs contrary to the plain lesson of the action as it links incident to form the plot. "For Tragedy is an imitation, not of men, but of an action and of life, and life consists in action, and its end is a mode of action, not a quality" (*Poetics* 6.9).

If we could learn nothing else from relating dramatic structure to critical theory, this alone would be a valuable lesson. Indeed, most analyses of Hamlet's character are based on his frustrated and therefore untrustworthy self-recrimination, or else on speculation about motives that presuppose off-stage incidents not

8.   Indeed, character may be superior to plot in Renaissance tragedy, but only with the idea that plot serves character and flowers ultimately in character and in personal decision or responsibility, a Christian doctrine that Aristotle could not be expected to consider. The critics to whom I refer have treated character in comparative isolation and not as the flowering of plot, which must mean that character is organized and given significance by plot.

shown to us or even referred to. Here we need Stoll's useful reminder that characters in art do not lead full and independent lives, both on and off-stage, of which we see in the presented episodes only the part of a whole. Quite literally, we see the whole of any dramatic character's life in the action and speech of a play. Nothing is left to silence, or to speculation to fill in. It is a fallacy to attempt to build critical theories on our reconstruction from the non-existence of a wraith.

But something more can be gained towards our understanding of *Hamlet* the play and Hamlet the man. I select only two of a number of points. The first must rest on simple statement, for discussion would be burdensome if not superfluous. The turning point of the play exhibits an action disobedient to divine command about a general rule of life, "Thou shalt not kill," and also, more specifically, an action that is contrary to a justice that must not involve crime if Hamlet is to remain a Heaven-selected minister. If this is so, Hamlet's earlier neutrality of action in respect to the revenge must be taken as showing obedience to God and therefore admirable. Certainly this is the way Tourneur's *Atheist's Tragedy* views a similar, though more didactic, hero. Thus it is strength, not weakness, that lies behind the delay, and it is a lack of fortitude that causes Hamlet to crack and to make his fatal blunder in the closet scene. In view of this clear lesson of the plot once an analysis is made of its parts, how ridiculous is Olivier's sepulchral introduction to his film, "This is the tragedy of a man who could not make up his mind." And how off the mark are all critics who take Hamlet's initial delay as a sign of confusion and of weakness rather than of strength.

Second, the significance of the catastrophe of a tragedy cannot differ from the significance of its climax. The way of the dénouement must seem to the audience to be the just consequence of the tragic error of the climax, or else, as Aristotle observed, the catharsis of pity and fear will not operate. Once again, statement must take the place of lengthy analysis. Let me suggest, therefore, that the end of Hamlet is a true death-in-victory, as analyzed in "The Death of Hamlet." Only by the assumption that Hamlet in some measure retrieves his error of the climax while paying the price of his life can the audience accept the justice of the final holocaust and undergo the catharsis that is essential. It is necessary, thus, to ask how Hamlet retrieves his climactic error. Is it only that he got the wrong man the first time, but succeeded in knocking off the right one at the end? This would be a trivial view indeed. The irony of the closet scene is that as a penalty for disobedience he kills the wrong man. He commits what turns out to be a useless murder, and must expiate this crime with his life.

A parallel can be drawn, I think, between *Hamlet* and Milton's *Samson Agonistes.* Samson fails in a charge given him by divine agency and is therefore alienated from God; but later, as a result of an insight previously denied him, he recovers his sense of original mission and carries out his charge. But his disobedience, although it has not, in fact, altered God's purpose for him, has changed the circumstances under which this purpose is achieved. Instead of a triumph that he will survive, his last victory over the Philistines requires his death in expiation for the consequences of his crime. God gives him the promised victory, but it is a death-in-victory. Nonetheless, we rejoice as does Samson's father when finally he sees in it the immutability of divine purpose and the justice of the ways of God to man.

In large part this formula applies to Hamlet. His disobedience in the closet scene when he seeks a private blood-revenge contrary to divine law seems to remove him as God's minister to enact justice. He recognizes that he is being punished by the murder of the wrong man, Polonius:

> *but heaven hath pleas'd it so,*
> *To punish me with this, and this with me,*
> *That I must be their scourge and minister.*

The recognition of his error is, in effect, his repentance, and it draws on signs of Heaven's reassertion of his original mission. We must not overlook Hamlet's own attribution of divine ordination to his wakefulness on shipboard, the discovery of the commissions, the circumstance that he could reseal them without discovery, and, finally, his rescue by the pirate ship.

When he returns, and Horatio warns him that the time is

short, Hamlet serenely replies that the interim will be his. This confidence in the successful outcome of his duty is backed by no known plan, and critics have never satisfied themselves why Hamlet should be so confident here. I suggest that he is confident because, like Samson, he feels himself once more reconciled to divine Providence. This time he will not repeat his tragic error but will wait for the proper opportunity to be given him, as indeed it later is given, both for him and for Samson. In this light, his denial of the omen of the pain about his heart that so alarms Horatio, and his refusal to follow Horatio's prudent advice to decline the fencing match, are as clearcut a hint of Hamlet's reconciliation as Shakespeare could give the audience: "we defy augury; there's a special providence in the fall of a sparrow. If it be now, 'tis not to come; if it be not to come, it will be now; if it be not now, yet it will come: the readiness is all." No more comprehensive words could be contrived to show Hamlet's faith that he is in God's hand.

As a consequence we can accept the justice of the catastrophe, content with Hamlet's death, because like Samson to whom God returned (although He had never departed), Hamlet dies in a victory that is the age-old demonstration of God's unchanging purposes as well as the symbol of a personal reconciliation and acceptance. This is a true Christian catharsis, superior to any possible for the Greeks, and it is important that we should not overlook its significance.

If, as has been suggested, an audience will accept the death of a tragic hero if it feels that in some manner his tragic experiences have given him a personal clarification and ennoblement, then the insight that comes to Hamlet, especially just before the fencing match, and his rectification in the same terms of his original error, constitute that ennoblement. Shakespeare is so concerned with this matter that he gives Hamlet the opportunity to flee when the omen strikes him. But when Hamlet rejects the omen and refuses to put his own will above that of divine purpose, even though it means his death, he wins through to final victory. Hamlet had erred in this manner once before, when he thought he detected the King behind the arras and had taken justice into his own hands in an action that could not be divinely appointed.

Now, at the end of the tragedy, he knows his previous error and he wills himself not to repeat it. This last action before the fencing match I take to be an important episode in the plot, one that serves to link the climax in significance to the catastrophe and to remove the final scene from the imputation of accident. Hence a reading of the plot may serve once again to let us see something of Shakespeare's larger purposes in this play.

If these suggestions I have made are correct, then we may see how salutary is a return to the analysis and comprehension of the significance of dramatic structure, which is to say, plot, as a service to accurate criticism. It is important, in my view, not to discuss any incident in vacuum but only as a part of the whole and only as it contributes to the effect of the whole, which must be clearly seen before the parts can be tackled. It is important, in my view, to analyze dramatic characters only after the plot and its intent are thoroughly comprehended, for these characters—as Aristotle remarks—have no life except in the action of the plot.

Finally, when dealing with great literature we must see that dramatic structure and the weight, or significance, of a play— what Galsworthy calls its "spire of meaning"—are mutually interdependent. One must check one's analysis of plot and its technical details by correlation with the ultimate significance of the action. In reverse, the structural parts of the plot cannot be distinguished clearly unless the significance, or meaning, of the play relates to them.

This double method offers a critical course that rests on what we may properly call evidence, not mere opinion or assertion; and we can trust its results, for the heart of a play lies in its action.

HAMLET'S "SULLIED"
OR "SOLID" FLESH:
A *Bibliographical Case-History*

ONE OF THE MOST DEBATED of all textual problems in Shakespeare is that of Hamlet's reference to his "too too solid flesh." Are we to read this as *sallied*, following the Second Quarto as well as the First? Are we to adopt the Folio's *solid*? Or are we to consider *sallied* as a misprint for *sullied* and boldly indulge in emendation?

The traditional reading is the *solid* of the Folio, but J. Dover Wilson has offered a vigorous defence of *sullied*. This, he argues, is what Shakespeare wrote, and he suggests that what he calls the misprint *sallied* was taken over by the Second from the First Quarto. He also points to the Second Quarto's *slight sallies* at 2.1.39 and to *unsallied* for *unsullied* in *Love's Labour's Lost*, 5.2.352—all, in his opinion, exhibiting the same error of *a* for *u*. *Sullied flesh* is for him the key to the soliloquy, for it shows Hamlet thinking of his mother's incestuous marriage as a personal defilement. *Solid flesh*, he declares, is absurd associated with *melt* and *thaw*, whereas on various occasions Shakespeare uses *sully* with the image, implicit or explicit, of dirt upon a surface of pure

From *Shakespeare Survey*, no. 9 (1956): 44–48; by permission of Cambridge Univ. Press.

white, like snow. An example would be *Winter's Tale*, 1.2.326–27, "sully the purity and whiteness of my sheets." [1]

The critical, or literary, argument in favour of *sullied* has, however, fallen short of acceptance. While Wilson is sure that *sullied* best fits the tone of the "To be or not to be" soliloquy, others are equally certain that this word ill fits the context and that *solid* was the adjective which Shakespeare had in his original manuscript.

When so much is a matter of opinion, little certainty can obtain. However, once we begin to pursue a somewhat different line of inquiry, certain strands of the problem may become clearer. That *sally* is a legitimate form of *sully*, and not a misspelling, seems to be the growing opinion of linguists. [2] Moreover, that the Oxford English Dictionary does not list *sally* is not real evidence that the word does not exist: almost surely the compilers overlooked the three occurrences in Shakespeare because they used edited modernized texts. And when we find the same form elsewhere in the sense of *sully*, in Dekker's *Patient Grissil*, "Then sally not this morning with foule lookes" (1.1.12), we can perhaps no

---

1.   The original arguments in *The Manuscript of Shakespeare's Hamlet* (1934), 2: 307–16, are summarized, with some addition, in the New Cambridge *Hamlet*, pp. 151–52 and, in the revised later printing, p. 294.

2.   However, the linguistic opinion is not based on strictly linguistic grounds. If I read Kökeritz aright (*Shakespeare's Pronunciation* [1953], p. 242 and n.), he is unwilling to take a definite position and cannot solve the problem. He starts by seeming slightly to favor the *unsallied* in *Love's Labour's Lost* as a misprint (he does not know of the Dekker *sally* and, curiously, fails to consider Polonius' *sallies*). He then splits the ticket and offers the opinion that this *unsallied* nevertheless suggests that the *sallied* of *Hamlet* should be interpreted as *sullied;* on the other hand, it may be an unrounded form of *solid.* Kökeritz's manifest confusion stems from the fact that such *u:a* alternative forms have not been recorded; hence as a linguist he would clearly prefer to find almost any escape.

In his review of Kökeritz in *Language* 29 (1953): 560–61, Professor Archibald Hill proved himself to be perhaps the first scholar willing to grasp the nettle firmly. At my request, he has subsequently amplified his position, which he describes only as "the evidence and a statement of the kind of method a linguist would use in attacking the problem." He continues in his private letter: "There is no sound change, dialectal or otherwise, which would result in giving variants in the shape of *sully-sally.* I would add only that since we don't know all about the history of English, it is always possible that we might find

longer appeal to coincidence in error, misreading of handwriting, and so on, but accept *sally* as a legitimate variant of *sully*, and not—as Wilson believed—as a misprint for it.

The early editors, who did not understand the relationship of the three *Hamlet* texts, could select Folio *solid* only on literary grounds. But the fact that some degree of corruption in the Second Quarto must be attributed to the influence of the First Quarto introduces other than purely literary considerations, and it is well to see how the case stands up to a somewhat more rigorous examination than is usually given it. Contamination from the First Quarto definitely exists in sheets B–D of the Second Quarto, which contain all but the last seven lines of Act 1. In his *Manuscript of Shakespeare's Hamlet* (1934), 1.159–61, Wilson gave it as his opinion that the Second Quarto compositor was well aware of the degenerate nature of the First Quarto text and that he consulted it only infrequently and with due caution when he could not decipher a reading in his manuscript. According to Wilson there are only twenty-five readings in Act 1 of the Second Quarto that have resulted from the First Quarto's influence. Most of these turn out to be eccentric spellings or punctuations, and Wilson selects only five in all that he feels represent actual corruption foisted on the Second from the First Quarto.

---

somewhere a dialect in which such a sound change occurred. What is involved is a sound change from *schwa*, which occupies the exact centre of the three columns and three rows of the nine English vowel phonemes, to the position in the centre of the bottom row. Such a change is therefore perfectly thinkable, but as I said above, remains unknown. . . .

"There are three examples of *sally* in Shakespeare involving three compositors and presumably two different batches of printer's copy. There is a fourth quite independent example in Dekker. To assume a misreading of *a* for *u* thus requires four separate assumptions.

"To assume an Elizabethan word *sally-soiled* is only one assumption and is therefore simpler. Since it is axiomatic that we cannot assume that we have recorded the whole of the Elizabethan vocabulary, there is nothing in such an assumption which is in any way radical—unless one believes that it is radical to postulate a word not recorded in dictionaries.

"If *sally* is a genuine word, it is not the result of sound change. It can, however, be explained as a borrowing from French *sale*, and its later disappearance in turn is explained by its homonymity with *sally*, 'issue forth to attack.'"

Of these five, three are really spelling errors (*horrowes*, 1.1.44; *cost*, 1.1.73; *sallied*, 1.2.129), and hence only two remain as real verbal contaminations (*of a most select*, 1.3.74; *interr'd*, 1.4.49), to which he later added three more.[3]

The six most prominent post-Wilson editors, all necessarily aware of the possibility for contamination in the Second Quarto from the First Quarto, are able to concur in only two of Wilson's five supposed substantive corruptions and in none of his added three; and since this concurrence is only in rejecting *horrowes* and *cost*, not much is proved.[4] Yet all save Craig-Parrott side against Wilson in believing that Folio *solid* must be correct. The fact is that in the twenty or so years after Wilson's pioneer monograph, five major editors (omitting Craig-Parrott as rigid followers of the Wilson hypothesis) have been able to agree only on *sallied* and thus have made it the single substantive contamination from the First in the Second Quarto text.

Viewed dispassionately, the textual situation does not enforce this word's being isolated as a manifest contamination any more than several other strong candidates; and certainly the Second Quarto's meaning is not so difficult or inappropriate as to force one to stretch textual probabilities unduly in order to avoid it. It may be that editors would have looked more kindly on *sullied* if Wilson had not mistaken the spelling as a misprint and hence listed *sallied* among the corruptions from the First Quarto. It was perilously easy, as a consequence, to feel that Wilson's arguments were partial and that the real contamination lay in the word itself and not merely in its spelling. This view would be the easier to hold since there is no evidence from their texts that the listed

3. In the New Cambridge edition Wilson adds *rootes* for *rots* (1.5.33); *Heavens* for *Heaven* (1.5.113); and the omission of *Looke you* before *I will goe pray* (1.5.132).

4. These six were Kittredge, Craig-Parrott, Harrison, Campbell, Alexander, and Sisson. For example, only Kittredge agrees with Wilson that the First Quarto has contaminated the Second Quarto in *roots* and that Folio *rots* is correct. Only three of the six (Kittredge, Harrison, and Alexander) concur that *interr'd* is a corruption taken over from the First Quarto and that Folio *enurn'd* is the true Shakespearean reading. More complete facts about the readings and their editorial treatment in Act 1 will be found in my "Textual Relation of Q2 to Q1 *Hamlet*," *Studies in Bibliography* 8 (1956): 64–66.

editors made any attempt to carry the facts about the First Quarto contamination beyond the rather unsatisfactory state in which Wilson had left them.[5] Hence it is clear that the bibliographical knowledge of the Second Quarto corruption from the First Quarto had no editorial influence on the post-Wilson state of the text save, ironically, to confirm editors in their critical preconception that *solid* was a better word than *sullied*.

Various considerations may be raised against this singular editorial treatment. A strong one is the fact that the peculiar form the line takes in the First Quarto shows that rightly or wrongly the actor reporting the First Quarto version (or the editor) thought it was *sallied*. When he recited "O that this too much grieu'd and sallied flesh   Would melt to nothing," we can be quite sure that *sallied* is no compositorial error or actor's simple mishearing for *solid:* the balancing word to *grieu'd* and one that participates in the modification by *too much* would be nonsensical as *solid*. If the First Quarto line is corrupt in this word, therefore, we must believe that the corruption arose when the actor lost his memory for *solid*, recovered it approximately as *sallied*, and thereupon twisted the line to suit the new meaning. On the other hand, if *sallied* is correct, we have this key word shaping the half-remembered form of the rest of the line.

Another strong consideration develops from the propositions we can now lay down. *Solid* can be defended only on one of two logical premises:

1. In Shakespeare's manuscript *solid flesh* was written much like *sallied* and was so misread by the scribe who copied the actor's part (and presumably the prompt book); and on the evidence of the First Quarto the actor was never corrected. When, therefore,

5. The evidence itself, without further interpretation, is sufficient to show that Wilson's explanation for the method of contamination is incorrect. It is interesting to see that though his treatment of the text was based on information about contamination from the First Quarto, a relationship unknown to the Old Cambridge editors, his choice of readings in this immediate connection did not differ materially from their traditional text. Of his original five corruptions the Old Cambridge editors had varied only in their preference for *solid* over *sullied*; and of the supplementary three found in his edition, only his choice of Folio *rots* disagreed with the Old Cambridge preference for *roots*.

at 1.2.29 the compositor of the Second Quarto came to read the word in what was presumably the same basic manuscript, he (a) made the same mistake, or (b) was uncertain about the word and consulted the First Quarto, taking its form from that document; and when, later, he came to 2.1.39 the same handwriting difficulty led him to mistake manuscript *sullies* for *sallies.*

Only a remarkably gullible person could believe this furious coincidence and persistence of error under variable conditions, the more especially since only in *Love's Labour's Lost* was the difficulty repeated. Hence only the second proposition remains:

2. (a) *Solid* stood in the manuscript behind the Second Quarto, and *sallied* in the First Quarto is an actor's memorial corruption. When the Second Quarto compositor came to 1.2.129, for one reason or another—dependent upon the theory held as to the exact means by which the First Quarto contaminated the Second Quarto—he picked up *sallied* from the First Quarto.

(b) When he came to 2.1.39, the sense was not especially clear to him and, either by misreading the handwriting or by misinterpretation—perhaps accompanied by his memory of earlier *sallied flesh*—he set the form *sallies* instead of *sullies.*

There are difficulties in this proposition. First, it is surely obvious that in dealing with such a rare word appearing twice in one play, we may not appeal to separate and divided error. It seems incredible that there is no connection between *sallied* at 1.2.129 and *sallies* at 2.1.39. Hence if *sallies* means *sullies*, as it surely does, *sallied* must mean *sullied.* To escape this conclusion one must believe (a) manuscript *solid* was misread *sallied* by the Second Quarto compositor and manuscript *sullies* was misread *sallies;* (b) *sallied* is a First Quarto corruption taken over by the Second Quarto, and *sallies* is an independent misprint for *sullies;* or (c) the corruption *sallied* influenced the Second Quarto compositor to misread *sullies* as *sallies.*

The odds against the first are certainly serious, and at best its improbability is marked. The second is not much more probable, since it offers two different causes to explain identical double error. The third is logically the most defensible but it can be demonstrated to be wrong. Once we depart from Wilson's view and accept *sally* as a quite possible variant spelling for *sully*, the whole idea of a misprint vanishes, and no reason exists to suppose that the first could have influenced the second. But there is evidence more relative.

We can now prove on physical evidence that no connection can possibly obtain. Bibliographical analysis now shows not only that sheet E in which (sig. E1v) the second *sally* appears in the Second Quarto was printed on a different press from sheet C containing on sig. C1 "this too too sallied flesh," each being machined at approximately the same time,[6] but also (as necessarily follows), that each was set by a different compositor.[7] Since the second *sally* was set by the second compositor from manuscript, the appearance of the first *sally* in *sallied flesh*, set by the first workman, can have had no possible influence on the other. Hence if one word is right, as must be so, the other must also be right as well, and the contamination explanation for *sallied flesh* fails as a matter of simple logical impossibility. If we cannot believe that *sallied* was picked up from the First Quarto in error, there is no argument by which *solid* can be maintained.

It stands that bibliographical research separating the typesetting and the printing of the two sheets as the work of two different compositors and presses can be applied directly to settle this celebrated Shakespearean crux. Double misreading of the handwriting by two compositors is improbable enough, but it is surely impossible in this case given the First Quarto's *sallied flesh*. Hence since Polonius' *sallies* must have been written in the manuscript, it is mere fantasy to hold that *solid* was present in the manuscript for Hamlet's soliloquy but by one cause or another the compositor corrupted it to the rare form *sallied*, and this by the purest chance was repeated by a different compositor from his manuscript in another sheet. On the evidence of the appropriateness of the black on white image for *sully* and of the *thaw* and *melt* for flesh compared to snow; on the belief that Hamlet's feeling his

6. Bowers, "The Printing of *Hamlet* Q2," *Studies in Bibliography* 7 (1955): 41–50.

7. John Russell Brown, "The Compositors of *Hamlet* Q2 and *The Merchant of Venice*," *Studies in Bibliography* 7 (1955): 17–40.

flesh to be soiled by his mother's incestuous marriage is not a far-fetched idea;[8] on the linguistic suggestion that *sally* is not a misprint for *sully* but a legitimate though rare form; on the evidence that the First Quarto actor remembered his part as reading *sallied*; and finally on the bibliographical evidence that the same word in its rare variant form was set by two different compositors in the same play and therefore the two appearances have no possible connection with each other,[9] one can now expose an error in criticism and by the application of the mechanical evidence of bibliography establish the text for an individual reading.

8. This stain from his mother attacks his natural honor. For the important distinction between natural and acquired honor in Elizabethan concepts, and the belief that acquired honor cannot be maintained if natural is destroyed, see my "Middleton's *A Fair Quarrel* and the Duelling Code," *Journal of English and Germanic Philology* 36 (1937): 40–65.

9. For example, if from the fact that the two occurrences in *Hamlet* of the spellings *somnet* (for *summit*) are set by different compositors we may establish that *somnet* was the manuscript spelling, the same principle should work for *sally*. It is interesting to contemplate that this same *somnet* form was rejected as a misprint in Thomas Pyle, "Rejected Q2 Readings in the New Shakespeare *Hamlet*," *ELH* 6 (1937): 114–46.

THE STRUCTURE OF *KING LEAR*

W HAT IS THE DRAMATIC, which is to say the technical, climax
of *King Lear*? If one asks a cheerful unsophisticate, a student, say, who has had minimal exposure to establishment criticism, the answer is prompt and invariable: Lear's division of the
kingdom. One then points out that the climax of an Elizabethan
play comes only after the rising action has peaked, this usually
in the third act; hence to select Act 1, scene 1 as the climax, with
no preceding action, offers some difficulties.

A sophisticated respondent, who has been reading the critics,
may suggest one or other of the storm scenes, perhaps the two
together as a unit if he has been reading a more aesthetically-
than dramatically-minded critic. These are properly positioned
in the third act. But if one pursues the question, and defines
climax as the turning-point of the plot, which leads inevitably to
the tragic or the comic catastrophe, then one must inquire in
what manner the tragic catastrophe—the events at the end of
the play—logically follow on the protagonist's decision in the
climax. That is, in terms of the plot, how does Lear's recognition
of his humanity in the second storm scene, and his willingness
to humble himself, lead to his own death (and the deaths of
Cordelia and Edmund) in the triumph—even at fearful cost—of

From *Shakespeare Quarterly* 31 (Spring 1980).

the forces of right. To this poser no dramatically satisfactory answer is likely to come forth.

Although framed in these deliberately crude terms to focus the problem, the question is of more than idle interest. In some knotty tragedies our understanding of Shakespeare's own view of the protagonist's character and of the crucial error that leads to a tragic instead of to a comic ending is completely dependent on the interpretation of the one place where a playwright must reveal his own insight—the climax. It follows that we can scarcely begin to analyze Shakespeare's intentions unless we can understand dramatic structure and isolate for critical examination those key episodes where any Renaissance dramatist must expose how he wants the audience to react. If he does not control this reaction he will commit the unforgivable dramatic sin of misleading his audience. Thus the posing of the problem of *King Lear*'s structure on a damned-if-you-do and damned-if-you-don't basis has more than a crude shock value. It is intended to remove, for the moment, any complacency about the answers that critics have given for this difficult play and to advocate a basic—indeed an ultra-elementary—examination before we try to put the pieces together again. For I make bold to suggest that critics have not yet provided us with the right answers because they have failed to ask the right questions.

To formulate these questions, we must first understand the conventional Shakespearean plot-formula, which is in fact the normal dramatic structure of English Renaissance five-act tragedy. In simple terms, we may say that the rising complications of the action culminate in a crucial decision by the protagonist, the nature of which constitutes the turning-point of the play and will dictate the nature of the catastrophe. In technical terms, this is the climax. We must avoid the partial view that the climax is necessarily some physical action that affects the subsequent plot. In drama, motive is everything. And decision is the culmination—the necessary spur to action—of motive. In a proper tragedy, not a melodrama, once the decision is taken, the embodying action follows as the night the day and will prove to be the physical implementation of the decision. The embodying action has a special importance, since it seals the decision. Up to the moment of this action, a decision can be changed and the consequences avoided. In theory, at least; in fact, the tragic decision is likely to be so momentous and the reasons for it so deep-rooted that change is improbable.[1] And in any event, the sealing action soon makes the decision irrevocable. It follows, then, that although the action that precipitates the tragedy is important in terms of the plot, the anterior decision that gave birth to the action is the more dramatically significant since it involves the tragic ethic. Without the reference back to this ethic there might be little significance to the action: it could be random, ill-motivated, and therefore melodramatic, not tragic.

What in fact enforces dramatic inevitability is the tragic ethic of the decision. In the world of tragedy a protagonist is ethically responsible for his actions, and particularly for the decisions that motivate these actions. The single most agonizing decision a tragic protagonist must make is that crucial, or climactic, one on which the whole tragedy rests—the decision which turns the play away from a possibly satisfactory to an unsatisfactory or tragic conclusion. The weight of the play as tragedy—its whole merit as a significant imitation of life that justifies its continued existence as a part of human experience, generation after generation—lies in the ethical import of the protagonist's decision and the logic of its working-out. The dramatic action that shapes the progress from climax to catastrophe may take different forms according to the ingenuity of the playwright, but it can never lead to a different fate for the protagonist. Part of the test of the playwright's art, then, is his manipulation of suspense by dramatic action between climax and catastrophe— suspense arising from the *how* by which the tragic ending will be brought about. The *why* and the *what* have been decided in the climax.

The climax, then, can be pinpointed as that incident in the

---

1. In theory (*pace* St. Paul) the crime of thought is not irrevocable until put into action from which consequences flow. This is the Elizabethan belief, and it has a legal validity. But in high tragedy decision and consequence are so ethically united as to leave no logical opportunity to withdraw and repair the rent in the moral fabric once the decision has been made.

play which constitutes its true turning point. The mistaken decision at that point taken must in a great tragedy be so ethically momentous as to justify the tragic ending. In this decision the protagonist seals his fate. After the climax, the suspense shifts. Since the die has been cast, it is no longer a question of *whether* the protagonist will come to a tragic end but only of *how* that end will be brought about. The protagonist's action that derives from the decision must therefore have irrevocable consequences, since only such a momentous action makes a tragic decision meaningful.

A playwright is most effective when he forges the highest possible logical sequence of post-climax events, leading by action and reaction from the irrevocable deed to the predetermined end in a manner that will satisfy the audience's sense of justice. The satisfaction that an audience feels at the end of a tragedy is twofold. The more powerful kind of satisfaction is the recognition of the justice of the end in light of the ethos of the climactic decision and its accompanying irrevocable action. The lesser, although still important, kind of satisfaction is the acceptance of the chain of events between climax and catastrophe as motivated, natural, and logically developed.

When we survey this pattern of Shakespearean tragedy we can see why the conventional analyses of the structure of *King Lear* fail to satisfy. One may freely grant that a turning-point in one respect does indeed take place in the humbling of Lear in Act 3, scene 4, the second storm scene. There is no gainsaying Lear's new consciousness of his participation in the common humanity from which in his pride he had thought himself exempt:

> *Poor naked wretches, whereso'er you are,*
> *That bide the pelting of this pitiless storm,*
> *How shall your houseless heads and unfed sides,*
> *Your looped and windowed raggedness, defend you*
> *From seasons such as these? . . .*
> *. . . Take physic, pomp;*
> *Expose thyself to feel what wretches feel,*
> *That thou mayst shake the superflux to them*
> *And show the heavens more just.*   (3.4.28–36)

This is a far cry from

> *The barbarous Scythian,*
> *Or he that makes his generation messes*
> *To gorge his appetite, shall to my bosom*
> *Be as well neighboured, pitied, and relieved,*
> *As thou my sometime daughter.*   (1.1.116–20)

Or from "Come not between the dragon and his wrath" (1.1.122). Or from "Better thou   Hadst not been born than not t'have pleased me better" (1.1.234–35).

It is consistent with this new recognition that Lear can kneel to Cordelia for her pardon, a most striking contrast with the blindness of his choleric pride when from his throne he had banished her at the beginning of the action. There is no need to emphasize the function of the storm in breaking down Lear's physical and mental defenses so that he can reverse his fault. In this there is common consent.

But two most serious problems remain. If this physical and moral revolution in Lear is the turning-point of the play, we must ask, first, in what respect it conforms to Shakespeare's established patterns for tragic climax, and, second, in what respect such a climactic "decision" implements itself in an action that directly leads to and causes the specific form of the catastrophe. Here we come up against the anomaly of *King Lear.* If the storm scene is the climax, how do we account for the fact that Lear's decision to release his humanity and suppress his pride-based choler is in fact regenerative and morally sound, not a violation of the ethical fabric? The injustice of Cordelia's death and the terror of the final events seemed in the late seventeenth century to be so little motivated by the storm scene that Nahum Tate's version with a happy ending[2] held the stage for well over a hundred years—

2. London, 1681. Most interestingly, when Nahum Tate turned *King Lear* into a tragicomedy, the storm scene became its rightful and fully technical climax; the "regeneration" of Lear therein led to his search for Cordelia and the happy ending of their union, completed by her marriage to Edgar. For further reference, see James Black, ed., *Nahum Tate: The History of King Lear,* Regents Restoration Drama Series, gen. ed. John Loftis (Lincoln: Univ. of Nebraska Press, (1975).

paradoxically providing the general sort of ending that Shakespeare had found in his source, the old play of *King Leir*. *King Lear* as a cosmic comedy is a concept that could be argued in a very special sense, but certainly it is not a Renaissance concept. And one should hesitate to graft such a vast philosophical *schema* on Shakespeare.

Shakespeare's tragic protagonists are one and all the victims of a "tragic flaw" (even though it is probable that Shakespeare had never read Aristotle on the drama). The tragic error of the climactic decision penetrates through the opening provided by this flaw, piercing the heroes' ethical armor. But in the storm-scene reconciliation of Lear with the real world of pity and mercy there is no flaw through which error enters. Quite the reverse. When we then try to connect the catastrophe—the death of Lear and incidentally that of Cordelia—with the supposed climax, we see no train of cause and effect. No matter what alteration Lear has suffered in the storm, its results have nothing to do with the defeat of the French, the mutual destruction of Goneril and Regan, the death of Cordelia, the victory of Edgar over Edmund, and Lear's own death. Whether an active and regenerated Lear in full possession of his powers could have rallied the country against Cornwall and Albany and insured Cordelia's victory is not only problematic but futile to ask. Shakespeare never allows any such suggestion of might-have-been to appear in the play (as he does ironically in *Hamlet*), and we have no right to insert it. Moreover, even if we were to permit this idle query, we should still have the problem of finding the necessary ethical error in the shattering of Lear in the storm that precedes Shakespeare's deliberately chosen tragic ending.

Where, then, do we stand? If the structural difficulties rule out a climax in the division of the kingdom in Act 1, scene 1, and the generally accepted turning-point of the play does not involve a tragic error that brings on the retribution of the catastrophe, what can we make of the structure of *King Lear* and its tragic form?

The answer that I suggest acknowledges the unique structure of *King Lear* among Shakespeare's tragedies. The problems that have here been raised about *King Lear* have all been caused by setting up the examples of such plays as *Hamlet, Antony and Cleopatra, Coriolanus, Romeo and Juliet, Othello*, and even *Macbeth* as the criteria against which *King Lear* should be evaluated. This will not work. These plays are conventional five-act, pyramidally-structured Renaissance tragedies. *King Lear* is unusual, indeed unique in Shakespeare, in its distinctive structure. But wherein lies the difference?

I suggest that we view *King Lear*, structurally, as a modified classical tragedy. I am well aware that it is bold doing to generalize about classical tragedy, because the preserved examples are by no means structurally uniform. Owing to the paucity of material to be studied, moreover, we cannot be so certain as we should like about whether the Greek trilogies were in general constructed on a relatively uniform pattern within which individual plays could vary. We now find most of the plays isolated from their overall framework. Aristotle did not raise this problem, perhaps significantly; instead, he examined his chosen plays as generally similar units. Admitting so much uncertainty, however, we can nevertheless discern in various Greek tragedies, and in Aristotle's commentary, a pattern to which critics have given the name of "fifth-act tragedy."

Literally, this should mean that the play devotes itself exclusively to the catastrophe and to the events immediately preceding it as dramatized in the fifth act of a typical Renaissance tragedy. Ordinarily what we find is this. In the fourth act of Shakespeare's tragic dramas the action and counteraction released by the third-act climax work out their respective forces to the point where the two are ready to start their collision course. Plans are drawn and actions proposed that will be set in motion in the fifth act to bring on the catastrophe. In *Hamlet*, for instance, the counteraction predominates in the fourth act. Hamlet is on the defensive and bends with the tide. He must voyage to England, but his letter to Horatio, read in Act 4, scene 6, indicates that what have been only suspicions ("I see a cherub that sees them," 4.3.47) are now certainties: a forward step. Then the madness and death of Ophelia give the last spur to Laertes' resolution so that, on the news of Hamlet's return, he joins the King in the plan that will prove successful against Hamlet's life.

The fifth act puts these movements into the action that culminates in the catastrophic holocaust.

If the classical drama is structurally a fifth-act tragedy, we cannot expect in it the formal climax that takes place in the third act of a five-act Renaissance drama. What corresponds to this normal Shakespearean climax occurs in Greek tragedy before the opening of the play, though whether in some antecedent play in the trilogy—as in the preserved *Oresteia*—we cannot always be certain. If we ask what is the tragic error that brought Oedipus to his doom, for example, we cannot be satisfied that it was his insistence on hearing the evidence of the herdsman. The crime Oedipus had committed that caused the pollution of Thebes occurred long before that, with the killing of his father at the crossroads, which led first to the marriage with his mother and then to his self-immolation and exile after the revelation that he had forced. In the total structure of the Oedipus story the patricide corresponds to the fatal decision and the fulfilling action in Renaissance tragedy.

Another example, closer to home, may be cited. Milton's *Samson Agonistes* is true to Greek tragedy in substantially concentrating its plot within the post-climax action of a Shakespearean play. If we ask what was the tragic fault for which Samson is punished—the turning-point in the whole story, that action which enforced a tragic ending—we would surely point to the loss of his reason to passion when Samson broke his vow to God and revealed to Dalila the secret of his strength. As in Sophocles' *Oedipus*, this crucial incident has taken place before the opening of the play, providing a structure that permits Milton to concentrate on the effects of the error and the preparation of Samson for his tragic expiation.

What we should now see is that if we analyze the total Lear story as we have done with *Oedipus* and *Samson*, the innocent view of its climax is indeed correct that assigns it as the division of the kingdom and the rejection of Cordelia. But it is important to emphasize that although this is the turning-point of the full Lear story, it is not the turning-point of the play in terms of its five-act dramatic structure. What Shakespeare has done is to move up into the first scene of his play what is the turning-point of the total story—instead of leaving it undramatized in the classical manner as a past event that must be narrated before the ensuing catastrophe can begin its course. If Shakespeare had structured the play entirely in the Greek form, as did Milton, we should recognize the genre and feel no difficulty. But because he has modified the form in order to dramatize this most significant episode, we are puzzled by the different structure of five-act tragedy that results.

The advantages of Shakespeare's innovation are obvious. Instead of the first half of the play being devoted to the rising action culminating in the kingdom's division, and then sliding with some rapidity down to the catastrophic consequences, Shakespeare allows himself almost the full length of the play to work out the far-reaching and complex results of Lear's tragic decision. This searching and detailed analysis of error and consequence gives the play its extraordinary weight and density. We should recognize, therefore, that the unique quality of *King Lear* among Shakespeare's tragedies is the direct result of the playwright's innovative modification of traditional Renaissance dramatic structure. It is no accident. The treatment and the powerful effect from the scope he is able to give to the retributive action arise from his blending of classical (in his case Senecan) and Renaissance dramatic tradition.

There is still one unanswered question. If the merging of classical with Renaissance produces in *King Lear* this curious amalgamated structure, which attempts to combine the best features of both traditions, what happens to the structural climax? Must we say that it truly occurs, most outlandishly, in Act 1, scene 1? I believe that a comfortable answer can be offered. If we inquire what the Greek tragic writers substituted for a climax, we see that they did have a form of turning-point where a decision was made—an episode that in terms of a fifth-act structure could act as a dramatic substitute for the proper climax of the whole story, which had occurred before the play opened.

If we revert once again to the peculiar nature and dramatic effect of the Shakespearean climax, we see that the ethical problem that turns upon it is invariably the great Elizabethan theme of the temporary conquest of reason by passion. The tragic decision made in this episode, when confirmed by action, requires the correspondingly tragic catastrophe.

If we argue that all turning-points of great drama must have an ethical import, even those of comedy (although that is subject to debate), it is legitimate to inquire what ethical turning-point the classical dramatists utilized instead of the climax of the story as a whole. In the most structured Greek and Senecan plays we may find this episode in a moment of decision, an incident that has been aptly named "the moment of final suspense" because of the theoretical possibility that the choice could go either way and correspondingly affect the final knot of the action. Oedipus is sufficiently warned against continuing the investigation of his birth. Concealing his decision under the guise of submission to the gods, Ajax nevertheless proposes suicide. Creon insists that the burial rites for Polynices, which the gods desire, must be punished, not condoned. In each instance, the essence of the moment of decision is that it continues the initial error and by its repetition confirms the justice of the punishment for the more important crime of which it is the consequence.

Oedipus' choler is the result of his pride. Stemming from pride, a similar manifestation of choler earlier led him to kill his father, though unwittingly, when precedence at the crossroads was in dispute. As the investigation of his birth begins to suggest that he was lowly born, it is his inverse pride that prompts Oedipus to continue and to reach the fatal truth. First he asserts that even if he were not of noble birth, he would have earned his throne by noble deeds. But the immediate spur to his insistence is his ironic misunderstanding of Jocasta's perturbation, which he imputes to shame at his birth; in fact, it is due to her glimpse of the dreadful truth of their incestuous marriage. Instead of submitting to the gods whom he has offended, and thereafter leading a life of peace, Ajax's pride reaffirms his original stubbornness. He therefore embraces suicide instead of submission. Creon's continued defense of his edict—leading first to his condemnation of Antigone, and then to his disregard of the warnings of Tiresias—confirms the offense to the gods involved in his first edict. The heart of such a moment of decision in Greek tragedy, then, is not the commission of an original error but instead the reaffirmation of the error on which the whole story has turned before the opening of the play. Since the protagonist has not learned from experience, the justice of the retributive ending is not arguable.

Something of the same sort of incident may appear in the five-act Renaissance tragedy, usually in the fifth act but rarely, as in *Macbeth*, in the fourth. Technically this moment is called the anticlimax. It may take various forms, but whether latent or overt it confirms the ethical significance of the climax. Coriolanus' blindness in rejecting Rome, for example, the turning-point of the plot, is confirmed when he performs the same act a second time in denying Menenius' suit for mercy. This is a true reproduction of the Greek moment of final suspense, which by repetition confirms the original error.

Naturally, in Elizabethan villain-tragedy the reaffirmation of error bulks large. Even in such a modification of the genre as we find in *Macbeth*, the order to murder Macduff's wife and children repeats the murder of Duncan and—if any sign were needed—demonstrates to the audience the impossibility of repentance. Similarly, it may be suggested that Faustus' cohabitation with a succubus, a demon in the shape of Helen, coming on top of the warning of the Old Man (and even the scene in which Faustus orders the torment of the Old Man)[3] indicates that repentance is impossible, a fact shown even more dramatically by the formal

3. (5.1). In the Marlovian scene Faustus merely orders Mephistophilis to "Torment sweet friend, that base and crooked age,   That durst disswade me from thy *Lucifer,*   With greatest torments that our hell affoords." Bowers, ed., *The Complete Works of Christopher Marlowe* (Cambridge: Cambridge University Press, rev. ed., 1981), 2.219, ll. 1753–55. If one could show that in the brief passage in which the devils enter to the Old Man (ll. 1791–96; a scene in the A-text only), they martyred him, then this would be murder on Faustus' part and a confirmation of his sin that would leave no room for repentance. But the text of the passage (almost certainly not by Marlowe) is ambiguous as to whether the devils attack the Old Man and carry him offstage or, as seems to be implied, are thwarted by his faith ("see how the heavens smiles   At your repulse"), with the two parties exiting severally. It is necessary, then, to ignore this tempting episode and to concentrate on the mortal sin, the ultimate lechery of flesh, of sexual intercourse with a devil as the final act that (in Marlowe's part of the play) binds Faustus' soul to hell.

departure of the Good Angel (although this last is probably in a non-Marlovian scene).

Let us now return to *King Lear.* As I have suggested, the division of the kingdom—for its dramatic effect moved out of the past and into the opening scene of the play—is the climax of the story but not of the play. But this modification of the classical structure still does not vitally affect *King Lear's* status as essentially a fifth-act tragedy worked out in Renaissance five-act form. It follows that, as in the Greek, *King Lear* will substitute for its climax what is instead the anticlimax of the conventional Shakespearean tragedy. This we may find in the second storm scene. A recognition of this adaptation of the classical moment of final suspense solves the problem I have sketched: relating the climax to the catastrophe in terms of action as well as of ethics.

In terms of action, the catastrophe of *King Lear* is indeed related by cause and effect to the story's climax, the division of the kingdom. After the gaping wound given to the body politic, to the concept and function of kingship, and to ethical justice in the rejection of Cordelia and the rewarding of Goneril and Regan (all these stemming from Lear's towering pride and its accompanying irascibility), the punishment of the catastrophe must be severe and of tragic proportions. As the play progresses we see the poisonous evil Lear has let loose in the land (and for personal reasons that are trivial in the extreme compared to the harm that follows), this evil infecting the whole social and political fabric. And we see that this evil can be expiated in tragic terms by nothing less than death.

Milton's word "levity" applied to the motives for Adam and Eve's fall from God is as applicable to the motives of Lear the ruler as to Antony the general-emperor. Great power carries great responsibilities which must take precedence over personal concerns. The weaknesses of a king in his private life (the lesser in importance of his two bodies) bring such harm to the kingdom as can be repaired only by the substitution of a ruler prepared to fulfill his role in both aspects. This is the lesson of *Richard II* and of *Antony and Cleopatra.* Even more devastatingly, it was the lesson of Sackville and Norton's *Gorboduc* (1565), to which *King Lear* is intimately related both in situation and in ethos.

The question still remains, however, of the function of the anticlimax, which in *King Lear*, as in classical tragedy, is substituted for the structural or dramatic climax. Here we must note immediately that in the Renaissance five-act drama, even more than in the Greek or Senecan, the anticlimax need have no cause-and-effect influence on the nature, the physical outcome, of the catastrophic action. Whether or not Macbeth's murder of the wife and children raised a determined revenger in Macduff, for example, Macbeth's fate was sealed by the murder of Duncan. Only the means, not the nature, of the catastrophe was determined by Macduff's motive for revenge. And given the terms of Coriolanus' climactic rejection of Rome, no motivation can be imagined that would justify his yielding to Menenius' pleas. The die has been cast: the second rejection merely confirms the first and leaves no room in the audience for a lingering sense of injustice to interfere with the ethical satisfaction to be derived from viewing the proper penalty for error (the basis of Aristotelian catharsis). Similarly, whether or not Lear is brought by the storm to a humane recognition so that his pride—while it still may flicker—is basically altered from what it was, the hellish evil that he has unleashed by the relaxation of his authority still demands its retribution, a retribution so terrible that it engulfs the innocent Cordelia as well as the guilty Lear. This punishment would have fallen on Lear with or without the moral change that he underwent in the storm. To that extent, so far as concerns the action that leads to his and Cordelia's death, the anticlimax acting as structural climax has no influence. The true turning-point for the story and its action, including the tragic fate of Lear, remains the division of the kingdom.

That the storm scene marks the turning-point of the play, taken as a dramatic unit, is nonetheless incontestable. The moral effect of the restoration of his reason over his passion (despite the ironic loss of his wits) does change Lear's character, even though no positive result on the action of the catastrophe can be traced to this change. With or without it, so far as we can see, Cordelia would have been defeated, Goneril and Regan would have exterminated each other, and Edgar would have killed Edmund. But a most powerful effect on the form of the catastrophe comes in the fact that Lear and Cordelia die reconciled, a direct product of the cracking of Lear's pride by the storm. What we have in the storm scene, then, is Shakespeare's use of the device of anticlimax as a means for effecting in the tragic close a reconciliation of protagonist and audience.

The classical protagonist confirmed his original error in the anticlimax and thereupon caused the audience to accept his tragic fate as an act of justice. What blindness he had exhibited in the decision that was the story's climax was repeated: it thereby became clear that the protagonist had failed to learn from experience and must suffer the consequences. The Greek and Roman was a pagan tragedy with no sense of redemption affecting the fate of its characters in the close of the play. Stoical acceptance of the justice, or injustice, of the gods was all that could be admired in the catastrophe. Good or evil, all men suffered death at last, and death was substantially the end of all. The gods had nothing to do with a dimly-perceived afterlife in which there were no rewards or punishments. Christian tragedy has this fundamental potential difference for a hero-protagonist: a good man who through some fault has failed but by repentance has altered the significance of his tragic end, even though death remains the temporal punishment he must suffer. In Renaissance Christian tragedy it therefore makes a great deal of difference whether the protagonist dies in a state of sin and alienation or in expiation, his sin forgiven.

The catharsis for the audience depends utterly upon its acceptance of the justice of the punishment, either spiritual or temporal. Shown a villainous protagonist, the audience observes with satisfaction the fulfillment of eternal law in the failure of his plots and the triumph of right. He has deserved his death in every possible respect, and no catharsis—no sense of fear mixed with satisfaction at the validity of law—would have taken place if he had escaped the consequences of his crime. The case differs when one sees a hero-protagonist entangled in the tragic toils, the Aristotelian good man led into error by a tragic flaw. Here a Renaissance audience (or a modern one, for that matter) distinguishes between the legal penalty of death to the body and the quite different matter of the religious penalty of death to the soul. It would be repugnant to an audience and would seriously affect the catharsis if a good man were punished eternally for a fault that was not typical of his whole life and character. In *Hamlet*, for example, unless angels were to sing the hero to his rest, the ending would leave a jagged wound, unhealed, and a profound sense of dissatisfaction. A Renaissance-minded audience wants to know that, despite his temporal punishment, the hero-protagonist has expiated his fault and will be accepted into grace. Only then can the full measure of pity and fear operate in a final judgment and the audience be released, enlightened as to the ways of justice, all passion spent.

In the Christian ethic, forgiveness for sin does not come unsought; it must be obtained. There is no substitute for repentance. States of mind in the drama must be shown in action. The hero, then, must repent, whether formally or not, and demonstrate his repentance by an action that removes the sting from his tragic fault. The anticlimax of the Renaissance drama is thus likely to consist of some incident in which the hero is faced with the same temptation that led to his climactic wrong decision. Because he now sees clearly (or intuitively) the nature of his fault, he responds in such a way as to prove that he rejects the opportunity to repeat the error of the climax, thereby reversing its most serious consequences. The penalty of temporal death is exacted, but the hero makes of this a willing expiation that satisfies justice and permits mercy to be extended.

Elsewhere I have suggested that in *Hamlet* this anticlimax is Hamlet's rejection of Horatio's temptation to delay the fencing match because of the omen feared in the pain about his heart. Hamlet responds with a fervent defense of his decision to put himself into God's hands, not seeking to affect the course of God's ordination. This precisely reverses his earlier fault, when he had set his own ego—his own impulse for instant retaliation—above the divine warning "Vengeance is Mine, I will repay," and killed Polonius in mistake for the King. In his response to Horatio, Hamlet shows that he has learned from experience and thus is redeemable. We see the same device operating in Milton's *Samson Agonistes*. By revealing his secret Samson has put his own desires above God's command. The punishment is swift and apparently final. But when a man has been chosen by God as an agent of justice, as with Hamlet and Samson, his error will not destroy God's plan, for divine intention can scarcely be thwarted by human means. The conditional means by which the agent succeeds in his ultimate act of justice will differ, but God's justice will still prevail. Meanwhile, however, the protagonist must pay the penalty of death that accompanies his victory. Hamlet succeeds in his mission, then, although in a very different way and with a different effect from that originally proposed. Similarly, in the interview with Dalila, Samson encounters the same temptation and reverses it by rejecting the wiles that had previously seduced him from his God. He is thereby prepared to destroy the Philistines, as in his original role of Israel's champion, even though at the willing sacrifice of his own life.

When Shakespeare does not treat his tragedies in this way, problems arise. *Macbeth* offers no difficulty because it is closely associated with the genre of villain-tragedy: Macbeth irremediably passes the point of repentance and expiation. *Othello*, on the other hand, has presented notorious difficulties. Because it lacks the guidance to the audience of this regenerative form of anticlimax, some critics have gone to the extreme of asserting that the audience receives its satisfaction from contemplating Othello's reception in the hell to which at the end he has consigned himself. This view seems to me to be seriously mistaken. To counter it, however, I cannot appeal to the details of the play's structure but only to the generally observed reaction of its audiences, which seem to lack no measure of the proper pity and fear at his expiatory suicide in the end.[4]

Although *King Lear* is laid in pagan times, its basic ethic is commonly accepted as Christian. Indeed, one need only compare *Coriolanus* and its strictly Roman standards with *King Lear* to see the difference in the power of the two catastrophes, stemming from the ethic that governs the anticlimaxes: the classical form of repeated and condemnatory error in *Coriolanus*, but what I

---

4. Structurally, the delay in Othello's understanding until the extended catastrophe seems to create the major problem since it merges anticlimax and catastrophe into one.

suggest is the Christian form of redemptive understanding and corrective action in *King Lear*.

The last extremity of the storm's cosmic strife is needed to confirm Goneril and Regan's ingratitude, the breaking of familial ties—the intrinsic knot that in microcosm represents the great kingdom that Lear's tragic decision has also brought to disruption and civil war. Without Lear's reversal, there could never have been the expiatory reconciliation with Cordelia, an action that sets the tone for Lear's exhausted death, the last consequence of his fatal decision. Reconciliation with Cordelia is, again, a microcosm of reconciliation with the kingdom, the body politic. It is this significant action that makes the ending of *King Lear* so different from that of its progenitor *Gorboduc*. In *Gorboduc* there is didactic terror but no pity. The wound to the body politic—the unleashing of disruptive power created by Gorboduc's division of his kingdom—will last for several hundred years of internecine strife before royal stability can once more painfully be won and the kingdom be at peace. In *King Lear*, as in *Hamlet*, the succession is assured, the kingdom's stability is provided for, and the wound is healed—a matter of grave concern to the dynastic-minded Elizabethans, and of concern still to us. In *King Lear* the personal reconciliation of Lear and Cordelia, succeeded by the political reconciliation that brings a strong young king to the throne,[5] lends pity to the fear that would otherwise have prevailed and demonstrates once more the validity of tragic catharsis in great drama.

At the end we see that such self-understanding as comes to Lear in the storm has no effect on the action leading to or within the catastrophe. Nevertheless, its effect is as powerful in shaping the ethic of the tragic close as is Hamlet's readiness-is-all speech. This distinction points up the real difference between climax and anticlimax as found in the five-act structure of *Hamlet* and the fifth-act, classically-structured tragedy of *King Lear*. For the climax that governs the action, *King Lear* substitutes the anticlimax,

5. With some deliberateness I choose the explicit Folio ending in which Albany defers to Edgar instead of what I take to be the memorial confusion of the Bad Quarto's ambiguous final speech assigned to Albany.

or ethical reversal, that governs the interpretation and reception by the audience of the action that follows on the tragic decision dramatized in the first scene of the play. This structure is unique in Shakespeare, and if we understand it we are brought a long way toward understanding the larger complexities of *King Lear.* Whatever other means a dramatist may employ for transferring his intentions to the audience—or, put another way, for controlling the reactions of the audience so that they will not go counter to his intentions—it is structure that as the basis always embodies the significance, the meaning, of great tragedy.

THEME AND STRUCTURE IN
KING HENRY IV, PART 1

THE POPULAR HISTORY PLAY of Elizabeth's reign was likely to
be a chronicle history. The name is applied not just because
the history in the play was taken from the chronicles, but because it was dramatized in the chronicle manner. History is not
an Elizabethan literary form. Some few examples of relatively
coherent history exist, as in Sir Thomas More's account of Richard III or Bacon's of Henry VII, but these are exceptional. A coherent history is written from a point of view; it concerns itself
as much with the *why* of an action as with its *how*. It delves into
causes and carefully traces their effects. It looks to men and to
the influence of their characters on action. It relates the event
to the whole: it sets the details of its narrative in proportion
against one another so that motivation and causality are apparent. In short, true historical writing shapes events to a higher
purpose of ultimate truth than simple factual narrative that has
not been analyzed to show the underlying purposes of affairs.

On the contrary, the favorite Elizabethan form was the chronicle history which has something to say about each year of a
reign, seldom in any pattern of coherence, and often attempts

From *The Drama of the Renaissance: Essays for Leicester Bradner*, ed. Elmer M.
Blistein (Providence: Brown Univ. Press, 1970), into which has been folded
"Hal and Francis in *King Henry IV, Part 1*," from *Renaissance Papers 1965*, ed.
George Walton Williams (Durham, N.C., 1966), by permission of the editor.

little more than a report of what seem to be the important events of that year, whether the birth of a five-legged calf, the rise of a civil war, the fall of hailstones in July, the onslaught of the plague, or the death of kings. Any notable event from a vast miscellany of choices is grist for its mill.

When Shakespeare first attempted the history, as in the *Henry VI* plays, one may watch him struggling to free himself from the dramatization of the chronicle—what happens next, what happens next. He was not immediately successful. Some attempts at a focus of events in the person of a single man may be seen in Talbot, of Part 1, for example; but the efforts never succeed in making out of historical fact what can be described as a plotted play. The focusing of events in one person reached its limit in *Richard III* but this elementary though successful technique could not be indefinitely repeated in all circumstances because the central factors of plot were missing. That is, an all-purpose plot requires conflict between two relative equals, action and counteraction of like weight, leading to a crucial decision put into action, and then its working out in inevitable terms to the final untying of the knot. This is how Elizabethan plays were ordered if they were true dramas, not dramatic representations.

However, sophisticated technique in plotting is useless unless the action is shaped to form something larger than itself in total effect. Literature cannot be literature if the dance is not of greater import than the dancer. *Significance* is a word viewed with a certain distrust today largely because of the simplistic view that it can be inserted on demand, as if Milton had written *Paradise Lost* and then put in the theology. *Meaning* may be a little better, although it is more neutral. Any writer except a hack must feel that the cumulative connections established between a series of events build into a design that gives them a meaning they would not have without this correlation. At what may often be a relatively high level of sophistication in drama, this sense of a pattern placed on the chaotic raw material of life may be enough, if it is so understood and so imaginatively presented by the playwright that it is transmitted as what seems to be true experience to his audience. Critics have not notably succeeded in basically finding much more than this in *Hamlet*.

But in literature of another order, what we may call a "theme" that shapes events may prove useful. Themes are not confined to less sophisticated forms of literature than *Hamlet* of course. The theme may be so powerful and universal as to soar above any possible limitations that might else have been placed on the imagination, as may be seen in *Paradise Lost*, and with more art in *Samson Agonistes*. Or what appears to be a theme may prove to be only the gateway to an experience that transcends the ostensible theme, as occurs in *King Lear*.

In his history plays, however, Shakespeare was to learn that the unifying force of a single central character was not adaptable enough to constitute a substitute for true plot. In the somewhat experimental play *King John* he found that too powerful a force, like the Bastard, could disrupt a play if he were not the central character or if he were not integrated into the plot. In its conventional definition, plot did not make a real history play (barring the case of *Richard III*) out of the chronicles until *Richard II*. *Richard II* brought the intractable material of history closer to the powerful shaping of a fictive imagination even though it was not an entire success in the meaningful presentation of action and counteraction generalized to what Galsworthy calls "a spire of meaning."

Shakespeare's most perfect English history play, *King Henry the Fourth, Part 1*, succeeds magnificently, where *Richard II* had partly failed, in the examination in dramatic terms of kingship, which is to say of power and its control. The title of a history play by convention is assigned to the name of the king in whose reign the events take place. But the king may or may not be the protagonist, even though the play is called after him. In a chronicle sense, the subject of the first part, and perhaps even more of the second part, is King Henry's suppression of a rebellion, thus ending the threat to the establishment of the Lancastrian dynasty to be carried on by his son. In any other sense, this is also what the play is really about. Richard II had let power slip from his careless hands; in contrast, Henry uses whatever means are suited to the situation to nurse his power; and he succeeds in imposing his will by breaking the back of a strong opposition to the extension of royal authority. On his death, his son can inherit an uncontested throne. Of all the history plays this one is most clearly and directly concerned with a theme close to Tudor hearts: the triumph of order through the imposition of centralized royal power as against the disorder of the fragmented rule of the nobles under the feudal system.

In that it is Henry who accepts the first challenge in this conflict, who is the sole and vigorous leader of his party, who orders and fights the war, *1 Henry IV* may be said to be about him. The main plot is certainly structured on this central action, and in it Henry is the protagonist. Who, then, is the antagonist? The easy answer would be Hotspur, but this is wrong. Important as Hotspur is to the action, it is not he who initiates the conspiracy against Henry, gathers together the aid of Mortimer and Glendower, and in the end precipitates the Battle of Shrewsbury. The true antagonist is Worcester, as Westmoreland in the first scene shrewdly declares: "This is his uncle's teaching, this is Worcester,   Malevolent to you in all aspects." Both at the start and at the end Hotspur is his uncle's factor (as unwittingly he becomes Hal's), almost his pawn.[1] Henry could have dealt with Hotspur, but not with Worcester, whom he recognizes as his true opposite in the parley before Shrewsbury.[2]

The rise and fall of the rebellion, then, is a contest essentially between Henry and Worcester. This is certainly the framework of the play's action; but no audience would agree that it com-

1.   Percy is but my factor, good my lord
            To engross up glorious deeds on my behalf;
            And I will call him to so strict account
            That he shall render every glory up.   (3.2.147–50)

2.   How now, my Lord of Worcester? Tis not well
            That you and I should meet upon such terms
            As now we meet. . . .
                    .   .   .   .   .
                        . . . will you again unknit
            This churlish knot of all-abhorred war,
            And move in that obedient orb again
            Where you did give a fair and natural light,
            And be no more an exhal'd meteor,
            A prodigy of fear, and a portent
            Of broached mischief to the unborn times?   (5.1.9–21)

prises more than the background for the central interest, which rests without question on the opposition of Hotspur and Hal. The result is a sophisticated plotting in which the two elderly men who hold the reins of power associate with their action and counteraction two strong young men to whom, in personal terms, the audience gives its main attention. Shakespeare had tentatively tried something like this in *King John* but had failed to unify the plot interest and the true issues involved in the action. The Bastard has no more future than Talbot of *Henry VI, Part 1*, except as the supporter of a king. The more independently he acts, the more in a sense he usurps the king's power without being able to supply a permanent solution to the troubles of the realm. But a firm unity is imposed in *1 Henry IV*, for Hal is himself the future and the solution. As the next king he will inherit Henry's power and continue the struggle against the divisive forces that endanger royal authority. Thus he thoroughly typifies the royal side of the struggle, and indeed represents it better than his father. He is the wave of the future, not the last struggle of the past. He is to be the hero king, Henry V, who united England and conquered France.

Unlike Faulconbridge, who had no true opponent, Hal's proper antagonist is Hotspur, who typifies the virtues of the feudal nobility as Hal typifies the virtues of the centralized monarchy. The elders are essentially schemers; the younger are men of action. The contrast of Hal and Percy comes to be central in the play as the power of each side swells to the conflict and to the meeting at Shrewsbury. It is an indication of the importance of these men to the central action that in a very real sense the battle is won and the rebellion broken by one episode alone, the single combat between Hal and Hotspur to which the whole play moves. Hal and Percy, then, are the true principals in the resolution of the play, its dénouement. In it past does not meet past; but future, future. It is no accident that both Hal and Percy are carefully kept apart from that action of the past whose consequences are being worked out in this play. Henry's seizure of the throne from Richard was aided by Northumberland and Worcester. Hotspur, indeed, has to be told of the events before he knows their details. The antagonisms of the past, then, center on Henry and Worcester. In their development these antagonisms bring in two active young men who had no part in the original episode. The rights and wrongs of this episode are so ambiguous and moreover are so further obscured by the present scheming of the elders, that no clear issue can be drawn from a conflict of Henry and Worcester. Right and wrong dissolve into expediencies. But with the younger men the case is different, for they are dissociated from this coil of the past. When, after Vernon's praise of Hal and a prophecy of the future greatness of England if he survives the battle,[3] Hotspur's sole reaction is the promise to kill the Prince,[4] something is being said that transcends past wrongs and battles long ago. Correspondingly, when Hal challenges Percy on the battlefield—"Why then I see   A very valiant rebel of the name"—an issue is being drawn that has little relation to whether Worcester and Northumberland were suitably rewarded and whether Henry broke his promise to them.

Both Henry and Worcester are too tainted, we may say, to be fit representatives for what becomes the central issue of the play—the shape and meaning that arise from the action—for which the rights and wrongs of Henry's claim to the throne have no true relevance. On the contrary, Hal and Hotspur can represent this issue. They have not met in the web of the dark past. They alone crystallize in their purest form the opposing principles of the power struggle in English history that was not to meet its resolution, according to the Tudor myth, until the crowning of Henry VII. In the turbulence of English history as Shakespeare, at least, saw it, the theme was the endlessly re-

3. One may compare the prophecy of Elizabeth's greatness that ends *Henry VIII*. Is it not probable that Hotspur's dying "O, I could prophesy,   But that the earthy and cold hand of death   Lies on my tongue" (5.4.83–85) also refers to Hal's future greatness?

4.   but let me tell the world,
        If he outlive the envy of this day,
        England did never owe so sweet a hope,
        So much misconstrued in his wantonness.
To this, Percy replies,
            be he as he will, yet once ere night
        I will embrace him with a soldier's arm,
        That he shall shrink under my courtesy.   (5.2.66–69, 73–74)

peated struggle between what came to be the modern Tudor principle of national patriotism resting on centralized royal authority, and the old system of diffused authority and personal loyalties represented by the feudal nobility.

Nowhere is this struggle more clearly pointed as a theme that illuminates the real significance of events than in *Henry IV*, where it controls the major structure of the plot and dictates the characterization. When on the field of Shrewsbury Hal challenges Hotspur—

> *I am the Prince of Wales; and think not, Percy*
> *To share with me in glory any more.*
> *Two stars keep not their motion in one sphere,*
> *Nor can one England brook a double reign*
> *Of Harry Percy and the Prince of Wales.*   (5.4.63–67)

—the issue is clearly joined. In Shakespeare's best dramatic manner, history has been concentrated in terms of men.

This principle behind the struggle for power between nobles and throne is what the history in the play is about. Like any good Elizabethan, Shakespeare saw the Tudor concept of kingship as allied with law and order; the challenge to this authority stems from fear and incipient chaos. It is no accident that though the rebels are brought together initially in the name of Mortimer, the least of their concerns is to put him on the throne of England. The country is marked up into three parts, and Mortimer is fortunate to secure a third. If the rebels were to triumph, before long Wales and Hotspur's new kingdom would be at war. The chaos of *Gorboduc,* of *King Lear,* would be repeated, and France would gobble up the weakened and divided realm. Shakespeare emphasizes the contrasts between the two parties. The King's party are united in a common cause under their lawful sovereign. Their councils are in agreement, no personal differences ruffle the accord. Shirley, Stafford, Blunt bravely sacrifice their lives to keep their king from danger. In contrast, the rebels bicker even in the meeting at which they seal their compact. The father Northumberland sacrifices his son by a diplomatic illness. Glendower is overruled by prophecies and breaks the compact, the powerless Mortimer with him. Hotspur and Douglas warily disguise the antagonism of Englishman and of Scot under effusive compliment, though the ancient enmity breaks out in Vernon. The council before the battle is angrily at odds, and indeed the battle is joined only because of a lie: every indication exists that Hotspur would have accepted Henry's composition if it had been truly reported. The bad cause corrupts the men. Vernon, who had protested to the Douglas that "If well-respected honour bid me on,   I hold as little counsel with weak fear," swallows his honor and agrees to support Worcester's false report of the King's offers: "Deliver what you will, I'll say 'tis so."

This lack of conscience about the effect on others as long as their own nests are lined is characteristic of the rebels. Worcester brings on the slaughter because he fears that Hotspur will be forgiven but he and Northumberland will suffer if peace is made; and Vernon has no thought of the men who will die to protect Worcester's personal welfare. Not so the King. It is one of his most royal characteristics that he holds himself responsible for the lives under him. His chief accusation directed at Mortimer's defection is that Mortimer deliberately engaged in a battle he intended to lose in order to be captured, and thus was the cause of the death of many English subjects. Before Shrewsbury, Hal's offer of a single combat is generously intended to prevent the slaughter. In condemning Worcester and Vernon to death, Henry in effect calls them murderers. Just as an evil king proverbially could not rule well, so an evil cause cannot produce good actions, and Worcester is a child of the times.

This is the significance of the history, and it is a sound one. But ideas must be incorporated into men. Henry and Worcester—though technically the principals—cannot embody the ideas of this play, and instead history comes to rest in the persons of Hal and of Hotspur, who represent the great opposing forces with which the drama is essentially concerned. This contrast is sharpened by making Hotspur of Hal's exact age, although in reality he was a contemporary of the King. The opposition of the two young men is handled with skill and suspense. Hotspur is early won to the conspiracy, and the action assigned him is devoted exclusively to this main line of the plot. Hal is brought over late: his official entrance into the main plot does not take place before the climax of the play. In fact, his joining his father to put down the revolt becomes his first *action* in opposing Hotspur, and since it is made the turning-point of the drama, it is thereby given major significance. The terms of this decision are such as to narrow the future action and to lead it inevitably to the single combat on the field of Shrewsbury, another of Shakespeare's inventions to emphasize the concentration of the play on these two figures, like the reduction in Hotspur's age. (History does not record how Percy died.)

In technical terms of the plot, the significance of this climax is profound. The implication is that the King alone may not be able to conquer the rebels; and indeed this doubt is emphasized when but for Hal the Douglas would have killed Henry in the battle and won the day. The entrance of the Prince into the main action, therefore, is the decisive factor that tips the scales. If the opposition had begun early—if, say, Hal had moved to counter Hotspur the moment the rebellion was formed—the peculiar effect of this climax-intervention would have been lost. As it is, the structure of the plot identifies Hal as the most powerful person in the play, on whose decision in the climax—the interview with his father—the form of the catastrophe, that is to say, the outcome of the play, will depend.

The dramatic effect of Hal's late coming to the main action emphasizes the strength of the future Henry V and, technically, adds a new interest to the events between climax and dénouement. The new interest depends in some part on the audience now having a clear-cut choice between two figures—Hal and Percy—within the same action. This is a little different from the choice that was latent previously, between an active Hotspur and an inactive Prince, each in a different plot. Before the climactic interview with his father, Hal existed as a potential force, only. After the climax-interview, Shakespeare rapidly builds the young Henry V to-be toward his fulfillment at Shrewsbury. This process is managed with considerable economy, for rather more lines are assigned to Hotspur's side, but it is perhaps the more effective because of the economy. In the interval the audience must detach its natural sympathy with Hotspur and transfer it to Hal. Shakespeare orders this process brilliantly. The more faulty the management of the rebels' cause and the brighter the prospects of the King's party from the union of son with father, the more impossible it becomes to accept any justice in the rebellion when contrasted with Hal's right to the throne and his acceptance of the engagement to defend it. Any sentimental leaning to the ideology of rebellion is now impossible; but as this sympathy is detached, Shakespeare carefully replaces it by building up the more admirable side of Hotspur's personal character. The frenetic choler, the inability to control his tongue, the abrasive effect of his pride on his companions exist no longer; and for the first time we glimpse the careful general, conscious of the relation of his words and actions to the morale of his soldiers, and so cautious of defeat that he would probably have composed with Henry if he had not been fatally deceived by Worcester. Thus as Hotspur's cause dwindles in its rectitude, until it reaches the nadir of Worcester's false report, Hotspur the man rises. By this means there is pity and justice in Hal's summation, first, "Why, then I see   A very valiant rebel of the name," and after the combat,

> *Adieu, and take thy praise with thee to heaven!*
> *Thy ignominy sleep with thee in the grave,*
> *But not rememb'red in thy epitaph!*   (5.4.99–101)

It was a pity that for one especial weakness a brave young man had been so misled as to seek the destruction of his country. The forces of law and order must strike him down when he threatens the public safety and will not be reconciled. The audience is brought into the right attitude of the *lachrimae rerum*, the pity of things in this mixed human condition of right and wrong. But the personal sympathy one may feel for Hotspur is detached from the ideological. One may admire his bravery, but he must not be allowed to kill the future Henry V to whom the divine right of rule will descend.

On the other hand, the delay in the association of Hal with the main plot presents some technical problems. If Hal were not to be introduced until the climax, or shortly before, the audience would be unacquainted with him, and a transfer of interest from a powerful Hotspur to the newcomer would be difficult to effect. Clearly, Hal must be a part of the play from the beginning; but if he cannot join the main action until the middle of the third act, Shakespeare must provide some other action for him and motivate it in a manner that will hold the audience's interest. This he does by emphasizing Hal in his potential aspect only, and by rationalizing the old stories of Hal's wild youth—the Bear's Son archetype traditional for a hero. The action representing Hal's wild youth, on quite another plane from the crudities of the old play *The Famous Victories of Henry the Fifth*, leads to the invention of Falstaff. The emphasis on Hal's potential is then rationalized by his relations first with Falstaff, then with his father, and finally with Hotspur. In the process of realizing his potential the progression moves Hal from his initial planned idleness with Falstaff to the climax of his decision to join the King, and on to the single combat with Percy at Shrewsbury. This is the shape of the action. But all three relationships are present from the start and are integral in Shakespeare's justification of Hal's idleness. We may summarize this rationalization by saying that Shakespeare puts tension into the tavern scenes when he transforms Hal's withdrawal from the responsibility of his position as Prince to make it, instead, a waiting period of preparation for his future greatness. This preparation takes the form of tests which Hal applies to each of the three ways of life he is under pressure to adopt. In the end, he chooses neither one nor the other—neither Falstaff's hedonism, Henry's political manipulation, nor Hotspur's crude ideals of honor—but rises superior to each by combining the best of all three to form a new synthesis of conduct that will guide the higher royalty of the Henry V to come.

Tests is too conventional a word to apply, perhaps. Three ways of life do indeed present themselves to Hal, dramatized in the persons of Falstaff, the King, and Percy, and what each one stands for. I suggest that there is a rising scale of difficulty here—it is hard to avoid the use of the word *temptation*, but its implications cast a false light on the picture. *Attraction* is perhaps better—a rising scale of attraction. I do not mean to imply that the attractiveness of any one of these ways is increased in the course of the action. I mean only that given the kind of man Hal is, the high place designed for him by his birth, and the higher by his ambitions, the attractiveness of certain elements in what Hotspur stands for is greater than what Falstaff stands for as a way of life.

All progression must be from lesser to greater, and thus it is appropriate to consider Falstaff first. Despite the fact that he is the least of the magnets that might pull the Prince from the fixed course of his future, the action devoted to his relations to Hal takes up more space than the others. This imbalance was forced on Shakespeare because the action involving the Prince and the King could not appear until the climax of the play, in the middle of the third act, and Falstaff must occupy Hal for roughly a half of the play. Hence Shakespeare forms of Hal and Falstaff the underplot, a device that involves a structural paradox, because Hal, who is to become the true protagonist of the play (in that the spire of meaning rises from him), transfers from the under- to the main plot to create the climax. At this point the underplot loses its structural identity; and though its characters continue in the action, they are now—from Hal to Bardolph—merged in the central action, the suppression of the rebellion.

The action of the underplot is exclusively concerned with the Gadshill robbery and its aftermath. This action has no independent ideological significance in itself, but in Shakespeare's usual manner it is brought into the larger unity as a form of parody of the main plot. In the inverted mimic world of the underplot an action is initiated against royal law and order, in earnest on the part of Falstaff but in jest on the part of the Prince. That the Prince is in but not of the Gadshill plot means that he can guide it, soften its impact, and ultimately, by the restitution of the stolen money, heal the wound given to the commonwealth. The conclusion of this jest coincides with the father's summons to Hal; thereafter no further action arises from the underplot, and its persons are absorbed into the main plot—Hal to take a preeminent part in its dénouement, Falstaff to continue the function of parody begun in the Gadshill affair.

Since the underplot—although complete in itself—parodies the main action of the rebellion in its war on law and order, it is not conducted without reference to the larger issues that are still in suspense. The parody of Hal's forthcoming interview with his father serves to bring the whole of the jest to a focus, and indeed its conclusion, or dénouement, marks the moment of Hal's decision to forsake the way of life that Falstaff represents. We shall come to this presently. In the interval a less clear-cut incident in the underplot needs analysis, for it contains the equivalent parody of the part that Hotspur represents.

As Falstaff owes his invention to a technical necessity of the action, so this scene—as important in its purpose as the mock father-son interview—has its origin in the need to bridge Falstaff's roaring exit from Gadshill and his entrance into the tavern where the Prince and Poins are prepared to round off the jest by his humiliation. The jest—it is clear—is not to be the robbery itself. Instead, the exposure of the monstrous lies Falstaff will tell to explain away his flight and the loss of the booty is the anticipated comic point of the episode. Between the end of Gadshill and the unmasking comes only a scene of Hotspur's departure for Wales, and then we shift to the tavern in Eastcheap where the dénouement has been prepared.

To bring Falstaff on at the very beginning of this scene is dramatically inadvisable: any audience takes pleasure in a tantalizing delay that raises suspense, provided the playwright infuses the anticipatory tension with some independent dramatic interest. Thus it is almost obligatory for Shakespeare to contrive a beginning to the scene that will allow the audience pleasurably to await the arrival of Falstaff, so long as it is not too long delayed and anticipation give way to overstretched impatience. What Shakespeare does is to bring on Hal, who ironically describes to Poins his drinking with the drawers of the tavern and learning their cant. This description concludes with Hal's assertion "I tell thee, Ned, thou hast lost much honour that thou wert not with me in this action."

In this part of the scene *honor* is a key word, since this virtue throughout the play is to be surveyed from varying points of view by Falstaff, Hotspur, the King, and by Hal. But "action" is not to be neglected. It means, substantially, a battle, an encounter, or some course that would lead to an important conflict. It is in this sense that Hotspur in the preceding scene abuses himself for trying to win to his party a cautious lord, "O, I could divide myself and go to buffets for moving such a dish of skim milk, with so honourable an action." Hal's words to Poins— "thou hast lost much honour that thou wert not with me in this action"—are intended to repeat Hotspur's phrase as a form of parody. "Action" is also on Falstaff's lips. As he enters at 3.3 he inquires of Bardolph, "am I not fall'n away vilely since this last action? Do I not bate? Do I not dwindle?" Here in the cant of the highway is another parody of the word, one that demotes its honorable and warlike connotations to the farcical engagement at Gadshill. Falstaff may not be wholly serious, but Hal's use of "action" (as of "honor") is clearly ironic and turned against himself, even though Poins is too stupid to recognize the fact, as Hal well knows. The action that Hotspur is engaged in is a dangerous assault on the throne itself. The heir to this throne has put himself into a position where his "action" can be only a drinking bout with the tavern boys. Thus his irony is a form of self-disgust and accusation, which sets the tone for the second "action"— although this is not so named—the individual encounter with Francis.

Hal suggests the joke in order "to drive away the time till Falstaff come," this last a partial apology to the audience for the delay. The encounter is tolerably crude in the hearty jest-book style of humor, "How the Prince and Poins made a tavern drawer to lose his wits by calling him from another room." If it had no other purpose than to delay the entrance of Falstaff, or to cause the less judicious in the audience to guffaw at poor Francis' plight, it would be an excrescence, a blot on the play. Indeed, puzzled critics have often considered it so, and have echoed Poins's bewilderment, "But hark ye; what cunning match have you made with this jest of the drawer? Come, what's the issue?" "Match," like Falstaff's use of "action," is highwayman's cant. What situation have you set up to your advantage, what was the point, in short, of this jest? Indeed, unfriendly critics who follow the fashion of interpreting the play as the training of a cold-blooded neo-Fascist king, like to seize on this episode as another of Hal's discreditable deeds. Kittredge, however, knew that the Elizabethans were not egalitarians, and he warned of the dangers of modern sensibility when he wrote, "And so this jest of the drawer comes to an end. Sentimental readers here and there feel that the Prince has treated the boy ill; but they need not distress themselves. When Francis grew up and became an innkeeper himself, we may be sure that he often told with intense self-satisfaction how he had once been on intimate terms with Prince Hal." This exhibits Kittredge's bluff commonsense; but he is misled, as are other critics, by Hal's answer to Poins's question: "I am now of all humours that have showed themselves humours since the old days of goodman Adam to the pupil age of this present twelve o'clock at midnight." Kittredge here comments, "Prince Hal informs Poins (and the audience) that there was *no point* except the mere fun of the game itself."

Let us grant that the unsentimental Elizabethan pit, and doubtless the galleries too, would have laughed at the jest of Francis, which—as I have remarked—might have come directly out of some jest-book. But is it truly a jest to the Prince, engaged in for the mere fun of the game itself? Hal does not laugh, and his mood in the scene is as ironic as his calling a drinking-bout an "action." When Poins returns, Hal repeats the Vintner's information that Falstaff has arrived, and abruptly inquires, "Shall we be merry?" We may grant that this query refers to the oncoming scene with Falstaff; but Hal is not holding his sides with laughter when he utters it. The irony is still present, with its tinge of bitterness, as in "honor" and "action"; he has just participated in an elaborate jest, and at the end he inquires, "Shall we be merry?" Clearly the actor of Hal must exhibit an impatience throughout this whole scene, something approaching to a sense of frustration. Hal's answer to Poins, then, is not entirely what Kittredge asserts, that there was no point except for the mere fun of the game. He does not, indeed, answer Poins at all except obliquely: the ironic gist is—"I contain within me every whim that the human race has ever conceived, and therefore I seem to have no rational purpose in the jest." If we may put a name to the mood that Hal has exhibited so far in this scene, and in this answer, it would be boredom; boredom and self-accusation, a show of disgust at his situation in words that only he can interpret.

However, it is wrong to take it that the explanation is complete with these lines. Francis re-enters, and to Hal's inquiry, "What's o'clock, Francis?" answers distractedly "Anon, anon, sir," as he runs off. Hal then turns to Poins with the real answer that explains his impatience, and culminates in a most unusual breakdown of all restraint when his voice rises to a shout, "I prithee, call in Falstaff. I'll play Percy, and that damn'd brawn shall play Dame Mortimer his wife. 'Rivo!' says the drunkard. Call in ribs, call in tallow." Yet a moment later he has imposed on himself his customary control as he demurely opens the match with, "Welcome, Jack. Where hast thou been?"

What the Prince says in between these two points is of crucial interest. Francis' "Anon, anon, sir" calls from Hal the ejaculation, "That ever this fellow should have fewer words than a parrot, and yet the son of a woman! His industry is upstairs und downstairs, his eloquence the parcel of a reckoning." This is a bitter comment under the joke that the son of a woman, a sex noted for its loquaciousness, should yield to a parrot in the limits of his vocabulary. What Hal is noting is the fact that Francis' training and occupation get nowhere and result in no more useful purpose than, say, an animal serving on a treadmill. The human activity that Francis' divine spark motivates is expressed in upstairs and down, the height (or depth) of futility for an "action." The speech by which his godlike reason (next to the angels') should be exhibited is lower than that of a mimic bird. This is what happens to the son of a woman—that is, a human being—when his activity is not rationally motivated and his occupation thus becomes a soulless one.

Hal then continues, "I am not yet of Percy's mind, the Hotspur of the North; he that kills me some six or seven dozen Scots at a breakfast, washes his hands, and says to his wife, 'Fie upon this quiet life! I want work.' 'O my sweet Harry,' says she, 'how many hast thou kill'd to-day?' 'Give my roan horse a drench,' says he, and answers 'Some fourteen,' an hour after, 'a trifle, a trifle.' I prithee call in Falstaff. I'll play Percy . . . 'Rivo!' says the drunkard."

We are not here dealing with a humour, or whim either, but with a coherent continuation of Hal's line of thought about the "action" of the drinking-bout and the subhuman activity of

Francis as an expression of the depths to which rational man can sink when governed only by his animal nature. "I am not yet of Percy's mind." This ironic "not yet" divorces Hal from Hotspur's way of life in two respects. In the first, Hal is not yet prepared to win his reputation in the slaughter of the battlefield. The numerical listing of Percy's victims by which Hotspur has gained his fame as England's first soldier is then linked by this "not yet" to the commentary on Francis. Francis was the son of a woman: he belonged to the human race. But the up-and-downstairs activity of his trade is certainly no better than that of a beast. And his speech, instrument of his rationally guided judgment, is inferior to the mimic sounds of a parrot. Withal, Francis is so stupid that he never thinks of breaking his indentures and running away to a better life; his "mind" is content with his trade.

When Hal rejects this concept of life as one without the operation of human reason, he simultaneously rejects Hotspur's "mind," which is—given only the difference in the plane of activity—identical with Francis'. Hotspur's slaughter of the Scots in private pursuit of the mere word "honor," which Falstaff remarks is only air, is fundamentally no more a rational, or noble occupation than Francis' treading the staircase in his endless round. Since the Elizabethans measured intelligence, or wit, by speech, and esteemed eloquence as the mark of wisdom, so Hotspur's inarticulate responses to his wife's breakfast-table chit-chat compare no more favorably as evidence for the operation in him of a human reason than does Francis' "Anon, anon, sir." If we laugh at Francis, we must laugh at Hotspur. His "mind," or inclination, or ideals, is not that of the balanced and rational man whom Hal can respect as a full equal. When the time comes for the future Henry V to break through "the foul and ugly mists of vapours" the "base contagious clouds" that have smothered up his "beauty from the world" will, "when he please again to be himself," overcome the senseless activity directed by an unintelligent mind that has given Hotspur a reputation above his true deserts.

Percy has been placed in his right perspective beside Francis, whose industry was "upstairs and downstairs" and his eloquence the parcel of a reckoning, no different from the itemizing of a parcel of some fourteen dead Scots. Hal is "not yet of Percy's mind," nor will he ever be.

If one seeks the cause for Hal's impatience, almost his frustration, in this scene, then, it is because the "action" that he knows is ahead is so slow in coming and he must still play his part in the taverns until the time arrives for him to demonstrate how the controlled strength for national good that reason directs is superior to the mindless activity of a Francis-Percy, who has never learned to exercise his godlike reason in speech or in deeds. Hotspur is the son of a woman, but his wit is no better than a parrot's when he seeks to "pluck bright honour from the pale-fac'd moon" by the destruction, not the protection, of his country.

The tavern parody of the King's interview with Hal is more obvious and thus less in need of discussion. What it does do, however, is to provide clear evidence that we do not need to wait for the famed rejection scene that ends Part 2 on Hal's return from his coronation. He rejects Falstaff here in the tavern, and all he stands for, no less decisively—and Falstaff knows it. Before this scene Hal's concentration of interest has been on Falstaff, but after it he turns to Percy, and Falstaff—though still entertaining him—is on the periphery of his real concerns.

This is not the place to discuss the complex relations of Falstaff to Hal except to remark that the conventional picture of an ancient Vice tempting an innocent young man is wide of the mark. Although we should not underestimate Falstaff's delight in Hal's wit—for his own followers are lamentably deficient in stimulating him to anything but abuse—the chief attraction of the young Prince is his position. Underneath the combats of wit, Falstaff is earnestly working to make himself so indispensable to the Prince that he will be protected and raised to high position when Hal inherits the throne. "When thou art king" comes to be something of a refrain, and the suggestion is more than casual that Falstaff has his eye on the office of Lord Chief Justice. For Hal the attraction is also the wit, which does not flower on his side of the fence either. This wit is more than the breaking of a few puns. On the one hand it is related to eloquence in its mastery of rhetorical devices and its comic inversion of logical modes of thought; on the other it is related to wisdom in the realistic view it takes of human imperfection, and in its satiric unmasking of inflated pretensions, as in the private joke about the Douglas and his marksmanship, all the more wise because its termination foreshadows the aftermath of Shrewsbury.

> *Falstaff.* Well, that rascal hath good metal in him, he will not run.
> *Prince.* Why, what a rascal art thou then, to praise him so for running!
> *Falstaff.* A-horseback, ye cuckoo! but afoot he will not budge a foot.
> *Prince.* Yes, Jack, upon instinct.   (2.4.383–89)

In defeat the Douglas' instinct is to flee. Instead of running "a-horse-back up a hill perpendicular" as in the joke, he

> *fled with the rest;*
> *And falling from a hill, he was so bruis'd*
> *That the pursuers took him.*   (4.5.20–22)

The equation is most apt.

In Hal's hands this wit is to become constructive, a sign of his superior intelligence applied to the welfare of his kingdom. In Falstaff's hands, however, it is essentially destructive since it serves chiefly to disguise self-seeking as in his determined efforts to bind Hal to him for his own profit. What happens to the kingdom is of no concern. It may be funny to accept bribes to relieve able men from military service and to cull out such dregs of the countryside as provoke Westmoreland's protest, "Ay, but, Sir John, methinks they are exceeding poor and bare—too beggarly," or to wear a bottle of wine into battle instead of a pistol. The one could lose a battle, and the other could kill Hal in his need. This abuse of wit therefore by a levity in dealing with serious situations—its failure indeed in an almost existential manner to recognize any action or human motive as necessarily serious even in emergency conditions—this distortion inherent in Falstaff's way of life under its surface charm is the very reverse of wisdom. In plain terms, Falstaff is as much an internal danger to law and order in the kingdom as Percy is an external danger.

Neither can be permitted. As long as Falstaff can be controlled under suitable conditions, as when Hal is prince, Hal will tolerate him and will pretend to be deceived about Falstaff's true intentions, though all the time defending himself by the exercise of his superior wit against the imposition of Falstaff's will. When Hal is king, the danger to the commonwealth by association with an incorrigible force for internal dissension cannot be tolerated.[5]

Throughout the first acts Hal defends himself from "when thou art king," and in the mock interview in 2.4 his warning is fairly given and fairly understood. Pretending to be Henry speaking to his dissolute son, represented by Falstaff, Hal turns Falstaff's self-praise into a diatribe on "That villainous abominable misleader of youth, Falstaff, that old white-bearded Satan." Falstaff defends his hedonism and ends with the plea to banish all companions but himself, for "Banish plump Jack, and banish all the world!" To this the Prince responds, "I do, I will." Properly acted this can send a shiver through the audience as its significance is recognized. Falstaff's "banish all the world" would instantly, in context, recall the constant Elizabethan association of the *world* with *vanity*, that is, with an excessive regard for the pleasures and rewards of mundane life. Hal's response is to that proposition as much as to Falstaff. He is forsaking the life of the taverns—in which he had sought refuge, as well as pleasure, according to the terms of the important "I know you all" soliloquy (1.2.219–41)[6]—and is taking up the life of duty required by his

5. No one can take seriously Falstaff's promise to purge and live cleanly if he is rewarded for the alleged slaying of Percy (5.4.166–68).

6. "The famous 'I know you all' soliloquy, at the very beginning of the play, effectively disposes of any dramatic suspense that might have developed from a genuine inability in the Prince to make up his mind about his future. From the start of the play, therefore, Shakespeare has deliberately cast off the legitimate suspense that might have been generated by a lack of Hal's firm commitment. The soliloquy shows Hal to be plain enough. He is amusing himself for the nonce. When an emergency arises he will break through the clouds like the sun and show himself in his true majesty. He is not in the least deceived by Falstaff, nor does he have more than a partial interest in their tavern life. . . . It is not a character speech at all, as Kittredge has observed, but a time-saving plot device, rather on the clumsy side, deliberately to remove from the audi-

birth. One must realize that when the fatal words sound, "I do, I will," Hal is only in small part playing the role of his father. He speaks in his own person directly to Falstaff, who knows it.[7]

As a final comment, it is proper to note that though Hal forsakes the taverns, he does not turn his back on what had been of value there, the pleasure-loving principle divorced from vanity. He is not a puritan like Hotspur. The well-rounded Renaissance ideal man should be deficient in no side of experience or appreciation so long as it is carefully kept under the control of reason. Falstaff's devotion to pleasure was so extreme that in any position of real authority he would have endangered the kingdom. To that extent he is irrational and governed by his passions. On the contrary, Hal—appreciating pleasure but in control of its excesses—is a supremely rational Renaissance man. His

---

ence any suspense that Hal was actually committed to his low-life surroundings" ("Shakespeare's Art: The Point of View").

To this, one may perhaps add the incentive Hal felt to remove himself from court during the critical time before he is to inherit the throne. That Hal amuses himself genuinely in the taverns is clear enough, but that he also chafes under the necessity is indicated in the Francis episode. Finally, Shakespeare goes to extraordinary lengths to keep Hal blameless. Falstaff's sly suggestion of sexual incontinence is promptly rejected (1.2.53–54), and it is clear that before Gadshill Hal had gone on no highway-robbery expeditions. In short, we hear talk about a dissolute life, but we see none of it except of the most harmless variety.

7. The moment the words are uttered, Bardolph runs in with the announcement of the arrival of the sheriff. Falstaff, who is surely in danger from this approach, is so concerned with answering Hal—also directly, though maintaining the fiction of the play—that he shouts him off. The Hostess then brings the same news. At this point Falstaff gives up the fiction of play-acting and addresses Hall without pretense: "Dost thou hear, Hal? Never call a true piece of gold a counterfeit. Thou art essentially mad without seeming so." These words can refer only to Hal's abuse of Falstaff in the role of the King, but particularly to the seriousness of "I do, I will," which Falstaff recognizes. (I must reject Kittredge's preferred alternative that they mean, "Believe what the hostess is telling you.") I am genuine gold, says Falstaff, not a sham. If you are serious in your proposal to reject me, you are truly insane, even though your surface demeanor would not suggest it. This is followed by Falstaff's direct challenge to Hal to let the sheriff come in and arrest him, the result being his execution as a highwayman. Hal does not accept this challenge.

wooing of Katherine of France shows how he had learned his lesson in London.

The actual interview with the King offers a problem. Henry is as intent on forcing a code of conduct upon his son as Falstaff had been. It is a legitimate inference that Hal's unwillingness to live by his father's code had been a primary factor in his flight from the court to the taverns, where he could be his own man in private life until the opportunity came to be his own man in public life. He is not Henry's image in temperament or in conviction. If he had lived as Prince of Wales, he could not have influenced his father's policy and thus would have been tarred with the same brush. It was easier to make a fresh start in imposing his own image on the kingdom by removing the false picture of himself as a ne'er-do-well than the false picture of himself as the Machiavellian son of a Machiavellian father.

Henry's mistake is a natural one. He rules, and most successfully, too, according to the terms of his own temperament. What he does not realize is that his formula does not fit all kings, and that Hal must rule according to the terms of *his* temperament and also the conditions he will encounter, which differ from those with which Henry must deal. On the evidence of Part 2 possibly Henry would have seen the distinction, since he recognizes that Hal will inherit a peaceful kingdom in contrast to the civil wars that beset him. But in Part 1 he is obsessed with his fear that Hal is another Richard II and will be overthrown by another Bolingbroke. Point by point, almost, his lecture to Hal has been refuted in the "I know you all" soliloquy, which has provided a blueprint to the audience for the plan of Hal's future actions. The son must listen, but he cannot agree that Henry's course is for him.

At the end of the tavern scene that concluded the Gadshill jest, Hal had recognized the altered part he must play now that Percy had made his move against the throne: "I'll to the court in the morning. We must all to the wars." Henry may think that he is pleading with a hostile son to join his party, but the decision has already been made. If it is the union of son and father that spells the failure of the rebellion, and if after this scene Hal joins the main plot as the great opposite to Percy, the spearhead of the menace to his kingdom, the decision made in this scene must form the climax or turning-point of the action. In an earlier essay I analyzed the scene from this point of view and argued that it was a climax that was not a climax. Indeed, that Shakespeare had constructed it so in order to make a dramatic point to the audience not easily contrived by another means. That is, Henry thought that by his last calculated insult he had won over an enemy son to his side; and thus he had every right to be pleased with the successful outcome of the highly calculated speech that had done the job. But the audience knew that Henry was deceived, that Hal had been won over all the time, and that the moment had come, in Hal's view, to thrust aside the dark obscuring clouds and reveal the sun of his royalty. That Hal throughout the play was in perfect control of every situation, that he was thoroughly his own man, and that this was the point of the play, I suggested, was demonstrated by the nonclimax. A true victory for his father would have implied a malleable son, and a conversion But Hal had never needed conversion, as shown by the "I know you all" soliloquy. All he needed, as he there recognized, was the arrival at some future time of the proper conditions in which he could step forward as himself.[8]

I think that this view is still substantially correct, but I will offer one modification that should have been presented before. That is, it is true that Hal's decision has been made on the rational, or intellectual, plane before the interview. The audience can be in no doubt that the King does not persuade Hal to join him, for no persuasion is needed. It seems to me now, however, that more emphasis should be placed on the implications of the really decisive part of the interview containing the King's calculated insult: "Why, Harry, do I tell thee of my foes,   Which art my nearest and dearest enemy?" This reference to Hal as his "enemy" is an obscure one to us, but not to the Elizabethans, who knew the whole story. It is referred to when Hal cries, "God forgive them that so much have sway'd   Your Majesty's good thoughts away from me!" but again, just as obscurely. We do not, in fact, find the true reference until Hal rescues his father at

8.   See "Shakespeare's Art: The Point of View," pp. 74–78 above.

Shrewsbury from the onslaught of the Douglas, and the King recants:

> *Thou hast redeem'd thy lost opinion,*
> *And show'd thou mak'st some tender of my life,*
> *In this fair rescue thou hast brought to me.*

At this, Hal cries, in reference to the same detractors,

> *O God! they did me too much injury*
> *That ever said I heark'ned for your death.*
> *If it were so, I might have let alone*
> *The insulting hand of Douglas over you,*
> *Which would have been as speedy in your end*
> *As all the poisonous potions in the world.*
> *And sav'd the treacherous labour of your son.*   (5.4.48–57)

These lines show the depths of the King's insult which—being the man he is—he does not deliver without having planned its effect. Its continuation, that he thinks it probable Hal will join Percy's forces and fight against his father, in fear of Percy's frowns, carries on the implication that thereby Hal will ascend the throne over his father's body, as a vassal of Hotspur. It is this implication, that he has planned to murder his father in the past and may take the opportunity to do so in the present, that fires Hal as much as the insult that he will join Percy's party through fear.

Henry's tactics succeed. Hal flares up:

> *Do not think so. You shall not find it so.*
>   .   .   .   .   .
> *I will redeem all this on Percy's head*
> *And, in the closing of some glorious day,*
> *Be bold to tell you that I am your son,*
> *When I will wear a garment all of blood,*
> *And stain my favours in a bloody mask,*
> *Which, wash'd away, shall scour my shame with it.*
>   .   .   .   .   .
> *This in the name of God I promise here.*   (3.2.129–53)

Small wonder that the King, in satisfaction at the success of his stratagem, replies, "A hundred thousand rebels die in this!   Thou shalt have charge and sovereign trust herein."

Is it possible to reconcile this real flareup on Hal's part, marking the success of his father's plan, with the fact that the King did not need to provoke him since the night before the interview Hal had announced he was joining the wars? Is it possible to make a climax out of this false or nonclimax? I think it is. Let us grant that insofar as the decision to join his father was concerned, Henry's provocation was unnecessary. He may think that he has succeeded in firing his son to come over to his party, but the audience knows otherwise. That the audience has heard Hal's previous decision prevents it from thinking that Hal was so reluctant to leave his wastrel life in the taverns, so little his own man that he had to yield to outside forces and be shaped by them in this crucial decision, instead of moving into his new role of his own volition. Such a feeling would be fatal to Shakespeare's concept of Hal as the future Henry V who rises superior to each way of life that is offered him and in the end combines the best of them all to form a new concept of royalty, far superior to what any one of the pressures put upon him could have conceived.

But since Hal is to join the King and thereafter take his place as the protagonist, as Hotspur's main opponent, between whom the real issue is drawn, the light-hearted and almost casual decision at the end of the tavern scene makes clear his intellectual acceptance but leaves unclear his emotional commitment. The Elizabethans believed that Plato's white and black horses of reason and of passion had to pull the chariot of the soul in tandem. Passion, or emotion, was bad only if it rose to an excess, overpowered reason, and caused the chariot to swerve. Hal's "I know you all" soliloquy has been an eminently rational document. The question in the minds of the audience about the corroborating strength of his passion, or emotion, has not been answered by the tavern action preceding this interview, however, even though some clue has been given in the Francis scene. If Hal is deficient in passion—if he is what we would call overintellectualized or, at worst, the sort of schemer whom Derek Traversi pictures—he is not a truly rounded man. He is not the future Henry V if the strength of his personal conviction does not equal his general intention.

The interview with his father, then, furnishes the dramatic spark missing from the previous action to demonstrate to the audience that Hal's emotional commitment equals his intellectual or rational commitment. What Spenser exhibits in the person of Guyon in *The Faerie Queene,* following the lead of Aristotle's *Nichomachean Ethics,* now inspires Hal. Previously he has shown a satirical skepticism about the legendary deeds of the Douglas and a contempt for the mindless code of honor built on the number of Scots Hotspur can slaughter before breakfast. But what Henry succeeds in doing, thereby justifying the dramatic climax of the interview, is to arouse Hal to what Spenser would have called "honest anger" at the threat of the rebellion to his country. This we have seen only in the partial glimpse offered in his impatience during the jest with Francis the drawer and in the emotional bitterness of his soliloquy before the entrance of Falstaff slides him back into the play-acting of his idle tavern nights. Useful as the Francis episode had been to show that Hal is not all intellect and that he balances wit with human emotion under control of his reason, it is not enough to motivate the full conviction of his opposition to Hotspur on personal as well as on intellectual grounds. The interview, then, is not a formality but a dramatic and indeed an ideological, or psychological, necessity. But its rationale must not be perverted by the easy belief that somehow the King has "converted" his erring son during its course. Simply, an emotional force has been added to a decision rationally undertaken long before.

This emotional fire so necessary to action having been provided, Hal is now ready to move on to the third test posed by this play—the pressure on him to adopt the code of honor represented by Percy, the universally admired soldier, the man who, in King Henry's words, is "the theme of honour's tongue"; the man who Henry at one time wishes might prove to be his own son, replaced by the changeling Hal in the cradle.

Shakespeare's art, not just in comprehensive characterization but in understanding the issues which alone give character meaning, is magnificently demonstrated in the mixed nature of Hotspur. A man of action, the greatest soldier of the kingdom, he is yet such a mass of contradictions that his very strengths turn to weaknesses because the ideal that moves his conduct is as outmoded as is a knight's armor against the anachronistic cannon introduced into the account of Holmedon. Shakespeare brings the play to rest on the theme of honor. This touchstone for action has been much in Falstaff's mouth, and is the subject of his famous soliloquy, "Honour pricks me on," with its pragmatic conclusion, "What is that word honour? Air . . . Who hath it? He that died a Wednesday. Doth he feel it? No. Doth he hear it? No. 'Tis insensible then? Yea, to the dead. . . . Therefore I'll none of it" (5.1.136–42). This theme is supported by his later conclusion, "Give me life; which if I can save, so; if not, honour comes unlook'd for, and there's an end" (5.3.63–65). Henry has tacitly taken up the subject in his account to Hal of how he secured and maintained his throne. Hal has satirically applied the word to the Gadshill action and to his drinking bout with the drawers.

Hotspur's code is simply stated. It associates honor exclusively with courage, with reaction to danger regardless of the cause that is involved. A distinct link exists here with the artificial code of the duello well understood by the Elizabethans. That is, as it was stated, a man who inherited natural honor as the son of an honorable father and mother had to maintain, in addition, his acquired, or artificial, honor. Acquired honor was gained and kept only by means of constant wariness against its being impugned. If a single act of cowardice was observed, the whole fabric of acquired honor collapsed and could not be restored, and with it went natural honor. This concept had no relation to the ethical source of action. The Elizabethans debated whether, if a man declined to fight because he was in the wrong, he could be called honorable. The answer was mixed. One side maintained that it was the higher honor to decline combat if one's cause was not just, since if one killed one's opponent defending the wrong, one's soul was inevitably damned. The other, and more powerful because more popular, side maintained that the code of honor required a man who was challenged to fight without regard for his cause, for otherwise who would know he was not a coward and therefore without honor? This is the code to which, in essence, Hotspur subscribed. At its heart was the concept that any one seemingly dishonorable action, no matter how motivated, could destroy the structure of honor painfully built up over years of effort. And once destroyed, acquired honor could never be restored. The Elizabethans noted this concept as pre-eminent among military men. Every action, therefore, must have as its central motive the defense of one's honor against any imputation that a temporizing action was taken from motives of cowardice.[9]

It is this code, as much as his natural choler, that makes Hotspur so touchy in Wales about the course of the river Trent as the boundary of his lands-to-be. It moves him to abuse the lord who failed to join the conspiracy as a frosty-spirited coward: "O, I could divide myself and go to buffets for moving such a dish of skim milk with so honourable an action!" (2.3.36–38). The lord had only pointed out, quite reasonably, that the "friends you have named [are] uncertain [as indeed they turn out to be], the time itself unsorted, and your whole plot too light for the counterpoise of so great an opposition." This is an accurate estimate of the conspiracy, but Hotspur's sole reaction is to accuse the lord of cowardice because he was unwilling to test himself against a danger.

The code of danger for its own sake as the sole test of courage, and thus of honor, is concentrated in Percy's reaction to Worcester's calculated warning that the conspiracy is

> As full of peril and adventurous spirit
> As to o'erwalk a current roaring loud
> On the unsteadfast footing of a spear.   (1.3.191–93)

To this Hotspur cries out, "If he fall in, good night, or sink or swim!" That is, the danger justifies the attempt without regard

9. For an examination of the Elizabethan code in this matter, see my "Middleton's *A Fair Quarrel* and the Duelling Code," *Journal of English and Germanic Philology* 36 (1937): 40–65. The question whether Hamlet believes he has lost his natural honor because of his mother, Gertrude's adultery and incestuous marriage, has earlier been mentioned.

for the outcome so long, he continues, as honor opposes danger. The well-known speech then follows, beginning,

> *By heaven, methinks it were an easy leap*
> *To pluck bright honour from the pale-fac'd moon,*
> *Or dive into the bottom of the deep . . .*

with its conclusion,

> *And pluck up drowned honour by the locks,*
> *So he that doth redeem her thence might wear*
> *Without corrival all her dignities.*   (1.3.201–7)

The only means known to Hotspur to maintain his honor is for him to endure no rival. This supremely selfish and personal code exhibits itself in various ways and throughout is carefully motivated as the conduct of a man governed chiefly by his passions. It leads him to a towering pride, for which Worcester reproves him. It also leads to various ungenerous actions, the most significant being his harsh refusal to listen to Vernon's praise of Hal and his bloodcurdling resolve to kill the Prince, just prophesied as his country's hope. Hotspur's narrow code denies his acceptance of any rival, whereas, in contrast, the Prince in the battle scenes is truly chivalric in his praise of Percy, except for one point.

Here we come to the heart of the problem. Hotspur's association of honor exclusively with warfare and danger denies all ethical and humane grounds for action in its exaltation of the single factor of risk. His honor, then, leads him to become a traitor to his country and to its proposed dismemberment as a nation. Self has been placed over country, not for Worcester's venal motives but in the pursuit of a private and artificial code divorced from all question of right and wrong. His actions are basically motivated by self-aggrandizement, but the prize in the form that he seeks it has been accurately described in Falstaff's word as "air."

In contrast, Hal's concept of honor is firmly rooted in cause. He is not smirched by the apparent dishonor of his low-life activities, because his mind is not placed there. His actions are just when he enters the battle since he has dedicated himself, in honest anger, to the preservation of his country. He praises his great opponent for all chivalric actions but one—his treachery to his country. His response to Percy's challenge, narrows the issue: "Why, then I see   A very valiant rebel of the name." He continues:

> *I am the Prince of Wales; and think not, Percy,*
> *To share with me in glory any more.*
> *Two stars keep not their motion in one sphere,*
> *Nor can one England brook a double reign*
> *Of Harry Percy and the Prince of Wales.*   (5.4.63–67)

These words differ from Hotspur's ungenerous refusal to acknowledge a personal rival: that is, in part, they deny a sharing of true glory with his rebellious leadership that has split the kingdom, spilled English blood, brought in the Scotch enemies, and endangered the country's external security. The reign that is in dispute, and that will be resolved by the single combat, is that of war and chaos and civil disorder as reflected in the passion-ruled Hotspur as against the order and law and national unity and glory as represented by the rationally-motivated Prince. Above all, however, it is an ideological statement about England's destiny and the new concepts that must rule the country. It is the contrast between patriotism and feudalism, between a new code of honor based on right and a discredited, outmoded code based on pride and personal glory.

Thus the honor that Hal wins from this combat cannot be called "air," because he serves a greater master than himself in the cause of justice. The patriotic fervor of the play *Henry V* is fully anticipated here. Its association of personal and of national honor in Hal as against their destructive opposition in Hotspur leads to the ultimate definition, transcending Falstaff's materialism, Henry's expediency, and Hotspur's fatal distortion. The education of the future hero king, Henry V, is complete.

MILTON'S *SAMSON AGONISTES:*
Justice and Reconciliation

I N HIS FIRST INVOCATION TO THE MUSE in *Paradise Lost,* and again
in subsequent invocations, Milton quite definitely sets himself
up against all previous epic writers as one who is determined to
outgo them. His stated reliance is on his Christian theme that
contains revealed truth unknown to the ancients and is therefore automatically superior to any subject they could have chosen for treatment. At the same time, Milton strove to outgo his
classical models not alone in theme but also in the art of literary
composition. That is, he deliberately invited comparison with
Homer and Virgil in his utilization of their structural and rhetorical devices, but always with a difference. The initial invocation is greatly extended and splendidly deepened, and, uniquely,
other and even more personal pleas for enlightenment and support are voiced at crucial intervals. The epic similes are enlarged
in scope as forms of prolepsis, irony, and characterization, and
they are carefully shaped to achieve a previously unenvisaged
coherence of elements in the two parts of the extended comparisons. Obviously, the formulas of epics needed to be enlarged to
do justice to Milton's great subject. Yet as a literary artist he de-

From *The Dress of Words: Essays on Restoration and Eighteenth Century Literature in
Honor of Richmond P. Bond,* ed. Robert B. White, Jr. (Lawrence: Univ. of Kansas
Libraries, 1978); by permission of the publisher.

liberately invited the reader's attention to the vitality and meaningfulness with which he had infused these traditional formulas that in lesser hands would have been palely imitative.

In the last paragraph of his preface to *Samson Agonistes*, also, he implicitly invites a comparison of his achievement with the dramas of Aeschylus, Sophocles, and Euripides by challenging only those readers to judge him who are acquainted with these "three Tragic Poets unequall'd yet by any, and the best rule to all who endeavour to write Tragedy." Milton would not have been Milton if he had failed to believe that in the view of judicious readers he would come off from the comparison not without honor, specifically, perhaps, in respect to *Oedipus at Colonus*. In matching himself against the Greek tragic writers Milton again trusted to his theme, which by the support of religious truth could not in his mind fail to surpass the dramatic subjects of the pagan world, its heroic history and its gods. But as he had done in *Paradise Lost*, one would expect Milton in *Samson* to adapt the various conventions of Greek tragedy to the superior grandeur of his theme and to inform them with new life, not alone from the influence of his biblical subject but also by means of his own artistic invention finding new and more meaningful variations on the formulas of classical tragic drama.

Milton's preface to *Samson Agonistes* is more respectful to the tragedy of the Greeks than the comparisons of his own work with classical epic in *Paradise Lost*. It is not inappropriate to speculate that his admiration for ancient drama was higher than for ancient epic: we must not forget that when early contemplating a work that would in effect justify his life of preparation, his first thoughts had turned to tragedy. At any rate, I take it that we do not observe in *Samson* so many of the technical innovations in traditional form that had marked *Paradise Lost*. Instead, we find within a framework of almost exact parallelism in external structure a conscious deepening of the significance, a new light on the means by which Greek conventions could be adapted to shadow forth the high significance of his theme, the relations of God to man in the working out of divine purpose. I suggest that in the end the new charge of energy that in *Samson Agonistes* runs through the old formulaic conventions transforms this dramatic structure by a sea-change in no less innovative a manner than the more technical alterations of epic formula with which he had experimented in *Paradise Lost*. Indeed, I am bold to assert that in its Christian vitalizing of ancient tragic form *Samson Agonistes* produced a greater and more original triumph than the Christian epic of *Paradise Lost*.

Two related problems face any critic of *Samson Agonistes*. The first is the precise nature of the misunderstanding that Samson and the other characters have of God's purpose for him after his blinding, a purpose not finally manifested until the catastrophe. The second is the exact means, as dramatically represented, by which the misunderstanding is eliminated and a reconciliation is brought about.

One minority group of critics, perhaps basing their thesis on Dr. Johnson's famous pronouncement that *Samson Agonistes* is a play wihout a middle, sees Samson as another Prometheus, the victim of extreme punishment, whose virtue is stoic or heroic suffering, simple endurance on the model of Job, until he recognizes the possibility for action offered by the feast of Dagon, seizes it, and achieves a mighty revenge for the indignities the Philistines had heaped upon him. Obviously, if this summary were true, the play would merely mark time by celebrating the virtues of stoic endurance up to the moment that Milton was ready to introduce what would have been the unmotivated catastrophe. That the ways of God to men would have been any further clarified by this dramatic program than in the relatively primitive and non-redemptive Old Testament ethos of the story of Job is doubtful, and that Milton would have engaged himself to such a theme that controverts the message of *Paradise Lost* and then had the effrontery to claim for it the reader's "new acquist of true experience from this great event" is scarcely to be credited.

Fortunately it is more often held that Samson earns his way back to a reconciliation with God and that the action dramatizes this reconciliation as the central theme of the play. This view makes of *Samson Agonistes* a redemptive tragedy not on the Greek but on the Shakespearean model, in which the hero after his tragic error wins through to a death in victory that justifies such a trust as Horatio's that flights of angels will sing Hamlet to his rest. Redemptive tragedy has its own special dramatic structure. However, at the moment the question is the nature of the misunderstanding that is turned to understanding in the reconciliation. That in the catastrophe God rescinds his estrangement and Samson once again becomes the champion of God and of Israel is certainly Milton's intention, one finally understood by Manoa and the Chorus and through them communicated to the audience in the magnificent close of the tragedy. What does not seem to be so clear to critics are the special terms of the reconciliation and the reason why these special terms impose the penalty of death on Samson.

The intention of *Samson Agonistes* does not differ from that of *Paradise Lost* in centering on the justification of the ways of God to men, a familiar quotation that can be read in two complementary ways: to make clear the justice of God's ways in dealing with man and to make clear to man the fact that God's ways are just. The lesson of *Paradise Lost* is that God's will cannot be controverted by Satan or by Adam. Since God's will is to good, what seems to be thwarting of that will by the success of evil is not a true thwarting. At best it is permitted and it is temporary, since the effect of evil is always to promote the good that obliterates the specific evil of the Fall and its effects on mankind up to the ultimate healing of the breach of faith in the Last Judgment when good will reign forever and evil be permanently imprisoned. *Samson Agonistes* has a more concentrated aim: to dramatize a concrete and derived example of Adam's disobedience and fall and the estrangement that follows. But the apparent thwarting by human means of God's Providence is here concluded in the triumphant demonstration that God always turns evil to good in a reconciliation with repentant man and in the resulting action that fulfills God's original purpose. As the first disobedience of Adam is a paradigm for Samson, so Samson may serve as a paradigm for any individual in the audience who must necessarily face the same problems of sin, punishment, and reconciliation.

In this paradigm there is a crucial element that mystifies man. This is the apparent severity of the punishment that is linked with estrangement when man fails in his mission of fulfilling God's purposes. Actually, it is not the severity of the punishment itself for failure so much as the harsh estrangement that puzzles man's understanding of the paradoxical ways of a loving God. Specifically, the estrangement appears to confirm God's abandonment of His purpose along with the rejection of His agent. If this is so, then of course no punishment could be too severe for a man who had failed in his high mission through willful and avoidable human weakness and thus prevented the success of God's plan for good. But if God abandons this fallen agent and seeks for another through whom he may work to the same end, punishment represents only retributive justice—retaliation for no other end than destruction. Man may admit the justice of this retaliation for having failed the Almighty, but uncomfortable problems are raised which Milton does not hesitate to face in *Samson*. If the Almighty selected an agent who in His foreknowledge He recognizes would fail so that the project had to be abandoned or a substitute put into the breach, the efficiency of such a system for getting the world's work done may well come in question, as well as the matter of equity in the excessive nature of the punishment that always seems to follow on the failure that, after all, had been foreseen even though not predestinated.

The only reason that Samson represents a special case is that he had been chosen for a specific mission, unlike the general run of mankind whose destiny is to serve by standing and waiting. Milton's great theme was that good always overcomes evil, that no special agent can ever thwart God's purpose in employing him, even though he may initially seem to fail and to be discarded. God's ultimate plan is immutable, although the means by which it is carried out are conditional. The days of miracles being past, according to Protestant thinking, only rarely does God intervene directly in human affairs but instead indirectly by the appointment of agents, who may be called His ministers. It is through them that He works to carry out His specific intentions within His Providential view for mankind. The mission may be to see that justice is done in human affairs, as in Hamlet's duty to bring justice to the murderer of his father, a concealed crime that the law was helpless either to detect or to punish. Or, as with Samson, some great step forward in the freeing of God's chosen people from servitude may be proposed, a mission that Milton also believed had been given to Cromwell. Through such agents the slow process of justice is built up in the world that will eventually culminate in a redemption and restoration in the person of Christ on the Day of Judgment.

In this process two great ends are served. First, the world is prepared by experience for its final apotheosis. Second, as a part of that experience the lesson is given that although man must strive for his perfection within the framework of God's Providence, he cannot fully succeed by his own efforts but only through Christ. The blindness of the Israelites in *Samson Agonistes* lies in some part in their expectation that Samson, although manifestly a divine agent, but also an inheritor of original sin, could achieve a physical loosening of their bonds without working in them a corresponding spiritual freeing which the Messiah alone was destined to provide. The nature of spiritual freedom may thus be exemplified as much in human failure as in human success; and over the long course of history man may be taught that although he must continually strive, the only possible fulfillment lies in Christ. In this manner the world may be prepared for its ultimate redemption by the cumulative understanding of the real nature of perfection. Within this context retributive or condign justice—meaning punishment with no other end in view but retaliation—was taken to be the fate of mankind in Old Testament days to break its stubborn spirit and prepare it for the acceptance of the salvation that was to be offered after the coming of the Messiah. In New Testament days the principle of salvation operates, since by exemplary, or redemptive, justice applied to error, each man may be taught to follow in the footsteps of Christ, which for Milton meant perfect obedience to the will of God. The purpose of punishment under the system of equity—mercy added to justice—that governs redemptive justice is to lead man to an understanding of the will of God when his own will has crossed divine purpose and alienated him from the supporting signs of grace. That man, so taught, can return to God's favor is the healing message of *Samson Agonistes* and its justification of the ways of God to man.

We may believe, then, that *Samson Agonistes*, is a redemptive tragedy, that in pulling down the temple Samson once more became God's champion and—although in death—won victory, indeed a victory that on the analogy of the Fortunate Fall may be taken to be greater than he would have achieved if he had not fallen. God's will thus has not been turned aside by the human weakness of His chosen minister. The justice of Samson's blinding and enslavement has proved redemptive, not retributive as originally believed by all characters in the play.

It is true that the general blindness of Samson and the others rests on the misapprehension that his fault has caused God to abandon him, and that the purpose for which he had been selected as minister is now aborted. So long as this doctrine of despair holds, reconciliation is impossible, for Samson will not have the understanding to perform his share of the reconciliation. The root of the misunderstanding spreads from the wrong interpretation of the evidence. No one in the play conceives of an alternative to Samson's return to his championship except on the original terms. Since an enslaved and blinded man, even though his strength is returning, is impossible to fit into the mold of the Samson who slew the Philistines with no other weapon than the jawbone of an ass, the present facts deny his championship; and any return in the future to his original role is envisaged only in terms of the restoration of his eyesight. In Milton's view, of course, what needs restoration is not the outer but the inner light that will support him in a new role. The whole basis for the theme of the blindness to the ways of God that permeates the tragedy is the accepted belief that reconciliation must come only from God, and not mainly from Samson, and that it must result in a return to the original conditions of Samson's mission. In these terms the only subject for debate is by necessity the question whether Samson's sin was so heinous that God cannot be expected to relax His punishment, or whether—like Apollo in *Oedipus at Colonus*—He will arbitrarily at some future time accept Samson's suffering as payment and, not without some degree of self-interest, restore him as he was before his fall.

This blindness illustrates the total lack of the Israelites' comprehension of God's ways in the balance between justice and mercy but particularly in the operations of His Providence in human affairs. Mercy is wrongly taken to be a total forgiveness that will restore Samson to the exact position he held before his sin. *Paradise Lost* demonstrates the opposite. Once sin enters and a minister falls by placing his own will in disobedience above that of God's, a conditional divine decree begins its operation that modifies the mission according to the changed conditions resulting from the fall. In *Paradise Lost* man is predestined to salvation, and mercy finds the means to achieve this great end in Christ's mediatory sacrifice. But Adam cannot work out his new destiny within the confines of the Garden of Eden as if the original sin that has now entered him were not. Spiritual death—which would be the utter condemnation of retributive justice—will be removed by Christ so that through the gateway of temporal death mankind will in the end be restored to a state of good that surpasses the state he would have achieved if he had never fallen. But the rules have changed. Although conditionally predestined for eternal life, just as if he had never sinned, man must first suffer the death that sin has brought. An Adam who will die has no place in the eternal perfection of the Garden of Eden. The original plan for his future, conditional upon his continued obedience, is now no longer operative and will never operate again on the same terms. Mercy that would wipe the slate clean and remove all consequences of sin without the satisfaction of the law is a sentimental and unrealistic proposition that controverts justice, in Milton's opinion. The road to Adam's restoration must now be trudged under very different conditions, even though the end will be his acceptance into glory, as before. That sin, although it will be forgiven, must first be punished according to the law, and that no agent of God who sins in disobedience will ever be restored to the exact terms of his original mission, is the heart of Milton's understanding, as it was of Shakespeare's.

If God has proposed a mission for an agent, however, and this agent fails in his mission through sin, God's purpose has not been turned aside: the mission will still be accomplished but in a completely different manner from that by an unfallen agent, the difference representing the conditions of sinlessness and the consequences of sin, of seeing evil through the eyes of good or good through the eyes of evil. The extension of mercy ameliorates justice but does not substitute for it. Mercy will modify the condemnation that justice demands, but justice must be satisfied even though forgiveness is extended. In redemptive tragedy whether of *Paradise Lost* or of *Hamlet*, the price that the agent must pay is his death, but it will be a death in victory because the mission will still be accomplished even though in a completely unexpected manner from that originally understood. In tragedy the different manner requires the expiatory death of the fallen but now regenerate hero and his willing acceptance of that death as the essential means of victory. This is the law that corrective justice teaches him so that he is prepared for reconciliation when he is caught up in or engages himself to the catastrophic event. Hamlet goes to his death after submitting his will to God in the knowledge that a man's life is not in his own hands but in God's and that for man the readiness is all. We must believe that a similar enlightenment comes to Samson when he finds some rousing motions in him that lead him to accept the Philistine summons.

The blindness in *Samson Agonistes* , then, is a double blindness. The first part has always been recognized—the despair that God has cast off Samson because of his sin of will. The second part has been less appreciated: the complete lack of understanding in the characters of the conditional alteration in the working-out of God's plan consequent upon Samson's fall, and thus of the changed terms on which God will still use him as His champion—the important difference being that Samson must pay the law by dying in order to win the victory, a champion once more.

If this is the theme of the play, as I suggest, then the means by which Samson comes to an understanding of his altered role and accepts the penalty in order to renew his mission must be the concern of the action. Within this action the significance of the three visitations (four if we count the Chorus) has been variously debated. A relatively crude view of the tragedy takes it that the visitations of Manoa, Dalila, and Harapha, which comprise the main action of the play framed between the entrance of the Chorus and the appearance of the Philistine Messenger, are not placed in a cumulative, or developing, sequence. This is the gist of Dr. Johnson's notorious complaint that the play lacks an Aristotelian middle "since nothing passes between the first Act and the last, that either hastens or delays the Death of Samson," a view that he repeats in other terms as "the intermediate parts have neither cause nor consequence, neither hasten nor retard the catastrophe." If this notion were to stand, the order of the interviews is random and they could be shuffled and transposed with no difference in their effect on the gathering of the forces that propel the ending.

The defence of *Samson Agonistes* attempts to find a rationale in the visitations that makes of them true dramatic incidents arranged in a significant order and leading to a motivated and therefore meaningful catastrophe. Unfortunately, this defence against Johnson's strictures does not speak with one voice. One school has found in the episodes the classic temptations of the World, the Flesh, and the Devil. There is much that is attractive in this way of looking at the visitors. Manoa can certainly represent the vanities of this world in the life of rest after toil that he paints for Samson as the only desirable or even possible sequel to his permanent defeat. The temptress Dalila adds to this life of sloth and gluttony the temptations of a sensual marriage bed as a form of nepenthe. Harapha tempts Samson by the sin of pride, which was the conventional gloss given to the Devil. The analogies are interesting and I think of some significance; moreover, they would represent an ascending order of trial. But in the end the explanation, although true at one level, is not wholly satisfying. Certainly it does not represent the ultimate answer since it fails to establish the relation of Samson's rejection of these temptations to his reconciliation with God and the renewal of his mission.

Another school argues, to quote William Riley Parker, that "Samson's will is responsible for the catastrophe. . . . 'Everything, therefore, which helps to determine Samson's will and to define his purpose leads to the catastrophe' [Jebb]. . . . As long as he doubts, as long as he questions, as long as he is anywise out of harmony with God's will, he is not a fitting instrument of God's purpose." This thesis is completely correct, so far as it goes, but it also is far too vague about the exact terms of the reconciliation as well as of the alienation. Moreover, in its charting of the preparation of Samson's mind for the decision that brings about the catastrophe, critics split as to the decisive incident. Some hold that the Dalila episode is the crucial one and that the whole point of Harapha's visit is not to provide a fresh temptation, with a corresponding enlightenment of Samson's will after he has successfully surmounted its trial. Instead, it is held, Samson is completely prepared after the successful conclusion of the Dalila episode except that he is necessarily passive in the absence of any indication of a line of action open to him. Harapha, then, provides the required spur to action. Others see the Harapha episode as the crucial one in the series of three and hold that Samson's reactions proceed not merely from an external spur to action suggested in the course of the incident but instead from the inner enlightenment provided by his sudden challenge to Harapha to combat in a trial of truth.

Such a serious difference of opinion about the structure needs to be resolved, of course. But even this need is subsidiary to the central question that does not seem to have found a satisfactory answer: precisely what is it that Samson and the other characters misunderstood about God's purposes, and how in the three visitations is Samson led to the truth that governs his catastrophic action. This can only be the truth that, transferred to Manoa and the Chorus from the action, brings forth the catharsis in them—and in the audience—of calm of mind, all passion spent; that is, the peace and support of understanding when the audience return to life after the fictive experience of the tragedy.

The first part of this question I have already endeavored to answer. The truth is that God punishes only irredeemable evil by retributive justice. Redeemable good, as in His ministers (scourges are quite another matter), is punished by corrective justice, the intent of which is to teach the way to an acceptance of reconciliation on the altered terms created by the new situation. That new terms are possible and that they will be extended to Samson is what no one in the play comprehends up to the point that the "rouzing motions" begin to fill his mind and—although he never says so—he sees for the first time and accepts the new truth. His enlightenment, then, is not merely the general recognition that God has not abandoned him, which is true, but the more specific recognition that if he is prepared to make the required expiation by a willing acceptance of the final and necessary corrective punishment of death, he can satisfy in a new manner the original requirement of his mission, although at the price of "Inevitable cause At once both to destroy and be destroy'd." The "rouzing motions ... which dispose To something extraordinary [his] thoughts" both are and are not his own, for any religious-minded member of the audience would recognize them as an impulse sent from God, the first time that God has communicated with Samson since his betrayal of faith. It follows that at this point Samson has in a sense earned the reestablishment of communication by the traditional way of having brought his will once more into harmony with God's.[1]

This harmonizing of wills, required before the catastrophe can hold any significance other than the terrible revenge on the Philistines for which Manoa at first mistakes it, has been recognized by critics like Parker. The difficulty is that although these critics have perceptively traced the rise and fall of Samson's moods in each interview and have shown him rejecting false interpretations both of his past and present conduct, little has been advanced that reveals how he may be successively coming closer to the specific truth that the rousing motions forecast. If each interview in some essential matter clarifies his mind so that he could not have met the test of the second without having surmounted the first, or encountered the third without conquering the second, then the play has a middle and the episodes are connected by a chain of cause and effect that may properly be said to motivate the catastrophe. If instead there is no successive and rising tide of clarification that prepares him to receive the "rouzing motions," then the criticism is true that places the greatest

---

1. However, the motion that leads Samson to follow the Messenger is only the first and incomplete step and its ultimate purpose is not understood except by the audience's acquaintance with the story. The real motion with its complete idea of necessary action to restore his championship comes later as he stands thoughtful in the temple.

emphasis on the Harapha incident and alleges that the interviews with Manoa and Dalila do little or nothing to advance the
action.

The prime difficulty I suggest comes in the disparity between
Samson's correct actions and the lack of conscious understanding
that he reveals about these actions. If it is a question of observ-
ing the development of his own enlightenment as manifested in
his words, one can easily see how Dr. Johnson and the other
critics like Chambers and Verity were misled. The basic response
Samson has to Manoa is that he cannot serve his nation or his
mission by sitting idle on the household hearth, a burdensome
drone

> *till length of years*
> *And sedentary numness craze my limbs*
> *To a contemptible old age obscure.*   (ll. 570–72)

On the other hand, he has no answer to Manoa's counter-
argument that he can scarcely serve his nation while in chains
as a slave, and he confesses himself deserted by Heaven:

> *Hopeless are all my evils, all remediless;*
> *This one prayer yet remains, might I be heard,*
> *No long petition, speedy death,*
> *The close of all my miseries, and the balm.*   (ll. 648–51)

The action here is right, for if he had obeyed Manoa he would
once more have interposed his will against God's by seeking to
cut short the punishment that justice had visited upon him. Yet
his resolve to remain drudge at the mill is instinctive, not rea-
soned, for the only end he foresees from his remaining is an earlier death than if he were to linger out his days in ease at home
with Manoa. The decision is a right one, but his reasons are un-
focused and despairing. Perhaps even more sharply, his sole interpretation of Dalila's visitation is that

> *God sent her to debase me,*
> *And aggravate my folly who committed*
> *To such a viper his most sacred trust*
> *Of secresie, my safety, and my life.*   (ll. 999-1002)

This is still taking himself as the recipient of retributive justice, the coming of Dalila prompted by God only to punish him further. His rejection of Dalila was well founded, for if he had accepted her form of comfort he could never have been received back into God's favor. But the action is not consciously taken and the grounds appear to differ little from his rejection of Manoa's appeal. If there is any advance in enlightenment between his reactions to the two visitations, the distance is imperceptible. That he has learned anything about himself that will aid him in correctly interpreting his relations with God can scarcely be demonstrated from his words. Neither abasement nor stoic suffering is enough, no matter how Promethean-like heroic, if it does not lead to enlightenment.

On the other hand, if we look not to Samson's own words but to the understanding by the audience of the inner significance of his deeds, even though performed in blindness, the case is altered. What Samson sees as retributive justice, offering no escape from punishment except death, the Christian audience interprets rightly as corrective justice, the intent to instruct not Samson alone but all Israel (and of course the audience) as to the conditions of redemption so that at the proper time God may once more send an impulse to His servant Samson. At the start of the play and the dialogue with the Chorus, Samson is aware of the heinousness of his crime. He accepts full responsibility and does not endeavor to shift the blame from himself, where it belongs. It was his weakness that led him to break his faith under a stress that could have been withstood. To this extent it is commonly recognized that the ground is prepared for eventual reconciliation; what holds it back is his despair. Critics make much of the progressive bringing of Samson's alienated will into harmony with God's, but they do not entirely face the question of how his will is out of harmony and how in the Manoa and Dalila episodes it moves toward harmony. That there is no harmony at the start between God's purpose to renew his championship and Samson's despair at being deserted is clear enough. It is a legitimate question, however, to what degree, if any, his will has altered between say, the entrance of the Chorus and the departure of Dalila so that a progression may be observed. Up to the coming of Harapha, the answer must be that there is none if we take only the evidence of Samson's own understanding. It is to his actions—the basis of all drama—that we must look for what is in fact happening. In one sense his responses to Manoa and to Dalila are negative in that he refuses to be swayed in any direction that will ameliorate his condition. He does not recognize what his refusals were aimed at: all he knows is that each suggested course of action would be a flight from his punishment. That his punishment has any other end than retaliation is not understood. What he does know, however, is that if God purposes to punish him, he would be setting his will against God's by attempting an escape. Thus his actions, though negative and without hope of redemption, are actually positive in their result, and from the point of view of the audience—though not of Samson—his state at the end of the Manoa episode differs from that at the beginning. I suggest that what the audience sees happening is a dramatization of the three stages of repentance as worked out in Book 1 of Spenser's *Faerie Queene* in accord with the conventional teachings of the church. We should remember that to Milton, Spenser was a better teacher than Aquinas.[2]

Like Samson, the Red Cross Knight after his breach of faith with Duessa and his encounter with Despair is in no condition to attempt the conquest of the dragon until he has been inwardly healed and thus qualified for the dispensation of mercy. Fidelia brings him to the first stage of this process of "trew repentance" by instructing him in the nature of sin so that

> That wretched world he gan for to abhore,
> And mortal life gan loath, as thing forlore,
> Greev'd with remembrance of his wicked wayes,
> And prickt with anguish of his sinnes so sore,
> That he desirde to end his wretched dayes:
> So much the dart of sinfull guilt the soule dismayes.   (1.10.21)

2. In *De Doctrina* Milton enumerates the progressive steps of repentance as "conviction of sin, contrition, and departure from evil, conversion to good" (see Maurice Kelley, *This Great Argument*. p. 169, and also p. 379). I take it, however, that Spenser has directly influenced him in *Samson Agonistes*. All quotations from *Samson Agonistes* conform to the first edition, London, 1671.

The difference between this dismay and the form allegorized in the earlier dispute with personified Despair is important. Red Cross had encountered Despair in full confidence but was abruptly brought low by arguments based entirely on the principle of retributive justice that offered no hope of forgiveness for what seems to be the irremediable heinousness of his sin. Against this argument he had no defense, for he lacked the protection of formal repentance against the hopelessness of his position now so pervertedly thrust home. It is true that, on the surface, under Fidelia's guidance Red Cross also feels a horror and an anguish that make him wish to end his life. But it is crucial that it is Faith who instills this recognition of the real nature of his crime and so the purpose is not retributive but, instead, the necessary preliminary to the redemptive process. By church teaching, a sinner can prepare himself for mercy only by first understanding the nature of his sin. This preliminary, I suggest, is represented in Samson's opening soliloquy in which he is assailed by his restless thoughts like a swarm of hornets. We must take it that despite his acceptance of full blame for his fall, Samson is not "repentant" in any fulfilled sense as Spenser saw it; and Milton powerfully illustrates his bewildered state of mind by the fevered questionings which foster only despair.

Spenser makes it clear that this same state of mind in the Red Cross Knight is only the preparation for repentance and by no means the start of the actual process. Red Cross sees no hope despite the comforting of Speranza, and Una is forced to beg Coelia for aid. Coelia fetches Patience, a doctor who has insight into the disease of grieved conscience, and only then does the cure begin. The words of wondrous might that Patience speaks to Red Cross do no more than reduce the emotional pain and confusion of his grief so that he may endure its burden. So far as his sin goes, Red Cross is still in a position wherein

> the cause and root of all his ill,
> Inward corruption, and infected sin,
> Not purg'd nor heald.   (1.10.25)

His diseased conscience is finally cured by the scourges of Penance and Remorse and by healing Repentance. When once more whole he is brought to Una, Spenser attributes the alteration to the ministrations of "wise Patience And trew Repentance." We must take it then that in his encounter with Despair Red Cross lacked this patience, and thus that the process of repentance could begin only when he was prepared to bear his burden with fortitude, not in a state of high and confused emotion as to the issues involved. Penance scourges his mind and Remorse his heart until his corruption is purged, while Repentance washes away his sins with the therapeutic salt water of tears. The distinction between penance (which contains remorse) and repentance is theologically a sharp one. Penance exhibits sorrow and contrition for sins, whereas repentance is won only subsequently by a thorough hatred of them and a change of mind, a firm resolve not to repeat the sins that have brought one low.

The first stage of purgation, the demonstration of patience, may be assigned to Samson's dialogue with the Chorus. Instead of the restless questions of the soliloquy, Samson now is comforted by the support of friends. His anguish remains but he is able to assert that the blindness he had bemoaned in his soliloquy as the worst now afflicts him least in comparison with shame at his betrayal of God. The discussion of ingratitude leads to Samson's conclusion that although he has been deserted by men and by God; men may not neglect God's proposed deliverance as they have now neglected him. In distinguishing between the blame to be attached to him and to his nation which failed as well, Samson has learned to accept with patience his guilt, but he properly refuses to accept more than his share. This is in fact an important clarification of his degree of responsibility and of guilt, and he thereupon is in a position to bear his own share with as much fortitude as can be mustered in his anguish.

The emphasis upon sorrow and contrition becomes more marked in the Manoa episode:

> *Appoint not heavenly disposition, Father,*
> *Nothing of all these evils hath befall'n me*
> *But justly; I my self have brought them on,*
> *Sole Author I, sole cause.*   (ll. 373–76)

Samson recognizes that the present

> *base degree to which I now am fall'n,*
> *These rags, this grinding, is not yet so base*
> *As was my former servitude, ignoble,*
> *Unmanly, ignominious, infamous,*
> *True slavery, and that blindness worse then this,*
> *That saw not how degenratly I serv'd.*   (ll. 414–19)

His action in refusing Manoa's offer of a retirement to soft ease is instinctively correct in that it is not his right to decide when the punishment shall end. Since Samson still sees the punishment as purely retributive, he intends to bear it until his hoped-for death, which alone will offer peace. On the other hand, the patience that he derived from his interview with the Chorus enables him to understand more clearly than before the exact nature of his crime, which he correctly imputes to effeminacy (or lack of fortitude) following on pride. By insisting on the endurance of his humiliation so long as God wills it, he is showing in the only way he knows his sorrow and remorse, and he has definitely moved into the second stage, that of penance.

The final stage of repentance, I suggest, is dramatized in the Dalila visitation where two very important decisions are made. The first consists of Samson's refusal to repeat his former sin, the effeminate subjection of his will to Dalila's. No more telling proof could be given of his repentance, his hatred of the sin that caused his downfall, than this rejection of the opportuniry to repeat the same temptation. This is the theological test of his fitness for redemption. To my mind, however, the second decision—the forgiveness of Dalila—is equally important, no matter how ironic the terms in which he delivers it. If Samson cannot forgive an enemy—the audience knows from the biblical injunction—God cannot forgive him. Samson has no hint of the true significance of this action, nor does he even recognize it as significant, perhaps, but it is crucial. Without it his salvation is impossible, for his hatred of his own sin must not be confused with an unforgiving hatred of the imperfect woman who tempted him to his fall. It is by no means entirely implausible that Milton had some understanding of the modern psychological doctrine that forgiving the one who brought disaster is forgiving oneself. As I understand it, this self-forgiveness means that a person is prepared to accept himself for what he is and has cleared his mind of the poison of self-punishment in excess of fact or responsibility, a deadly neurosis. In this self-understanding frame of mind one can deal with the consequences of an act without attempting to free oneself by blaming others or else by imprisoning oneself in a mental labyrinth from which no escape is possible except into a breakdown and from which no action except for suicide can evolve. As Adam and Eve must forgive each other before they can seek a reconciliation with God, so in forgiving Dalila Samson has finally healed the running sore of despair; by this change of mind he has prepared himself, though unwittingly, for the further change that is to take place in the Harapha episode.

That Samson is without self-consciousness of this rise from fortitude to penance and then to repentance is no evidence that Milton was not working within this general theological scheme. In the first place, Milton is a dramatist and as a dramatist he is properly more concerned with action than with exposition. It is the duty of the audience to interpret the action and to recognize the ironic gaps between speech and apparent motive and the true test of action. In a play so laced with irony it is a structural irony that correction and redemption come to Samson almost completely unawares, in the sense that—contrary to the audience—he has no inkling of the formal process through which he is progressing, and thus his actions are instinctive rather than coherently planned to win his reconciliation. Secondly, the church's teaching of the formal process of sin, punishment, and redemption is a strictly Christian concept, and in the Old Testament story of Samson it would be highly anachronistic to portray Samson as consciously following a Christian path. On the other hand, Milton's Christian audience was accustomed to interpreting Old Testament stories as types of New Testament things to come. Hence there is nothing anachronistic in Milton's presentation of underlying Christian concepts natural and familiar to the reading audience as the basic facts from which the interpretation of the action must derive although these principles are unknown to the dramatic characters involved. The formalities of the system may vary between Old and New Testament, but the continuum of men's relations with God is unbroken.

The test of the theological basis for this progression comes in the Harapha episode, about which there has been real confusion. Those critics who believe the Dalila incident to be the crucial one hold that Samson's mind is then settled and he thereupon needs no more than the opportunity and the spur to action to demonstrate the plateau of understanding, or enlightenment, that he had there reached. If this is so, the climax of the play has passed, and Samson's reactions to Harapha will follow as the anticlimax, the natural and indeed inevitable effect of the cause— the turning-point in his understanding reached in the interview with Dalila. Another school holds that the Harapha episode is itself the true turning-point, and that a temptation and trial exist in this scene comparable to and perhaps greater in severity than those represented by Manoa and Dalila, and that it is in the passing of this final test that the highest level of enlightenment is reached.

The truth lies somewhere between these two extremes. If one argues structurally, it is difficult to think of a temptation more important than the renewed circumstances of the original tragic error which Samson, now in full understanding of the nature of that error, refuses to repeat. It was his pride, he states, that led to his effeminate subjection to Dalila and the betrayal of his secret. If Harapha represents a trial by pride, then the reversal of the order produces seriously diminished returns. Samson's effeminacy did not lead to pride, but pride to effeminacy. On the other hand, if in some manner Harapha offers a rising scale of trial, there is little unanimity, or even any credible specific suggestions, as to the nature of the temptation that makes it more important than the trial offered by Dalila, a repetition of the original error. True, the three-part encounter with the World, the Flesh, and the Devil has a superficial attractiveness. Pride is certainly taken to be the greatest of the Seven Deadly Sins from which all the other six flow. But Pride can be elevated to the climactic interview only at the expense of downgrading the theological significance of the hatred of sin accompanied by a resolve never to repeat it which forms the basis of repentance. If in fact Samson

has unwittingly repented in rejecting Dalila, though with forgiveness, Pride has no true theological place in an ascending order of temptation. In short, if the final temptation of Pride must
be surmounted before Samson's mind is fully illuminated, then
the system of Patience, Penance, and Repentance is either non-
existent or is subsidiary to another and more important progression, the nature of which is obscure. Moreover, how Samson
surmounts the sin of Pride in the Harapha episode is by no
means clear.

Fortunately it is possible to reconcile these two opposites on
the basis that the Dalila episode is structurally the climax of the
play. Nevertheless, the dramatization of the encounter with Harapha needs analysis for what it actually contains. We may divide
it into two main parts to which the coda of Samson's reaction is
attached. The first part consists of the usual preliminaries to
battle, each character describing his own prowess in an attempt
to gain a psychological advantage over his enemy. What is important for our purposes is that it is a purely personal encounter
of two fighting men representing their respective warring na-
tions. Harapha scorns Samson's present degradation and boasts
that he would have defeated Samson even in his prime. Samson
defends his present state as brought about by Philistine guile,
not prowess, and challenges Harapha to a single combat man to
man. This part ends when Harapha declines the proposal and
suggests that Samson's past invincibility was given him by magic.
Samson's answer introduces the second part of the encounter. In
the first, it will be noted, Samson offers combat as a private man,
not as a representative of his nation or of his God. But Harapha's
sneer produces a vital reaction. His strength, Samson returns,
came not from magic but from God and had been divinely given
to God's champion and minister. A challenge now follows on very
different terms: Samson's indignation leads him to offer himself
in a combat for a trial of truth. Judicial combat is a formal and
well-recognized means of determining truth in cases where evidence is too uncertain for the legal process to decide. Thus in
extremity two antagonists place their truth in the hands of God,
and the result of the official combat is taken to represent God's
decision. (The case is best known to most of us in the procedures

for the aborted combat for trial of truth between Bolingbroke and Mowbray that opens Shakespeare's *Richard II.*) The significance of this shift of ground from Samson as private to Samson as public champion is emphasized by the series of three challenges which he delivers in this new role. In the first, he challenges Dagon in the person of Harapha to stand up to the test against Israel's God in him. On Harapha's response that his God has deserted him, Samson is led to the new position that confident of final pardon he can issue a second challenge to combat. This second defiance leads to a dispute about Samson as a murderer and a member of an enslaved nation, to which he responds disclaiming responsibility for the venality of his countrymen and asserting that he has never been a private person but an agent assigned by Heaven. On this basis the third challenge follows, which Harapha turns aside before he retreats, leaving Samson exhausted and discouraged at the apparent failure of his action.

Critics have been prompt to point out the shift in the first and second of this series of challenges in which, stung by Harapha's taunts, Samson in answering them is led to a partial assertion of his continued championship in the first and a tacitly full assertion in the second:

> *yet despair not of his final pardon*
> *Whose ear is ever open; and his eye*
> *Gracious to re-admit the suppliant;*
> *In confidence whereof I once again*
> *Defie thee to the trial of mortal fight,*
> *By combat to decide whose god is God,*
> *Thine or whom I with Israel's Sons adore.*   (ll. 1171–77)

Because this is the first statement of any confidence of pardon, and because it links with no earlier statement in the first two visitations, the theory has been proposed that Harapha acted as the spur, and that nothing in the nature of a trial is present in the episode. In defending the purity of his God, Samson is automatically led into a defense of the purity of his own divinely prompted actions up to his betrayal, and thence, in the heat of the challenges, to a confidence that in this confrontation he will still—though blinded—be able to act as champion. This is a fair

statement of the position and if, as commonly, Samson's returning confidence in himself as agon is taken as an enlightenment,
it is impossible to find in the latter part of the episode the overcoming of any temptation to pride. On the other hand, an argument might be raised that in his challenge as a private person
Samson differs from the position he adopts in the series of three
that follows. If this were Milton's intention, however, the language effectively conceals it. Certainly it is proper to ask what
response other than his first disgusted challenge to a boaster one
would expect from him, and what pride is shown in it. Milton
distinguishes the private from the public defiances, but as a dramatic device to show how Samson under pressure passes from a
simple to a complex reaction in his understanding that this trial
has implications beyond a simple man-to-man fight.

There are only two options. If God has sent Harapha as a punishment for a further and ultimate humiliation, then Samson is
indeed lost and only retributive justice can be heaped on him
until his death. This was his former attitude about Dalila's visitation. I suggest that, again instinctively for himself but with the
full knowledge of the audience as to the issues, the crucial test
of Dalila has in fact strengthened him to admit the other option,
the possibility that the punishment has been corrective and that
God will pardon him in the end if he will act correctly in accord
with God's will. The distinction between the two sets of challenges, then, marks the transition to an understanding that Harapha, like Dalila, was sent for other reasons than aggravation of
his fault. He closed the Dalila episode with forgiveness. If Harapha has any element of test, Samson meets the test by passing
from a private to a public challenge. If one were to work hard at
it one might find some suspicion of an escape from pride in the
new terms, but if so it would appear to represent only a latent
danger, not a visible one. In a sense Samson does pass from failure to triumph in thus shifting his ground, but that does not
signify that the audience would need to disapprove of his first
challenge as an error. Admittedly it is incomplete and not ethically based. Nevertheless I take Milton's arrangement to represent more a dramatic motivation than a testing ground on which
Samson's fate wavers in the balance between sin and virtue. The

transition marks the difference between alienation and partial reconciliation, of course. In the first two interviews, supplementing the dramatic treatment of the opening choral dialogue, without Samson being conscious of it God has moved closer to him.[3] In the second series of challenges Samson makes his first conscious step toward God, but not toward God's purpose for him.

The question now follows: was Samson's enlightenment complete when he hoped for pardon and in that confidence challenged Harapha as two representatives of their gods? The answer must be, no. Granting that Milton was not prepared to rewrite the Bible story, let us speculate on the effect if under the new terms Harapha had accepted combat and Samson had killed him though suffering his own mortal wound in the process. Would the understanding of Manoa and the Chorus, and the final catharsis for the audience, be substantially the same? If the answer is yes, then Milton's invention of Harapha and his retreat would be only a desperate expedient to retain the biblical ending: an arbitrary foreclosing of an impossible situation like the rescue of the Lady in *Comus* before the brutalizing drink is forced between her lips. Such a reductio ad absurdum shows us that something is still wrong. Samson's discouragement when Harapha escapes him is like his exhaustion at the end of the Dalila episode and its comment no more to be trusted as to what the audience is to think than in the episode before. The case may be clarified perhaps by inquiring whether any audience would take it that Samson's hope for an ultimate pardon that will enable him to fight Harapha as God's champion is prompted by himself or by God. The whole weight of the evidence suggests that this affirmation is self-prompted, Samson's own move toward a waiting God. Any other view, in fact, would destroy the religious and dramatic impact of the "rouzing motions" that later change his mind about following the Messenger to the Philistine festival.

Samson has attested to the communication of God with him

3.   In a divinely ordered world, God *had* in a sense sent Manoa and Dalila to him. One may profitably recall Milton's discussion in *De Doctrina*, chap. 8, of good temptations, *John Milton: Complete Poems and Major Prose*, ed. Merritt Y. Hughes, p. 988.

through impulses, as in the marriage with the Woman of Timna. There can be only one impulse in this tragedy: it must be that which leads Samson to obey his fate and complete the reconciliation by the expiation of a death in victory. According to this point of view Samson's own positive action toward reconciliation, the second set of challenges, is necessary and admirable as a recognition of the difference between retributive justice and the corrective justice that has actually been visited on him, but it falls far short of full enlightenment. In the nature of the case this final illumination or impulse should come from God and must therefore be adumbrated by the "rouzing motions" which he feels only at a later time. Critics have usually held that the true enlightenment was his assertion that he would fight Harapha as God's champion, confident in his hope of pardon. Redemptive as Samson's challenge is, it leads to no dramatic action, for Harapha skulks off with futile menaces and Samson is back where he started for an opportunity to act. This ending to the episode is itself the firmest evidence that what Samson proposed was not acceptable to God and therefore was not full enlightenment.

The reason for Milton's treatment is clear. In challenging Harapha to combat, whether as private or as public contestants, Samson was attempting to recreate the past in the exact terms of his former mission, and he hoped for success despite the seemingly insurmountable obstacle of his blindness. This thinking is in line with the blindness of Manoa and the Chorus throughout the play in believing that God will forgive Samson, if He does, by some miracle that will restore his sight so that everything would be as it was before Samson's betrayal. As I have remarked, this frame of mind shows no understanding of the way in which God works to repair evil. Adam's expulsion from Eden was necessary as well as symbolic. The consequences of original sin will be removed by Christ's sacrifice, but the effects of the sin will remain in the form of temporal death until the Day of Judgment. Things can never be identical once evil has corrupted. Good will counterbalance the evil, and more than counterbalance it, but the death that Adam ate will not be lifted. Physical death, however, will ultimately turn into spiritual victory over Satan in the immortality of man within the body of Christ.

The theme of retributive tragedy known to the Greeks celebrated the heroic endurance of the protagonist, because there was little else to celebrate in a pagan world. Even in *Oedipus at Colonus*, which comes closer than any other Greek tragedy to the ethos of *Samson Agonistes*, much closer than *Prometheus Bound*, the tragic stoicism merely tries to seal off man's responses to ill and thus to glorify fortitude in adversity, for life would otherwise be intolerable. The greatness of human character is manifested by Promethean resistance to irreparable external situation. On the contrary, redemptive tragedy is almost exclusively a Christian phenomenon, with its own rules. It is a tragedy of error, too, but of error repaired by willed action that alone is positive and meaningful and that alone can reaffirm God's mercy and justice. The two great lessons that *Samson Agonistes* teaches are that God's justice is redemptive, not retributive, and that good will always overcome evil according to a larger design which cannot be altered by the human failure under stress of an agent selected for a special mission in God's Providential system. For Manoa and the Chorus the stunning cathartic enlightenment that closes the tragedy is revealed as the unerring power of divine good working through fallible man. The only terms of reconciliation previously envisaged had been appropriate to the Old Testament and had been little different from the arbitrary lifting of retributive justice after heroic suffering in the *Oedipus at Colonus*. All characters in the play conceive of Samson's future in the single terms of the original mission. When this mission is aborted by his tragic error and his blinding and enslavement, no other repair of the damage is dreamt of except a relaxation of the punishment at some future time—and a miracle to restore Samson to his former state so that the mission can then continue as if it had never been interrupted.

In this context the Harapha episode—for action—is a dead end. In it Samson has spoken to God but God has not yet spoken to Samson. The spur to action provided by Harapha is both wrong and impossible as Samson responds to it: it is still his

understanding that history is repeating itself. Although handi-
capped by blindness, he proposes to fight on the same terms as
before his fall and to conquer his enemies by force of arms in
open combat. This proposal marks an incomplete enlightenment
as to God's purposes and it would have proved unacceptable, one
reason why it must not take place. Yet we are not to suppose that
by this wrong interpretation of experience, Samson has failed
God again; it merely signifies that corrective punishment has not
provided the full lesson. Milton presents the episode as the final
reach of what the unenlightened human understanding, in an
Old Testament context, could comprehend of divine purpose before the principle of sacrificial mercy, not arbitrary mercy, was
announced in Christ. Non-Christian human reason is not
enough, for it misses the essential truth that one cannot go
home again. No more than Adam can escape the penalty of
death for sin can Samson escape his blindness and be restored to
vigorous championship in combat, or even to a blind-man's victory over Harapha. His fall from grace did not alter God's purpose to crush the Philistines, but conditional upon his fall the
means must necessarily change by which that purpose will in the
end be unerringly fulfilled.

The changed means involve the grand principle of reconcila-
tion through expiation. Within the framework of free will, men
on earth fulfill divine purpose, particularly those special agents
like Samson who have been set apart as ministers of Providence.
Although Samson fails and believes that he has been cast off,
God's purpose remains unwavering. However, human reason has
difficulty in understanding this unfaltering divine purpose because men expect the purpose to fulfill itself in the identical
terms of the original plan. But Samson's fault changes these
terms, though not the essence of the plan. The original victorious end will still be fulfilled but it will be altered to a quite
different action that will require Samson's expiatory death as the
willing payment for reconciliation. It is this final transformation
that Samson glimpses in its "rouzing motions," the return of
communication with God in the divine impulse that in the past
had prompted his ministerial actions. The command of the Mes-

senger is correctly interpreted as the opportunity to follow God's will, not Samson's own,[4] and in the holocaust that follows the pulling down of the temple, Samson fulfills his original mission—despite his neccssary death—more terribly than by any symbolic victory over Harapha. His challenges of Harapha had not been incited by God, but in the new action at the temple Samson is a God-guided man once more. The knowledge that this exchange of expiatory death as the price of victory is just, and redemptive, reconciles the audience to the tragic penalty that justice must always exact for sin even though forgiven. Indeed, the forgiveness lies in the terms of the penalty for reconciliation. The victory achieved in death, then, is the visible sign of the final reconciliation of the hero with his God, and of divine acceptance of the results of his mission. The function of mercy to ameliorate justice by the acceptance of sacrifice is the *true experience* that Manoa and the Chorus learn; and through them the audience can understand the fulfillment of Old Testament history in the New,[5] for the profound effect of the catharsis in the audience is of course powerfully Christian. The ending not only shows that God's ways are justifiable to man, that divine purpose will work itself out inevitably even though obscurely to human eyes, but that the requirement of sacrifice from men is not retributive but redemptive. What the audience knows as the last measures of the kommos fall on their ears is the exaltation of the Christian experience working itself out through the range of human history.

4.   This interpretation highlights Samson's challenges to Harapha as proceeding from his own will. The final pardon, as there viewed, would enable a blind man to defeat an active opponent. But God has other plans, and Samson is not yet in tune with divine disposals before the "rouzing motions." The transmitted impulse is, of course, by no means specific except that the Messenger's command seems to be reinforced by something more than the Philistine threats and thus requires hopeful obedience. It is only when in the temple he stands between the pillars that he understands he has been given by ordinance the means by which he may retrieve himself as champion.

5.   Long before the Renaissance Samson had been explained as a type of Christ, but Milton is not working with such a pattern. Instead, his concern with such typology for Samson is concentrated on the Old Law repetition of Adam's fall and his future redemption under the New Law.

All is best, though we oft doubt,
What th'unsearchable dispose
Of highest wisdom brings about,
And ever best found in the close.
Oft he seems to hide his face,
But unexpectedly returns
And to his faithful Champion hath in place
Bore witness gloriously; whence Gaza mourns
And all that band them to resist
His uncontroulable intent,
His servants he with new acquist
Of true experience from this great event
With peace and consolation hath dismist,
And calm of mind all passion spent.